Ethics and Professional Practice for Paralegals

SECOND EDITION

S. Patricia Knight

emp
2010
Emond Montgomery Publications
Toronto, Canada

Emond Montgomery Publications Limited
60 Shaftesbury Avenue
Toronto ON M4T 1A3
http://www.emp.ca/highered

Printed in Canada.
Reprinted July 2012.

We acknowledge the financial support of the Government of Canada through the
Canada Book Fund for our publishing activities.

The events and characters depicted in this book are fictitious. Any similarity to
actual persons, living or dead, is purely coincidental.

Acquisitions and development editor: Peggy Buchan
Marketing manager: Christine Davidson
Director, sales and marketing, higher education: Kevin Smulan
Supervising editor: Jim Lyons
Copy editor: Sarah Gleadow
Production editor: Cindy Fujimoto
Proofreader: Jamie Bush
Indexer: Paula Pike
Cover designer: John Vegter

Library and Archives Canada Cataloguing in Publication

Knight, S. Patricia
    Ethics and professional practice for paralegals / S. Patricia Knight. — 2nd ed.

Includes bibliographical references and index.
ISBN 978-1-55239-326-0

    1. Legal assistants — Ontario — Textbooks. 2. Legal assistants —
Professional ethics — Ontario — Textbooks. 3. Practice of law — Ontario —
Textbooks. I. Title.

KEO168.L43K56 2009   340.023'713   C2009-903918-4
KF320.L4K56 2009

For Martha Schuler Higgins

Contents

Acknowledgments

The original version of the Office Procedures Manual excerpted at Chapter 7 is the work of William J. Kirton and Krista-Maria Wall, 2009 graduates of the Paralegal program at Sheridan Institute. It is reproduced here in a modified form with their kind permission, for which I thank them.

I would also like to thank Peggy Buchan for her patience and encouragement while this book was being written, and Sarah Gleadow for her thorough, careful editing and many helpful suggestions.

CHAPTER 1

Paralegal Governance in Ontario

LEARNING OBJECTIVES

After reading this chapter, you will understand:

- The basic features of paralegal governance in Ontario.
- Who must be licensed.
- Exemptions from licensing.
- Authorized areas of practice for P1 licensees.

BACKGROUND

In Ontario, **paralegals** have been practising as independent, non-lawyer agents providing paid legal services to the public for several decades. In many cases, the legal services offered by independent paralegals were authorized by statute. For example, paralegals were authorized to appear before various courts and tribunals by statutes that expressly permitted a defendant or accused in a quasi-criminal or criminal proceeding, or a party in a civil or administrative proceeding, to be represented by counsel or "an agent." Prior to April 30, 2007, the *Courts of Justice Act*, the *Statutory Powers Procedure Act*, and the *Provincial Offences Act* all contained such provisions. Section 800(2) of the *Criminal Code* continues to authorize representation of defendants in summary conviction proceedings "by counsel or agent."

Because of their affordability, a demand developed for paralegal services. In response to this demand, and in the absence of any form of governance prescribing the role of paralegals, independent paralegals began providing legal services in areas of law where there was no statutory or other legal authority for them to do so. These areas included family law, corporate law, wills and estates, and real estate. From the outset, the legal profession opposed this practice. However, the public needed affordable legal services, and independent paralegals met that need. Independent paralegals were inexpensive, and therefore accessible to people who did not have a lot of money to spend on legal services.

Many independent paralegals were honest and competent, and handled their clients' cases to a professional standard. They formed professional associations, complied voluntarily with good character requirements and professional codes, and carried errors and omissions insurance. **Errors and omissions insurance** is a form of liability insurance that is intended to reimburse clients for loss or damage suffered as a result of negligence or wrongdoing by a legal representative.

In the absence of any legislated form of professional governance, membership in paralegal professional associations and compliance with their requirements was voluntary. In reality, anyone could set up an office and provide legal services to the public as an independent paralegal. Independent paralegals were not required to have any formal legal training. They were not required to be of good character, to comply with a code of professional standards, or to carry errors and omissions insurance. If a paralegal firm was not insured, a client who had suffered damage as a result of a paralegal's incompetence or negligence could not look to an insurer for compensation. Instead, the complainant would be forced to sue the defendant paralegal firm for redress. Many independent paralegals incorporated their businesses. A successful plaintiff often found himself or herself trying to enforce a judgment against a **shell corporation**—that is, a business with no assets to enforce a judgment against.

This situation raised issues of consumer protection with the Ministry of the Attorney General and the **Law Society of Upper Canada**, which governs the legal profession in Ontario in the public interest. In the absence of regulatory legislation, the Law Society had been confined to prosecuting paralegals on a case-by-case basis, as complaints came to its attention, for offences contrary to the *Law Society Act* and the *Solicitors Act*. This ad hoc approach to disciplining rogue paralegals was not a very effective way of protecting the public interest. As the Ontario Court of Appeal noted in a much-quoted passage from *R. v. Romanowicz* (at paragraph 88):

> A person who decides to sell t-shirts on the sidewalk needs a licence and is subject to government regulation. That same person can, however, without any form of government regulation, represent a person in a complicated criminal case where that person may be sentenced to up to 18 months imprisonment. Unregulated representation by agents who are not required to have any particular training or ability in complex and difficult criminal proceedings where a person's liberty and livelihood are at stake invites miscarriages of justice. Nor are de facto attempts to regulate the appearance of agents on a case-by-case basis likely to prevent miscarriages of justice.

Although *Romanowicz* was a criminal matter, there were similar concerns about the potential for harm if uneducated, uninsured, and unregulated persons continued to be permitted to provide legal services to the public in other areas where there was statutory authorization for non-lawyer agents to do so, such as Small Claims Court, provincial offences court, and before administrative boards and tribunals.

REGULATION BY THE LAW SOCIETY OF UPPER CANADA

On May 1, 2007, the *Law Society Act* was amended to make the Law Society of Upper Canada the regulator of the paralegal profession in Ontario. The following is an overview of some key features of paralegal regulation in Ontario.

How Did the Law Society of Upper Canada Become the Regulator?

In 2001, then Ontario Attorney General David Young advised the Law Society that the Ministry of the Attorney General was interested in developing a framework for paralegal regulation. By that time, paralegals had been providing legal services in Ontario for roughly two decades without regulation. Two things were clear:

- there was public demand for paralegal services, and

- some form of regulation was urgently required if paralegals were to continue to provide legal services to the public.

Although the Law Society had previously resisted invitations to regulate the paralegal profession, in response to the Attorney General's invitation it formed a working group of legal organizations, including advocacy groups for lawyers and paralegals. In 2002, the Working Group on Paralegal Regulation published a consultation paper, whose recommendations elicited a storm of protest from paralegals and lawyers alike.

In the absence of consensus, the government took no further action on paralegal regulation. Then, in January 2004, at the invitation of then Attorney General Michael Bryant, the Law Society set up a Task Force on Paralegal Regulation. In its September 2004 *Report to Convocation*, the Task Force made its final recommendations for paralegal regulation. Most of the essential points outlined in the 2004 Report were incorporated (some in modified form) into Schedule C of Bill 14, the *Access to Justice Act, 2005*, an omnibus bill that was introduced to the legislature on October 27, 2005 by then Attorney General Michael Bryant. The rationale for Schedule C was that regulation of paralegals would improve access to justice by giving consumers more choice in qualified legal services while protecting people who seek legal services from non-lawyers. The *Access to Justice Act, 2005* became law on May 1, 2007, amending the *Law Society Act* to establish the Law Society as the regulator of the legal and the paralegal professions in Ontario.

Among the amendments to the *Law Society Act* were a new definition of the Law Society's function (s. 4.1) and a statement of its principles (s. 4.2). Pursuant to s. 4.1, it is the Law Society's function to ensure that:

(a) all persons who practise law or provide legal services in Ontario meet standards of learning, professional competence and professional conduct that are appropriate for the legal services they provide; and

(b) the standards of learning, professional competence and professional conduct for the provision of a particular legal service in a particular area of law apply equally to lawyers and to paralegals.

Section 4.2 states that the Law Society shall have regard to the following principles when carrying out its functions, duties, and powers under the Act, which include the implementation and administration of paralegal regulation in Ontario:

1. The Law Society has a duty to maintain and advance the cause of justice and the rule of law.

2. The Law Society has a duty to act so as to facilitate access to justice for the people of Ontario.

3. The Law Society has a duty to protect the public interest.

4. The Law Society has a duty to act in a timely, open, and efficient manner.

5. Standards of learning, professional competence and professional conduct for licensees and restrictions on who may provide legal services should be proportionate to the significance of the regulatory objectives sought to be realized.

How Does Paralegal Regulation Affect the Role of Paralegals in Ontario?

In some Canadian jurisdictions (British Columbia, for example), a paralegal's role is very similar to that of a legal office assistant or a law clerk in Ontario. In those jurisdictions, a paralegal may perform a wide range of law-related tasks—some very complex—but may not give legal advice to a client. The paralegal's work is always done under the supervision of a lawyer, who is accountable for that work.

The role of paralegals in Ontario was, until 2007, unique, with paralegals assuming a wide range of roles depending on the nature of their work. Some worked as **independent paralegals**—that is, non-lawyer agents who provided legal advice and other legal services (including appearances before courts, statutory boards, and tribunals) to the public for a fee. Others worked as **supervised paralegals** in roles similar or identical to those of legal office assistants or law clerks. Supervised paralegals worked under the supervision and direction of lawyers or other managers, who were accountable for the quality of their work, in a range of law-related venues, including law firms, court offices, Crown offices, municipal prosecutions, government ministries, children's aid societies, and legal aid clinics.

Effective May 1, 2007, both lawyers and paralegals were required to be licensed. The *Law Society Act* set up the framework for governance of the legal and paralegal professions, while the by-laws, the Paralegal Rules of Conduct, and the Paralegal Professional Conduct Guidelines implemented that framework. **Convocation**—the governing body of the Law Society—became responsible for drafting and revising the rules of conduct and the by-laws (*Law Society Act*, ss. 61.2 and 62). Licensing categories, requirements, and exemptions came under the governance of the Act and By-law 4.

The licensing model set up by the *Law Society Act* and By-law 4 abolishes the old distinction between independent (unsupervised) paralegal advocates and supervised paralegals. You cannot assume, because you are working under the supervision of a lawyer, that you are exempt from the licensing process. To determine whether you are providing legal services—and therefore need a license—you must refer to the *Law Society Act*, By-law 4, and any relevant information in the "Paralegals" section of the Law Society website (www.lsuc.on.ca). It is an offence to provide legal services to the public without a licence.

In the former, unregulated environment, paralegals provided legal assistance in any area of law where there was a demand for their services. Effective May 1, 2007, a P1 (paralegal) licensee is authorized to provide legal services in areas of law authorized by the by-laws for that class of licence. It is an offence for a paralegal licensee to provide legal services in areas of law not authorized for the holder of a P1 licence.

Licensing

A **paralegal licensee** is a person who is licensed to provide legal services in Ontario. A person **provides legal services** if she engages in conduct involving the application of legal principles and legal judgment to the circumstances or objectives of another person (*Law Society Act*, s. 1(5)). By-law 4, s. 5 establishes the P1 (paralegal) class of licence, which allows P1 licensees to provide legal services in Ontario.

Lawyers are licensed to practise law as barristers and solicitors in Ontario. By-law 4, s. 2 establishes the L1 and L2 categories of licences for lawyers.

REQUIREMENTS FOR ISSUANCE OF A P1 LICENCE

Effective July 1, 2010, all programs offering a paralegal curriculum in Ontario must be accredited by the Law Society. By-law 4, s. 13 sets out the requirements for a P1 licence for graduates of accredited paralegal programs who apply for a licence after June 30, 2010. The applicant must have graduated from a legal services program that was accredited at the time the applicant graduated from it. The applicant must have applied for, and successfully completed, the applicable licensing examination(s) set by the Law Society. The applicant then has three years to apply for a P1 licence.

BOX 1.1

What Is an Accredited Legal Services Program?

An **accredited legal services program** is defined at By-law 4, s. 7 as a legal services (paralegal) program in Ontario that is approved by the Ministry of Training, Colleges and Universities and accredited by the Law Society. The curriculum of accredited programs must, at a minimum, contain 18 legal services courses mandated by the Law Society and meet the requirements for minimum instructional hours for those courses. It must also cover and evaluate all of the competencies established by the Law Society for a paralegal education program, and meet the learning outcomes established by the Ministry of Training, Colleges and Universities for a paralegal curriculum.

Prior to regulation, community college programs that delivered a paralegal curriculum were called Court and Tribunal Agent programs. Many accredited programs have changed their name to Paralegal, while other accredited programs continue to call themselves Court and Tribunal Agent programs.

All applicants who apply for a paralegal licence after June 30, 2010 must have graduated from an accredited Paralegal or Court and Tribunal Agent program. A list of accredited paralegal programs can be found at the Law Society website. ◇

By-law 4, s. 8(1) outlines the basic procedures and requirements for the issuance of any class of licence under the *Law Society Act*, including a P1 licence. These are summarized below.

1. The applicant must complete and submit the application for a licence.

2. The applicant must pay the applicable fees, including the application fee.

3. The applicant must be of good character.

4. The applicant must take the applicable oath. (See By-law 4, s. 21(2) for the oath required for P1 licence applicants.)

5. The applicant must provide to the Society all documents and information required by the Society relating to any licensing requirement.

The Paralegal Licensing Process Policies provide supplementary rules and procedures for licensing applications. They should be read in conjunction with By-law 4. The following is a brief discussion of some key points.

FALSE OR MISLEADING REPRESENTATIONS

A **misrepresentation** is a statement or conduct by a person that is misleading or false, and that is intended to deceive another person. A deliberate failure to disclose accurate information is also misrepresentation.

It is essential that applicants be truthful and forthright, and comply with the Licensing Policies when completing the various steps in the licensing process. An applicant who makes a false or misleading statement or declaration is deemed not to meet the requirements for the issuance of any licence under the *Law Society Act* (By-law 4, s. 8(2)).

A person who makes a false or misleading statement (1) when applying for the licensing examination; (2) when requesting issuance of a paralegal licence; and/or (3) when registering as a P1 licensee with the Law Society, is deemed not to meet the requirements for that step in the process, and that step plus any previously completed steps will be deemed void (Licensing Policies, Part VII).

A failure to disclose relevant information (for example, a conviction for fraud or an unpaid judgment in a civil proceeding) is also misrepresentation for purposes of By-law 4, s. 8(2) and Part VII of the Licensing Policies.

GOOD CHARACTER REQUIREMENT

Under the *Law Society Act*, an applicant for a licence must be of good character (s. 27(2)).

Part VIII, s. 8(1) of the Licensing Policies restates the good character requirement, while s. 8(2) authorizes the Law Society to require applicants to provide information and/or supporting documentation regarding good character. In particular, as an applicant you must disclose any of the following if they apply to you (the list is not exhaustive):

1. You have been convicted of any offence other than speeding or parking infractions.

2. You are the subject of criminal proceedings.

3. You have had judgment rendered against you in an action for fraud.

4. You have an unpaid judgment against you in a civil action.

5. You have been in contempt of a court order.

6. You have been dismissed from employment for cause.

7. You have been suspended, disqualified, censured, or otherwise disciplined as a member of a professional organization.

8. You have been denied a licence or permit, or had a licence or permit revoked, for failing to meet good character requirements.

9. You have been refused admission as an applicant or member of any professional body.

10. While attending a postsecondary institution, you had allegations of misconduct made against you, or you were suspended, expelled, or penalized by a postsecondary institution for misconduct while attending that institution.

11. You were petitioned or assigned in bankruptcy or made a proposal to creditors under the *Bankruptcy and Insolvency Act*, or have been bankrupt or insolvent under any statute.

12. You have been disciplined by an employer or been a respondent in proceedings related to a *Human Rights Code* violation.

13. You have been sanctioned or had a penalty imposed upon you by a court, administrative tribunal, or regulatory body.

If one or more of the above applies to you, you must make the appropriate disclosure on the Paralegal Application Form in the good character section. The Law Society will then conduct an investigation. If the investigation reveals that there are grounds for concern with regard to your character, the matter will be referred to the Law Society Hearing Panel for consideration. Section 27(4) of the *Law Society Act* states that a person may not be refused a licence without a hearing before the Hearing Panel.

If an application for a licence is refused, another application may be made at any time, based on **fresh evidence** or a **material change in circumstances** (s. 27(6)). Fresh evidence is evidence of something that has happened since the first hearing, or has come to the applicant's knowledge since the hearing and could not by reasonable means have come to her knowledge before that time. A material change in circumstances is a change in the applicant's circumstances since the first hearing, a change that may justify a variation of the original order.

The Instruction Guide for the Paralegal Application Form states that the following are exempt from disclosure in the good character section of the application:

1. You were found guilty of an offence under the *Young Offenders Act* or the *Youth Criminal Justice Act*, the disposition was an absolute discharge, and it has been one year since you were found guilty.

2. You were found guilty of an offence under the *Young Offenders Act* or the *Youth Criminal Justice Act*, the disposition was a conditional discharge, and it has been three years since you were found guilty.

BOX 1.2

What Do You Need to Disclose in the Good Character Section of the Paralegal Application Form?

Scenario

During Samuel Brown's first semester in an accredited paralegal program, he was discovered using unauthorized materials on a final exam. After an investigation, Samuel's professor was satisfied that a breach of academic honesty had taken place. It was his first offence. Samuel received zero on the exam, and a breach of academic honesty letter was put on his file. He passed the course with a D.

Samuel is now in his third semester of the program. He has committed no further breaches of academic honesty. He is applying to the Law Society to write the paralegal licensing exam. He has read the Licensing Policies and is aware of the contents of Parts VII and VIII.

When completing the good character section of the application, Samuel does not disclose the breach of academic honesty. He figures that there is no way the Law Society will ever find out that he cheated on an exam in first year.

Question: Has Samuel made a false or misleading representation to the Law Society?

Discussion: Yes. Part VIII of the Licensing Policies requires that a candidate disclose any allegations of misconduct made against him while attending a postsecondary institution, or any sanctions for misconduct imposed on him by a postsecondary institution while he was attending that institution. In college, Samuel was caught cheating and was penalized. Since this falls within required disclosure under Part VIII, Samuel's failure to disclose this information to the Law Society is a misrepresentation.

Question: What are the consequences of Samuel's misrepresentation if it is discovered?

Discussion: A person who makes a false or misleading statement when applying for the Paralegal Licensing Examination is deemed not to meet the requirements for taking the examination, and any successful completion of the examination will be deemed void (Licensing Policies, Part VII). If Samuel's misrepresentation is discovered after he has taken any subsequent step in the licensing process, the voiding of the licensing exam will void the subsequent steps as well.

Question: What would have happened if Samuel had disclosed the breach of academic honesty?

Discussion: If Samuel had disclosed the breach of academic honesty, the Law Society's investigation would have revealed that it was a first offence, that he was sanctioned for it, and that there were no further breaches—that is, there is no pattern of dishonest conduct. Samuel was honest and forthright about disclosing the incident to the Society, and he complied with the Licensing Policies. While academic dishonesty is a serious offence, the absence of recidivism together with the act of disclosure would likely convince the Law Society that they need have no concerns about Samuel's present character.

Question: Why does disclosure matter here, since it is unlikely that Samuel will ever get caught?

Discussion: Professional conduct is not about what you can get away with. It is about compliance with the rules and standards established by the Law Society for the paralegal profession. ◇

3. You were found guilty of a summary conviction offence under the *Young Offenders Act* or the *Youth Criminal Justice Act*, and it has been three years since all dispositions in respect of the offence were made or completed.

4. You were found guilty of an indictable offence under the *Young Offenders Act* or the *Youth Criminal Justice Act*, and it has been five years since all dispositions in respect of the offence were made or completed.

Provision of Legal Services

A person who provides legal services in Ontario must be licensed in accordance with the *Law Society Act* and the by-laws. A person provides legal services if she engages in conduct involving the application of legal principles and legal judgment to the circumstances or objectives of another person (*Law Society Act*, s. 1(5)). Section 1(6) further defines what constitutes the provision of legal services:

1. advising a person about the legal interests, rights, or responsibilities of the person or another person;

2. selecting, drafting, completing, or revising, on behalf of a person,

    (vi) a document affecting the legal interests, rights, or responsibilities of a person in areas of law authorized for paralegals, or

    (vii) a document for use in a proceeding before an **adjudicative body** (defined in s. 1(1) as a body that hears evidence or legal argument, and makes a decision affecting the legal interests, rights, or responsibilities of a person, including (a) a federal or provincial court, (b) an administrative tribunal, (c) a statutory board, and (d) an arbitrator);

3. representing a person in a proceeding before an adjudicative body; or

4. negotiating the legal interests, rights, or responsibilities of a person.

Representing a person in a proceeding includes (*Law Society Act*, s. 1(7)):

1. making decisions about service and filing of documents relating to a proceeding;

2. deciding what persons to serve a document upon or with whom to file a document;

3. deciding when, where, or how to serve or file a document; and/or

4. engaging in any other conduct necessary to the conduct of the proceeding.

By-law 4 sets out **authorized areas of practice** for paralegals. These are legal services that P1 licensees are authorized to provide to the public. At present, P1 licensees may provide legal services in the following areas (By-law 4, s. 6(1)):

BOX 1.3

What Is a "Person"?

Ordinarily, the word "person" means a human being. For legal purposes, a **person** is any entity that is recognized by law as the subject of legal rights and obligations, including the right to sue and be sued. For example, a corporation is a legal person. ◇

1. Small Claims Court,

2. provincial offences court,

3. summary conviction court,

4. statutory boards and tribunals, and

5. Statutory Accident Benefits Schedule matters under the *Insurance Act*, s. 280, 280.1, 282, 283, or 284.

Authorized activities for P1 licensees include (By-law 4, s. 6(2)):

1. giving a party advice on legal interests, rights, or responsibilities with respect to a proceeding;

2. representing a party in Small Claims Court, provincial offences court, summary convictions court, before statutory boards and tribunals, or in Statutory Accident Benefits Schedule claims under the *Insurance Act*;

3. making decisions about service and filing of documents relating to a proceeding (including deciding what persons to serve a document upon or with whom to file a document, and deciding when, where, or how to serve or file a document); conducting an examination for discovery; and/or engaging in any other conduct necessary to the conduct of a proceeding, pursuant to the *Law Society Act*, s. 1(7);

4. selecting, drafting, completing, or revising a document for use in a proceeding, or helping someone else to do so;

5. negotiating a party's legal interests, rights, or responsibilities with respect to a proceeding; and

6. selecting, drafting, completing, or revising a document that affects a party's legal interests, rights, or responsibilities in a proceeding, or helping someone else to do so.

OFFENCES

If you do not have a P1 licence in the Province of Ontario, according to the *Law Society Act* (s. 26.1) you are not permitted to:

1. provide legal services in Ontario, or

2. hold yourself out or represent yourself to other persons as someone who may provide legal services in Ontario.

If you are a P1 licensee, you are not permitted to:

1. provide legal services that are not prescribed by the *Law Society Act* or the by-laws, or

2. hold yourself out or represent yourself to others as a person who may provide legal services without specifying the restrictions on the areas of law that you are authorized to provide legal services in and the legal services that you are authorized by law to provide.

Specifying the areas of law in which you are authorized to provide legal services and confirming that the client's matter falls within one of these areas is usually done during the initial client interview, and confirmed in writing in the retainer agreement or engagement letter. A **retainer agreement** is a contract between the client and the paralegal confirming that the paralegal has been hired to provide legal services to the client, and outlining the terms on which she has been hired. An **engagement letter** is a letter to the client from the paralegal that confirms the retainer and the terms of the retainer.

If you fail to comply with s. 26.1, you are guilty of an offence and subject on conviction to the following penalties (*Law Society Act*, s. 26.2):

(a) for a first offence, a fine of up to $25,000; and

(b) for a subsequent offence, a fine of up to $50,000.

Exemptions from Licensing

The general rule is that anyone in Ontario who practises law or provides legal services must be licensed. Section 1(8) of the *Law Society Act* states that certain categories of persons are deemed not to be practising law or providing legal services, and accordingly are not required to be licensed. They include:

1. a person who is acting in the normal course of carrying on a profession or occupation governed by another Act, which regulates specifically the activities of persons engaged in that profession or occupation (the Law Society has taken the position that this exemption applies only to regulated professions where membership in the relevant regulatory body is mandatory in order to practise in the profession);

2. an employee or officer of a corporation who selects, drafts, completes, or revises a document for the corporation's use or a use to which the corporation is a party;

3. an individual who is acting for himself in relation to a document, a proceeding, or otherwise;

4. an employee or volunteer representative of a trade union acting on behalf of the union or a member of the union in a grievance, a labour negotiation, an arbitration, or a proceeding before an administrative tribunal; and

5. any person or persons exempt from licensing under the by-laws (see below).

By-law 4 sets out additional categories of persons who may provide legal services without a P1 licence. They include:

1. in-house paralegals employed by a single employer, such as municipal prosecutors (s. 30(1)1);

2. persons who are not in business as legal services providers and occasionally assist friends or relatives at no charge (s. 30(1)5);

3. articling students (s. 34);

4. employees of legal clinics funded by Legal Aid Ontario (s. 30(1)2);

5. employees of non-profit organizations that provide free services to low-income clients, provided certain criteria as to their non-profit status and funding are met (s. 30(1)4);

6. Aboriginal court workers;

7. staff of the Office of the Worker Adviser (s. 31(2));

8. staff of the Office of the Employer Adviser (s. 31(3));

9. constituency assistants working in MPP offices (s. 30(1)6);

10. law students working in student legal aid services' societies, provided they are supervised by a lawyer and covered by the lawyer's insurance (ss. 30(1)2, 3);

11. Injured Workers Outreach Services (s. 31(4));

BOX 1.4

Do You Need a Licence?

Even if you are working under a lawyer's supervision, you may require a licence in certain circumstances. When determining whether you require a P1 licence, you should ask yourself the following questions.

Step One

Question: Are you providing legal services?
Discussion: To determine whether you are providing legal services, begin with the definition of "provision of legal services" in the *Law Society Act*, ss. 1(5) and (6).

Question: Are you giving a person advice with respect to that person's legal interests, rights, or responsibilities (s. 1(6)1)?
Discussion: If the answer is yes, then you must have a P1 licence. Non-licensees (other than articling students) are prohibited from giving legal advice to the public.

Question: Are you selecting, drafting, completing, or revising, on behalf of a person, a document that affects a person's legal interests, rights, or responsibilities (s. 1(6)2(vi)), or a document for use in a proceeding before an adjudicative body (s. 1(6)2(vii))?
Discussion: If the answer is yes, then you must have a P1 licence. Non-licensees (other than articling students) are permitted to draft routine correspondence and documents only. All other documents should be reviewed by a licensee.

Question: Are you representing a person in a proceeding before an adjudicative body (s. 1(6)3)?
Discussion: If the answer is yes, then you must have a P1 licence. Non-licensees (other than articling students) are permitted to appear before tribunals on routine scheduling and other administrative matters only.

Question: Are you negotiating a person's legal interests, rights, or responsibilities (s. 1(6)4)?
Discussion: Non-licensees (other than articling students) are permitted to carry out routine negotiations only, with the client's consent and subsequent review by a licensee. In any other circumstances, you must have a P1 licence.

Step Two

Question: Does your role fall within one of the exemptions set out in the *Law Society Act*, s. 1(8), or By-law 4, s. 30, 31, or 32?
Discussion: If you fall within a category that is not captured by the *Law Society Act* or one of the exemptions set out in By-law 4, then you may provide legal services to the public. ◈

12. Ontario Federation of Labour staff and consultants representing union members in workers' compensation matters (under the Occupational Disability Response Team), including representation of the families of deceased workers (s. 32(2));

13. trade union representatives acting on behalf of retired persons who were formerly members of the trade union, and while providing services to another local of the same union (s. 32(2));

14. union representatives assisting families of deceased workers at coroners' inquests (s. 32(2)); and

15. members of the following voluntary standard-setting associations: the Human Resources Professionals Association of Ontario, the Ontario Professional Planners Institute, the Board of Canadian Registered Safety Professionals, the Appraisal Institute of Canada, and the Canadian Society of Professionals in Disability Management (s. 30(1)7).

Other Features of Paralegal Governance

CONVOCATION

The benchers, sitting as Convocation, govern the affairs of the Law Society. Under the *Law Society Act*, as amended by Bill 14, the composition of the **elected benchers** sitting on Convocation is as follows:

1. 40 lawyer licensees (s. 15), and

2. 2 paralegal licensees (s. 16).

In addition, there may be eight lay benchers, who are appointed by the Lieutenant Governor in Council (s. 23). A **lay bencher** is a non-licensee who sits on Convocation.

PARALEGAL STANDING COMMITTEE

The Paralegal Standing Committee is established by Convocation and is responsible for developing, for Convocation's approval, policy options on matters relating to the regulation of P1 licensees (*Law Society Act*, s. 25.1).

The composition of the Paralegal Standing Committee is as follows (s. 25.1(3)):

(a) five paralegal licensees, elected in accordance with the by-laws;

(b) five lawyer licensees, who are elected benchers; and

(c) three lay benchers.

Pursuant to By-law 3, s. 130, the Paralegal Standing Committee is responsible for developing policy options on the following:

1. the classes of licence for the provision of legal services in Ontario issued under the Act, the scope of activities authorized under each class of licence, and the terms, conditions, limitations, or restrictions imposed on each class of licence;

2. the licensing of paralegals in Ontario, including the qualifications and other requirements for licensing and the application for licensing;

3. the regulation of paralegal licensees with respect to the handling of money and other property, and the keeping of financial records;

4. the rules of professional conduct applicable to paralegal licensees;

5. the requirements to be met by paralegal licensees with respect to indemnity for professional liability;

6. the professional competence of paralegal licensees, including

    i.   the requirements to be met by such persons with respect to continuing legal education, and

    ii. the review of the professional business of such persons;

7. Guidelines for professional competence applicable to paralegal licensees;

8. the provision of legal services through professional corporations;

9. the provision of information to the Society, and the filing of certificates, reports, and other documents relating to the Society's functions under the Act, by paralegal licensees;

10. the election of five paralegal licensees as members of the Committee;

11. the election of two paralegal licensees as benchers; and

12. the appointment of the chair of the Committee.

REPORTS REGARDING REGULATION OF PARALEGAL LICENSEES

The *Law Society Act* provides for a two-year review of paralegal regulation (s. 63.0.1(2)) and a five-year review of paralegal regulation (s. 63.1). Both review periods began to run on October 19, 2006, the day Bill 14, the *Access to Justice Act, 2006* received royal assent.

Report After Two Years

For the two-year report, the *Law Society Act* (63.0.1(2)) states that the Law Society shall (1) assess the extent to which the by-laws made during the review period with respect to paralegal licensees are consistent with the principles set out in the 2004 *Report to Convocation*, (2) prepare a report of the assessment, and (3) give the report to the attorney general within three months of the end of the two-year review period.

The Law Society's two-year report on the implementation of paralegal regulation, dated January 2009, was tabled in the Ontario legislature in early 2009. As of that date, more than 2,300 paralegals were licensed and insured.

In a Law Society media release dated March 30, 2009, the treasurer of the Law Society of Upper Canada, W.A. Derry, was quoted as saying:

> We believe the Ontario government's commitment to the regulation of paralegals is visionary. Thanks to regulation, licensed paralegals are now held to the same high standard of professional conduct as lawyers, must pass a licensing examination, and carry liability insurance. They are now providing a range of important legal services within a recognized, regulated profession.

The 2009 Report concluded that the by-laws implementing paralegal regulation made by Convocation during the two-year period from October 19, 2006 to October

18, 2008 were consistent with the principles set out in the 2004 *Report to Convocation*. The 2009 Report (at 48) also noted that, because of the large number of applicants for licensing, the paralegal regulatory model is self-funding:

> The funding model was originally based on the Law Society underwriting the cost of the creation of the paralegal regulatory model with a contribution from grandparent paralegal applicants. This was projected to generate a deficit in the start-up costs of approximately $1.6 million, to be funded by the Law Society and recovered over a number of years from an annual levy on licensed paralegals. However, the actual number of paralegal applicants far exceeded the expected number contained in the budgetary estimates so that the start-up costs have been fully recovered from paralegals.

Reports After Five Years

The five-year review (*Law Society Act*, s. 63.1) provides for two reports on paralegal regulation—one by the Law Society, and another by a non-licensee appointed by the attorney general.

For the five-year report, the Law Society shall (1) review the manner in which paralegal licensees have been regulated under the *Law Society Act* during the five-year review period, and the effect that regulation has had on paralegal licensees and on members of the public; (2) prepare a report of the review, ensuring that part of the report is authored by the Paralegal Standing Committee; and (3) give the report to the attorney general within three months of May 1, 2012, the end of the five-year review period.

In addition, the attorney general shall appoint a person other than a lawyer licensee or a paralegal licensee to (1) review the manner in which paralegal licensees have been regulated under the Act during the review period, and the effect that regulation has had on paralegal licensees and on members of the public; and (2) prepare a report of the review and give the report to the attorney general within six months of May 1, 2012.

CHAPTER SUMMARY

On May 1, 2007, the *Law Society Act* was amended to make the Law Society of Upper Canada the regulator of the paralegal profession in Ontario.

The governance model set up by the Act and the by-laws requires that any person who provides legal services in Ontario be licensed to provide those services. This includes (1) advising a person about the legal interests, rights, or responsibilities of the person or another person; (2) drafting documents on behalf of a person affecting that person's legal interests, rights, or responsibilities; (3) drafting documents on behalf of a person for use before a court, tribunal, board, or arbitrator; (4) representing a person in a proceeding before a court, tribunal, board, or arbitrator; and (5) negotiating the legal interests, rights, or responsibilities of a person.

Paralegal licensees are restricted in the areas of law in which they may provide legal services. Permitted areas include Small Claims Court, provincial offences court, summary conviction court, statutory boards and tribunals, and Statutory Accident Benefits Schedule claims under the *Insurance Act*.

The *Law Society Act* and By-law 4 deem certain classes of persons not to be practising law or providing legal services. Persons whose activities fall within the specified exemptions need not be licensed.

If you are not a P1 licensee, you may not provide legal services or represent yourself to other persons as someone who may provide legal services in Ontario.

If you are a P1 licensee, you may not provide legal services that are not prescribed by the Law Society Act or the by-laws, and, in offering legal services, you must specify what legal services you are authorized by law to provide. If you fail to comply with these requirements, you are liable on conviction to a fine of up to $25,000 for a first offence and up to $50,000 for a subsequent offence.

KEY TERMS

paralegal	fresh evidence
errors and omissions insurance	material change in circumstances
shell corporation	adjudicative body
Law Society of Upper Canada	representing a person in a proceeding
independent paralegal	person
supervised paralegal	authorized areas of practice
Convocation	retainer agreement
paralegal licensee	engagement letter
provide legal services	elected bencher
accredited legal services program	lay bencher
misrepresentation	

REFERENCES

Courts of Justice Act, RSO 1990, c. C.43.

Criminal Code, RSC 1985, c. C-46, as amended.

Insurance Act, RSO 1990, c. I.8.

Law Society Act, RSO 1990, c. L.8, as amended.

Law Society of Upper Canada (LSUC), *By-Laws* (Toronto: LSUC, 2005); available online at http://www.lsuc.on.ca/regulation/a/by-laws.

Law Society of Upper Canada (LSUC), Instruction Guide for the Paralegal Application Form (September 2008); available online at http://rc.lsuc.on.ca/pdf/licensingprocessparalegal/pa08mem_ParaAppFormGuide.pdf.

Law Society of Upper Canada (LSUC), Paralegal Licensing Process Policies (November 2007) ("the Licensing Policies"); available online at http://rc.lsuc.on.ca/pdf/licensingprocessparalegal/pa17pol_ParaPolicies.pdf.

Law Society of Upper Canada (LSUC), "Paralegal Regulation Sets Precedent for Consumer Protection" (March 30, 2009); available online at http://www.lsuc.on.ca/media/mar3009_paralegal_reg_precedent_en.pdf.

Law Society of Upper Canada (LSUC), *Report to the Attorney-General of Ontario on the Implementation of Paralegal Regulation in Ontario Pursuant to Subsection 63.0.1(2) of the Law Society Act* (Toronto: LSUC, January 2009) ("the 2009 Report"); available online at http://www.lsuc.on.ca/media/mar3009_paralegal_regulation_en.pdf.

Law Society of Upper Canada (LSUC), Task Force on Paralegal Regulation, *Report to Convocation* (Toronto: LSUC, September 23, 2004); available online at http://www.lsuc.on.ca/media/convsept04_paralegal_report.pdf.

Provincial Offences Act, RSO 1990, c. P.33, as amended.

Romanowicz, R v. (1999), 45 OR 506, [1999] OJ No. 3191 (CA).

Solicitors Act, RSO 1990, c. S.15.

Statutory Powers Procedure Act, RSO 1990, c. S.22.

REVIEW QUESTIONS

1. What are the functions of the Law Society of Upper Canada, as set out in the *Law Society Act*? Provide the statutory authority for your answer.

2. What principles must the Law Society have regard to when carrying out its functions, duties, and powers, according to the *Law Society Act*? Provide the statutory authority for your answer.

3. Define "person who is authorized to provide legal services in Ontario." Provide the statutory authority for your answer.

4. Define "provision of legal services" and give five examples. Provide the statutory authority for your answers.

5. What are the authorized areas of practice for P1 licensees? Provide the statutory or other authority for your answer.

6. You are a librarian. Your mother's best friend asks you to help her draft simple wills for her and her husband. She says she phoned some lawyers, but the lowest fee quoted was $1,000. You've known her all your life, and have always called her and her husband "aunt" and "uncle." You obligingly draft up wills and the powers of attorney. You and your mother witness their signatures on the wills. You don't charge them anything.

   When answering the following questions, give reasons for your answers, referring to the *Law Society Act* and By-law 4.

   a. Are you providing legal services when you draft the wills and powers of attorney?

   b. Have you committed an offence? If yes, what are the penalties?

7. You are a P1 licensee. Your mother's best friend asks you to help her draft simple wills for her and her husband. She says she phoned some lawyers, but the lowest fee quoted was $1,000. You've known her all your life, and have always called her and her husband "aunt" and "uncle." You obligingly

draft the wills and the powers of attorney. You and your mother witness their signatures on the wills. You don't charge them anything.

When answering the following questions, give reasons for your answers, referring to the *Law Society Act* and By-law 4.

a. Are you providing legal services when you draft the wills and power of attorney?

b. Have you committed an offence? If yes, what are the penalties?

CHAPTER 2

Professionalism

LEARNING OBJECTIVES

After reading this chapter, you will understand:

- How to read the Paralegal Rules of Conduct.
- Standards for paralegals.
- How to use the Paralegal Professional Conduct Guidelines.
- The general duty of integrity and civility.
- Management of outside interests and public office.
- The role of the paralegal as mediator.
- The obligation to fulfill undertakings.
- Application of the Ontario *Human Rights Code* to paralegal practice.
- The role of the Discrimination and Harassment Counsel.

INTRODUCTION

The Paralegal Rules of Conduct, which establish standards of professional conduct for paralegals in Ontario, were approved by Convocation on March 29, 2007. As a paralegal, you must know the Rules and comply with their standards for professional conduct. Non-compliance may result in disciplinary action by the Law Society. More importantly, unprofessional conduct brings the reputation of the paralegal profession in Ontario into disrepute.

When reading the Rules, you should always keep rule 1.03, Standards of Paralegals, in mind. This rule sets out the principles according to which you should interpret the Rules, namely:

(a) As a paralegal, you have a duty to provide legal services and to carry out all responsibilities to clients, tribunals, the public, and other licensees honourably and with integrity.

(b) As a provider of legal services, you play an important role in a free and democratic society and in the administration of justice. You are responsible for recognizing the diversity of the Ontario community, protecting the dignity of individuals, and showing respect for Ontario's human rights laws.

(c) You have a duty to uphold the standards and reputation of the paralegal profession, and to assist in the advancement of its goals, organizations, and institutions.

(d) The Rules are intended to express the high ethical ideals of paralegals to licensees and to the public.

(e) The Rules are intended to specify the bases on which paralegals may be disciplined.

(f) The Rules cannot cover every situation that may arise, but your conduct in such situations should reflect the principles underlying the Rules, with due regard for the public interest and the integrity of the paralegal profession.

When reading and interpreting the Rules, you should refer to the Paralegal Professional Conduct Guidelines, the by-laws, and any relevant case law or legislation. The Guidelines are intended to assist paralegals with the interpretation and application of the Rules and the by-laws.

When reading the Guidelines, you should keep the following principles in mind:

1. The words "shall" or "must" indicate that compliance is mandatory—that is, you must implement the practice or policy.

2. The words "should" or "should consider" indicate a recommendation that a practice or policy for maintaining or enhancing professional conduct be implemented.

3. The words "may" or "may consider" indicate that you have discretion to decide whether or not to implement a particular practice or policy, taking into account your particular circumstances, your areas of professional business or clientele, and/or the circumstances of a particular client or client matter.

PROFESSIONALISM (RULE 2; GUIDELINE 1)

Integrity and Civility (Rules 2.01(1), (2))

INTEGRITY (RULE 2.01(1))

Integrity means honesty and moral uprightness. Rule 2.01(1) requires that a paralegal's conduct maintain the integrity of the paralegal profession—that is, its reputation for honesty and adherence to high moral standards. A paralegal who does not conduct himself with integrity may cause harm to his clients, and will certainly damage both his own reputation within the paralegal profession and the reputation of the paralegal profession within the community.

CIVILITY (RULE 2.01(2))

Rule 2.01(2) requires that a paralegal behave with courtesy and civility, and act in good faith toward all persons with whom he has dealings in the course of his practice. **Acting with courtesy and civility** means being polite, respectful, and considerate of others, including clients, opposing parties, other paralegals and lawyers, support staff, judges and tribunal officers, court and tribunal staff, and Law Society representatives.

BOX 2.1

Integrity and Civility

Scenario: You run a small paralegal practice consisting of yourself and a part-time legal assistant, Christopher, who has been working with you for four months.

One afternoon, you have a meeting with a client to review her evidence in a matter that is going to a hearing the following week. You are in court that morning longer than you expected, and return to your office an hour late. The client is waiting for you in the reception area.

When you go into your office, the client file is not on your desk. You go back out to reception and say, "Where's the file?" Christopher gives you a panicky look and says, "The file? I don't think I've seen it."

While the client waits, Christopher starts going through everything on his desk and in his filing cabinet, looking for the file. You smile apologetically at the client, and say to Christopher, "I might be able to get stuff done around here if you got organized." Then you go back into your office, where you check your file trays and the filing cabinet. Finally, you find the file under some papers on your desk, where you must have left it the last time you phoned the client.

You go out to the reception area and tell Christopher, "It's okay, I found it where you buried it." You look at the client, shake your head, and say, "You can't count on anyone, can you? He's new. I guess he'll learn."

You've been so busy that you haven't had time to review the file. You quickly go through it, making notes. By the time you ask the client into your office, she has been waiting almost 45 minutes.

Question: Have you complied with rule 2.01?
Discussion: Rule 2.01(2) requires that you be courteous and civil to all persons with whom you have dealings in the course of your practice, including support staff. You made a remark to Christopher disparaging his professional skills in the presence of a client. You also blamed him, again in front of the client, for mislaying the client's file. Even if these remarks are justified, they should be made in private, not in front of another person.

Did you breach rule 2.01 when you were late for the client's appointment? Possibly. This is a time management issue. If practicable, you should consider scheduling client appointments for days when you do not have court appearances. If you must

attend at court on a day that you have also scheduled client meetings, you should notify your office if you are going to be delayed, with instructions to notify the client and reschedule the meeting, if that is feasible.

After you got back to the office, you kept the client waiting while you searched for the missing file, and then continued to keep her waiting while you reviewed its contents. You can avoid losing and misplacing files by having procedures in place requiring that when files are pulled from file storage, they must be returned to file storage when you are finished with them, and no later than the end of the day.

As discussed, you should consider scheduling client appointments for days when you do not have court appearances. This will permit you to set aside time to review files and prepare your notes before clients arrive for their appointments. In this case, your conduct in this regard was inefficient, and was inconvenient for your client. Whether it was also discourteous is open to question, and depends to some extent on your client's perception of the situation. These things happen sometimes, especially when you are trying prepare for and schedule meetings with clients around court appearances.

Question: Were you justified in blaming Christopher?
Discussion: You are ultimately responsible for all business entrusted to you, including training your staff in legal office procedures. In this case it was you who mislaid the file, not Christopher. If you had proper file management systems in place, this would not have happened. While you are not required to confess to the client that you mislaid the file, you should have found a way to handle the situation without humiliating your legal assistant in the client's presence. You could have gone back to reception, announced calmly that you had found the file, and advised the client that you would need a few minutes to review it before meeting with her.

Further Comment: You and your staff must hold all client information in the strictest confidence. Client files should not be discussed with staff in public areas, such as reception. Client files should not be left lying around in any area to which the public has access. ◇

Acting in good faith means making legitimate and honest efforts to meet your obligations in a given situation, without trying to mislead other persons or parties or attempting to gain an unfair advantage over others, through legal technicalities or otherwise.

Paralegals must make their legal services available to the public in a way that commands respect and confidence, and is compatible with the integrity and independence of the paralegal profession.

You cannot provide quality legal services to the public unless you are knowledgeable about the areas in which you provide those services and have the skills necessary to apply your knowledge. In addition, in order to provide your services efficiently and with a minimum of inconvenience to your clients, you must be organized in your practice. You may be an expert in a particular area of law, but if your practice is disorganized (without proper file management, time management, record-keeping, and other procedures in place) you cannot make your legal services available in a timely, cost-effective way. Sound practice management is the bedrock upon which effective client service rests.

Outside Interests and Public Office (Rules 2.01(3), (4); Guideline 2)

A paralegal who engages in another profession, business, occupation, or other outside interest, or who holds public office at the same time as she is providing legal services, shall not allow the outside interest or public office to jeopardize her integrity, independence, or competence as a paralegal (rule 2.01(3)). In addition, she shall not allow her involvement in an outside interest or public office to impair the exercise of her independent judgment as a paralegal on behalf of a client (rule 2.01(4)).

Guideline 2 states that the term **outside interest** covers the widest possible range of activities. It includes activities that may overlap or be connected with the provision of legal services, such as acting as a director of a corporation or writing on legal subjects. It also covers activities in areas loosely connected or unconnected to the provision of legal services, such as business, politics, or the performing arts. The question of whether and to what extent it is proper for the paralegal to engage in the outside interest will be subject to any applicable by-law or rule of the Law Society.

When acting in her outside role, a paralegal must continue to fulfill her obligations under the Paralegal Rules of Conduct. She must refrain from acting in a manner that would bring her or the paralegal profession into disrepute. Her conduct must be characterized by integrity and civility. She must continue to provide legal services to her clients to an acceptable standard of professional competence, avoid conflicts of interest, and maintain confidentiality.

According to guideline 2, it is the paralegal's responsibility to consider whether her involvement in the outside interest may impair her ability to act in the best interest of her clients, either because of an existing or potential conflict of interest, or for some other reason. A **conflict of interest** is any interest, financial or otherwise, that may negatively affect your ability to exercise your independent judgment on behalf of the client. A conflict will arise when (1) you are representing, or connected with, two or more persons whose interests are adverse, and/or (2) your ability to act in your client's best interest is compromised by a personal interest.

The paralegal must also consider whether involvement in the outside interest will adversely affect her professional competence by, for example, taking up so much of her time that she is unable to attend to her clients' interests properly.

A paralegal who finds herself in a situation involving a conflict of interest must decide whether she will withdraw from representation of the client or cease her involvement in the outside interest.

Acting as a Mediator (Rule 2.01(5))

Mediation is a non-adversarial process in which a qualified and impartial third party (the **mediator**) helps the parties to a dispute to resolve their differences. A mediator has a duty to be neutral in relation to the participants in the mediation—that is, the mediator must have no preconceived opinions or biases in favour of or against one party or another.

If you or a member of your firm has provided legal assistance to a party, you must recuse yourself from mediating in that dispute or any related dispute. **Recusal** means removing yourself from participation to avoid a conflict of interest. Similarly, if you have mediated a dispute and a party to the dispute later seeks legal assistance from you or another member of your firm in a legal matter related to the issues mediated, you and the other members of your firm must refuse to provide that assistance. The party should be referred to another paralegal or to a lawyer.

A paralegal who acts as a mediator shall, at the beginning of the mediation, ensure that the parties to the mediation understand that he is not acting as a representative for either party, but as an impartial third party whose role is to help the parties resolve their dispute (rule 2.01(5)). A paralegal mediator should also advise the parties that he cannot represent either or both of them in any subsequent legal matter related to the issues mediated.

Undertakings (Rules 2.02 and 6.01; Guideline 3)

GENERAL

In a legal context, an **undertaking** is an unequivocal, personal promise to perform a certain act.

Undertakings given by licensees are matters of the utmost good faith and must receive scrupulous attention (*Towne v. Miller*, at paragraph 11).

Rule 2.02(1) states that a paralegal shall fulfill every undertaking given, and shall not give an undertaking that cannot be fulfilled. Except in exceptional circumstances, undertakings shall be made in writing at the time they are given, or confirmed in writing as soon as possible thereafter (rule 2.02(2)). Unless the language of the undertaking clearly states otherwise, a paralegal's undertaking is a personal promise, and it is the paralegal's responsibility to fulfill the undertaking (rule 2.02(3)).

The language of undertakings should be clear and unambiguous. Documents that are to be produced should be described with a reasonable degree of specificity. Tasks to be performed should be clearly described. Deadlines for completion of undertakings are recommended, and should be stated in writing. If performance of the undertaking depends on certain events, the undertaking should clearly state what those events are, and what will happen if they do not occur—for example, does the obligation become null and void, or does it continue to exist, in a modified form? Licensees who give undertakings should identify themselves as licensees on the undertakings.

If you receive written undertakings from others, you should review them carefully to ensure that they reflect your understanding of what you asked for. If they do not, clear up any discrepancies as soon as possible, and confirm any revisions in writing.

Diarize for any deadlines for completing undertakings, including undertakings to be completed by other parties. To **fulfill an undertaking** means to complete the requirements of the undertaking. To **diarize** means to note a deadline or other important date (for example, a date set for a motion or a hearing) in your tickler system, along with a series of bring-forward dates to remind you that the deadline is approaching. A **tickler system** is a paper or electronic system that gives you notice of upcoming deadlines (including limitation periods) or tasks to be completed.

It is good and courteous professional practice to fulfill your own undertakings as soon as possible after they are given, regardless of whether there is a stated deadline or not. If other parties fail to fulfill their undertakings by a stated deadline (or, where there is no stated deadline, in a timely fashion), you should follow up with them immediately in writing.

You must not give an undertaking that you cannot perform. If you know that you cannot fulfill an undertaking, because it is unreasonable or for some other reason, do not give the undertaking.

Best Efforts Undertakings

Sometimes you will be asked for an undertaking that is reasonable, but is not in your power to fulfill. An example would be a request by another party for documents that are relevant to issues in the matter and that may be available to your client, but have not been produced to you. You cannot take personal responsibility for production of the documents, because their production is not in your control—it is in your client's control. In such a case, where honouring the undertaking depends on the actions of another person, you should undertake to make best efforts. **Best efforts** means that you will make good-faith efforts to see that the undertaking is fulfilled, but you will not assume personal responsibility for answering it.

BOX 2.2

What Are "Best Efforts"?

Giving another party a best efforts undertaking does not absolve a paralegal from making a good faith effort to ensure that the undertaking is fulfilled. As the court noted in *Gheslaghi v. Kassis* (at paragraph 7):

> The words mean that [a licensee] and his/her client will make a genuine and substantial search for the requested information and/or documentation. The undertaking is not to be taken lightly—a cursory inquiry is not good enough. … If a party and/or [licensee] is not able to discover the subject of the undertaking, [they] must be able to satisfy a court that a real and substantial effort has been made to seek out what is being requested by the other party. ◇

Using the phrase "on behalf of my client" in an undertaking will not release you from personal responsibility for fulfilling it (guideline 3; see also commentary to rule 6.03(10) of the Rules of Professional Conduct for lawyers).

Undertakings may be enforced by a court or a tribunal. A paralegal may be required to appear before a court or tribunal to explain why an undertaking was not fulfilled, and may be ordered to take steps to fulfill the undertaking or pay any damages resulting from the breach of undertaking. A **breach of undertaking** is a failure to fulfill an undertaking.

UNDERTAKINGS GIVEN TO THE LAW SOCIETY (RULES 6.01(8), (9))

In certain circumstances, a paralegal or a non-licensee may be required to give an undertaking to the Law Society.

A paralegal whose licence to provide legal services is suspended may be required to give an undertaking to the Law Society not to provide legal services. In this case, the paralegal shall not (rule 6.01(8))

(a) provide legal services, or

(b) represent or hold himself out as a person entitled to provide legal services.

A paralegal required to give an undertaking to the Law Society to restrict his provision of legal services shall comply with the undertaking (rule 6.01(9)).

Failing to comply with undertakings given to the Law Society could result in disciplinary action.

PROFESSIONAL CONDUCT AND THE ONTARIO *HUMAN RIGHTS CODE*

Harassment and Discrimination (Rule 2.03; Guideline 4)

GENERAL (RULES 1.03(B) AND 2.03(1), (2))

Rule 1.03 sets out standards for interpreting the Paralegal Rules of Conduct. Rule 1.03(b) highlights the paralegal's responsibility to recognize the diversity of the Ontario community, to protect the dignity of individuals, and to respect Ontario's human rights laws.

Rule 2.03(1) incorporates the principles of the Ontario *Human Rights Code* and related case law into the interpretation of that rule. This means that rule 2.03, the *Human Rights Code*, and any relevant case law applying and interpreting the Code must be read together. A term used in rule 2.03 that is defined in the *Human Rights Code* has the same meaning as in the Code (rule 2.03(2)).

THE ONTARIO *HUMAN RIGHTS CODE*

The Ontario *Human Rights Code* gives everyone equal rights and opportunities without discrimination in the following areas:

- services, goods, and facilities;
- accommodation (housing);
- contracts;
- employment; and
- membership in vocational associations and trade unions.

Prohibited Grounds

The Code (s. 1) prohibits discrimination or harassment of persons with respect to activities in any of the above areas on any of the following **prohibited grounds**:

- Race or colour. There is an exemption for special service organizations.

- Ancestry and place of origin. **Ancestry** refers to family descent. **Place of origin** means country or region of birth, and includes regions in Canada.

- Ethnic origin. **Ethnic origin** relates to cultural background.

- Citizenship. Citizenship refers to citizenship status, including landed immigrant, refugee, or non-permanent resident. Discrimination on the basis of citizenship is allowed in the circumstances set out in s. 16 of the Code.

- Creed. **Creed** means religion or faith. The Code prohibits a person from trying to force another person to accept or conform to a particular religious belief or practice. As well, it may require an employer to make a reasonable accommodation for the religious beliefs and practices of an employee, such as allowing breaks for prayer at certain times. An **accommodation** is an action taken or a change made to allow a person or group protected by the Code to engage in any of the activities covered by the Code—for example, employment.

- Sex. For a woman, the right to equal treatment on this ground includes the right to equal treatment without discrimination in the event she is or may become pregnant (Code, s. 10(2)).

- Sexual orientation. Sexual orientation includes heterosexual, lesbian, gay, bisexual, transgendered, transsexual, and intersexed people.

- Age. Age means 18 years or more.

- Record of offences. A **record of offence** is a *Criminal Code* conviction that has been pardoned, or a provincial offence (Code, s. 10(1)). Discrimination against a person with a criminal offence for which no pardon has been granted is legal.

- Marital status or family status. **Marital status** refers to the status of being married, single, widowed, divorced, separated, or living with a person in a conjugal relationship outside marriage (Code, s. 10(1)). **Family status** governs parent and child relationships (Code, s. 10(1)). A parent may be a biological parent, an adoptive parent, or a legal guardian.

- Disability. The definition of disability in s. 10(1) of the Code encompasses a broad spectrum of conditions, including (1) a physical disability or disfigurement caused by injury, illness, or birth defect; (2) psychiatric disability; (3) a disability for which benefits were claimed or received under the workers' compensation system; (4) substance abuse (addiction to drugs or alcohol); (5) past and presumed disabilities (Code, s. 10(3)); and (6) in the context of housing only, receipt of public assistance (Business Practices Permissible to Landlords in Selecting Prospective Tenants for Residential Accommodation, s. 4).

Paralegals provide legal services to the public. Paralegal firms provide employment to other persons. Paralegals have a legal and ethical duty to ensure that they do not withhold legal services or provide inferior legal services to clients on any of the prohibited grounds (rule 2.03(6)). Paralegals must also ensure that their employment practices comply with the Code (rule 2.03(7)).

DISCRIMINATION (RULES 2.03(4), (5))

Discrimination means treating a person or group differently or negatively based on a prohibited ground of discrimination under the Code. It includes comments or actions that relate to a person's race, age, religion, appearance, marital status, or sexual orientation. Note that the standard is objective. A person who makes discriminatory comments or engages in discriminatory conduct may not consciously intend to be discriminatory. However, if they ought reasonably to have known that their conduct would not be welcomed by the recipient, their conduct is discriminatory.

Discrimination includes **constructive discrimination** (sometimes referred to as **adverse impact discrimination**), defined in the Code as a requirement, qualification, or factor that is not discrimination on a prohibited ground but that results in the exclusion, restriction, or preference of a group of persons who are identified by a prohibited ground of discrimination (Code, s. 11(1)).

Rule 2.03(4) states the general duty of a paralegal to respect the requirements of human rights laws in force in Ontario. It also states that paralegals shall not discriminate with respect to employment of others or in dealings with other licensees or any other person on the prohibited grounds stated in the Code, with the exception of family status. The exclusion of family status from the prohibited grounds in rule 2.03(4) complies with the nepotism policy exemption in s. 24(1)(d) of the Code. **Nepotism** is favouritism based on family relationships. This exemption in the Code permits a paralegal employer who prefers not to have closely related employees in the workplace to implement hiring practices that prohibit spouses, children, or parents of employees from being hired. Without the exemption, such hiring practices would be discriminatory.

Paralegals should take reasonable steps to prevent or stop discrimination by any staff or other person who is subject to their direction and control.

HARASSMENT (RULE 2.03(3))

Rule 2.03(3) states that a paralegal shall not engage in sexual or other forms of harassment of a colleague, staff member, client, or any other person on any of the prohibited grounds.

The Code defines **harassment** as "engaging in a course of vexatious comment or conduct that is known or ought reasonably to be known to be unwelcome" (s. 10(1)). Harassment is a form of discrimination. It includes unwelcome comments or behaviour that might reasonably be expected to cause insecurity, discomfort, offence, or humiliation to another person. Harassment includes, but is not limited to, behaviours such as name calling, racial or religious slurs and jokes, sexual slurs and jokes, sexually suggestive conduct, and demands for sexual favours.

Sexual Harassment

Guideline 4 defines sexual harassment as one incident or a series of incidents involving unwelcome sexual advances, requests for sexual favours, or other verbal or physical conduct of a sexual nature, when one or more of the following circumstances are present:

(a) such conduct might reasonably be expected to cause insecurity, discomfort, offence, or humiliation to the recipient;

(b) giving in to such conduct is a condition for the supply of legal services by the paralegal, whether the condition is spoken or unspoken;

(c) giving in to such conduct is a condition of employment by the paralegal, whether the condition is spoken or unspoken;

(d) giving in to or rejecting such conduct affects the paralegal's employment decisions regarding an employee (including but not limited to assigning of files to the employee, promotion, salary increases, job security, and employee benefits);

(e) such conduct is intended to interfere or results in interfering with a person's work performance; or

(f) such conduct creates a work environment that is uncomfortable, unfriendly, or unpleasant.

Guideline 4 and the commentary to rule 5.03 of the Rules of Professional Conduct for lawyers give the following examples of behaviour considered sexual harassment (refer to the Code and the case law, as the list is not exhaustive):

- sexist jokes causing embarrassment or offence;
- sexist jokes causing embarrassment or offence, told or carried out after the joker has been advised that they are embarrassing or offensive, or that are by their nature clearly embarrassing or offensive;
- the display of sexually offensive material;
- the use of sexually degrading words to describe a person;
- the use of derogatory or degrading remarks directed at a person's sex or sexual orientation;
- the use of sexually suggestive or obscene comments or gestures;
- unwelcome comments or inquiries about one's sex life;
- unwelcome sexual flirtations, advances, or propositions;
- leering (giving another person sexual looks);
- persistent, unwanted contact or attention after the end of a consensual relationship;
- requests for sexual favours;

- unwanted touching;
- verbal abuse or threats; and
- sexual assault.

Section 7(2) of the Code specifically prohibits employers, agents of employers, and other employees from harassing employees because of sex.

Section 7(3) of the Code deals with sexual solicitations from persons in a position of authority. Every person has a right to be free from: (1) a sexual solicitation or advance made by a person in a position to confer, grant, or deny a benefit or advancement to the recipient of the solicitation or advance, where the person in authority knows or ought reasonably to know that the sexual solicitation or advance is unwelcome (s. 7(3)(a)); or (2) a reprisal or threat of reprisal for the rejection of a sexual solicitation or advance, where the reprisal or threat of reprisal is made by a person in a position to confer, grant, or deny a benefit or advancement to the person who rejected the sexual solicitation or advance (s. 7(3)(b)).

In *Janzen v. Platy Enterprises Ltd.*, Chief Justice Brian Dickson addressed the deleterious effects of sexual harassment in the workplace (at paragraph 56):

> Without seeking to provide an exhaustive definition of the term, I am of the view that sexual harassment in the workplace may be broadly defined as unwelcome conduct of a sexual nature that detrimentally affects the work environment or leads to adverse job-related consequences for the victims of the harassment. It is … an abuse of power. When sexual harassment occurs in the workplace, it is an abuse of both economic and sexual power. Sexual harassment is a demeaning practice, one that constitutes a profound affront to the dignity of the employees forced to endure it. By requiring an employee to contend with unwelcome sexual actions or explicit sexual demands, sexual harassment in the workplace attacks the dignity and self-respect of the victim both as an employee and as a human being.

BOX 2.3

Is It Harassment?

Scenario: Doug owns a busy paralegal practice. Recently he hired a young woman associate, Anne, to help out with the Small Claims and residential tenancies matters. One day Anne is talking to Doug about a trial she has coming up in a couple of days. It is Anne's first trial. "I'm really nervous," she tells Doug. "I'm well prepared, everything is ready to go, but I keep thinking, what if I blow it and my client loses big time?"

"Don't worry about it," Doug says, grinning at her. "Dress for success. Wear high heels, a short skirt, and a low-cut blouse. If the judge is a guy, you'll win."

As it turns out, Anne gets a very good result for her client. When she tells Doug about it, he says, "See? I told you it would work." When Anne tells him that she wore a business suit and that the judge was a woman, Doug says, "You girls. You always stick together." Anne is upset and offended, but she doesn't say anything because she does not want to put her job at risk.

Question: Is Doug's conduct sexual harassment?

Discussion: Doug's "dress for success" comments imply that Anne's success at trial depends on a sexually provocative appearance, not on the quality of her work. His "girls sticking together" comment suggests that she won at trial because she is a female appearing before a female judge, not because of the quality of her work. His remarks denigrate her performance as a paralegal based on her sex.

With reference to guideline 4, Doug's conduct might reasonably be expected to cause insecurity, discomfort, offence, or humiliation to Anne. In addition, Anne believes that accepting such conduct may be a condition of her employment, and that rejecting it might affect Doug's employment decisions regarding her. If Doug continues with this course of conduct, it may interfere with Anne's work performance, and it may also create an uncomfortable, unfriendly, or unpleasant work environment for Anne, if it has not done so already. ◇

Other Harassment

The definition of harassment in s. 10(1) of the Code is not limited to sexual harassment. Any form of harassment in the workplace is forbidden by s. 5 of the Code. Guideline 4 gives the following examples of non-sexual harassment (refer to the Code and the case law, as the list is not exhaustive):

- the display of offensive material, such as racial graffiti;

- leering (giving another person malicious looks);

- repeated racial slurs directed at the language or accent of a particular group; and/or

- verbal abuse or threats.

POLICIES AND PROCEDURES

A paralegal shall ensure that no one is discriminated against on a prohibited ground with respect to the provision of services (rule 2.03(6)). A paralegal shall also ensure that her employment practices do not offend rule 2.03 (rule 2.03(7)). The Law Society has developed a series of best practices and model policies to assist paralegals and lawyers in promoting equity and diversity in all areas of their practice, including employment and provision of services. Guideline 4 recommends that paralegals implement these policies and procedures in their practice. They include:

- preventing and responding to workplace harassment and discrimination;

- promoting workplace equity in their firms;

- providing pregnancy/parental leaves and benefits;

- providing accommodations with regard to flexible work arrangements (subject to undue hardship); and

- providing accommodations with regard to religious beliefs, gender or sexual orientation, and disabilities (subject to undue hardship).

The Equity Model Policies, Publications, and Reports can be found in the "Practice Resources" section of the Resource Centre at the Law Society website. The Law Society also provides education and training to legal service providers regarding equity and diversity issues.

All members of your paralegal firm, including support staff and field placement students, should be familiar with your workplace policies and procedures. Copies should be included in your office procedures manual, and should be readily available to everyone in the workplace.

Paralegals should encourage all members of their firm—including other paralegals, support staff, and students—to participate in the education and training regarding equity and diversity issues provided by the Law Society.

DISCRIMINATION AND HARASSMENT COUNSEL

The Law Society Discrimination and Harassment Counsel provides service free of charge to lawyers, paralegals, students, and the Ontario public. The Counsel confidentially assists anyone who may have experienced discrimination or harassment by a lawyer or paralegal, or within a law or paralegal firm. Although funded by the

Law Society, the Counsel is completely independent of the Society. Contact information is posted at the Law Society website.

The Counsel provides advice and support, and reviews options with complainants. These may include:

- filing a complaint with the Law Society,

- filing a complaint with the Ontario Human Rights Tribunal, and

- allowing the Counsel to mediate a solution in cases where all parties agree.

CHAPTER SUMMARY

The Paralegal Rules of Conduct establish standards of professional conduct for paralegals in Ontario. As a paralegal, in order to avoid disciplinary action by the Law Society and to avoid bringing the reputation of the paralegal profession in Ontario into disrepute, you must know the Rules and comply with their standards for professional conduct.

The Paralegal Professional Conduct Guidelines, rule 1.03 (Standards of Paralegals), the by-laws, and relevant case law or legislation will provide additional guidance as you read and interpret the Rules.

According to the Rules, a paralegal's conduct must maintain the profession's reputation for honesty and adherence to high moral standards. Paralegals who do not conduct themselves with integrity may harm their clients, and will damage their reputations within the paralegal profession as well as the reputation of the profession within the community.

Paralegals must make their legal services available in an efficient and convenient way that commands respect and confidence, and is compatible with the integrity and independence of the paralegal profession. Members of the public should be able to find with a minimum of difficulty and delay a paralegal with expertise in the area in which they are seeking legal service; the paralegal should be able to provide the required services efficiently and without unnecessary inconvenience to the client.

Paralegals who engage in another profession, business, occupation, or other outside interest, or who hold public office at the same time as they provide legal services, shall not allow the outside interest or public office to jeopardize their integrity, independence, or competence.

A paralegal who acts as a mediator shall ensure that the parties to the mediation understand that she is not acting as a representative for either party, but as an impartial third party whose role is to help the parties resolve their dispute. She should also advise the parties that she cannot represent either of them in any subsequent legal matter related to the issues mediated.

Undertakings given by licensees are matters of the utmost good faith and must receive scrupulous attention. Except in exceptional circumstances, they should be made in writing at the time they are given, or confirmed in writing as soon as possible thereafter. Unless the language of an undertaking clearly states otherwise, a paralegal's undertaking is a personal promise and it is his responsibility to fulfill it.

Paralegals must respect the requirements of Ontario human rights laws. The principles of the Ontario *Human Rights Code* and related case law must be applied when interpreting rule 2.03.

Paralegals shall not discriminate with respect to employment of others, or in dealings with other licensees or any other person on the prohibited grounds stated in the Code. They shall not engage in sexual or other forms of harassment of colleagues, staff members, clients, or any other person on any of the prohibited grounds. They shall ensure that no one is discriminated against on a prohibited ground with respect to the provision of services.

Paralegals are encouraged to implement the best practices and model policies developed by the Law Society to assist them in promoting equity and diversity in all areas of their practice.

The Discrimination and Harassment Counsel provides confidential assistance to anyone who may have experienced discrimination or harassment by a lawyer or paralegal, or within a law or paralegal firm.

KEY TERMS

acting with courtesy and civility

acting in good faith

outside interest

conflict of interest

mediation

mediator

recusal

undertaking

fulfill an undertaking

diarize

tickler system

best efforts

breach of undertaking

prohibited grounds

ancestry

place of origin

ethnic origin

creed

accommodation

record of offence

marital status

family status

discrimination

constructive discrimination

adverse impact discrimination

nepotism

harassment

REFERENCES

Business Practices Permissible to Landlords in Selecting Prospective Tenants for Residential Accommodation, O. Reg. 290/98.

Gheslaghi v. Kassis, [2003] OJ No. 5196 (SCJ).

Human Rights Code, RSO 1990, c. H.19, as amended.

Janzen v. Platy Enterprises Ltd., [1989] 1 SCR 1252.

Law Society of Upper Canada (LSUC), Equity Model Policies, Publications & Reports; available online at http://rc.lsuc.on.ca/jsp/equity/policies-publications-reports.jsp.

Law Society of Upper Canada (LSUC), Paralegal Professional Conduct Guidelines (Toronto: LSUC, 2008) ("the Guidelines"); available online at http://www.lsuc.on.ca/paralegals/a/paralegal-professional-conduct-guidelines.

Law Society of Upper Canada (LSUC), Paralegal Rules of Conduct (Toronto: LSUC, 2007, as amended) ("the Rules"); available online at http://www.lsuc.on.ca/paralegals/a/paralegal-rules-of-conduct.

Law Society of Upper Canada (LSUC), Rules of Professional Conduct (Toronto: LSUC, 2008, as amended); available online at http://www.lsuc.on.ca/regulation/a/profconduct.

Towne v. Miller, [2001] OJ No. 4241 (SCJ).

REVIEW QUESTIONS

1. Define the following words and phrases. For review and study purposes, it is a good idea to note the source of your definition, and the section or rule number.

    a. accommodation;

    b. acting in good faith;

    c. acting with courtesy and civility;

    d. best efforts;

    e. breach of undertaking;

    f. conflict of interest;

    g. discrimination;

    h. fulfill an undertaking;

    i. harassment;

    j. mediation;

    k. mediator;

    l. outside interest;

    m. prohibited grounds;

    n. sexual harassment;

    o. undertaking.

2. a. You are asked for an undertaking to produce a document to an opposing party in a proceeding. The document is relevant to issues in the proceeding. You have it in your case file at your office. Should you give the undertaking?

    b. You are asked for an undertaking to produce a document to an opposing party in a proceeding. The document is relevant to issues in the proceeding. You do not have the document in your possession. Your client says she may be able to obtain a copy from another person. Should you give the undertaking?

3. One of your paralegal colleagues has a calendar on the wall in her office. It is in a corner behind a bookshelf. It cannot be seen from the door of her office, but it can easily be seen by anyone who approaches her desk, including other paralegals, staff, students, and clients. The calendar shows pictures of male firefighters posing in various states of undress, from shirtless to completely naked except for a very skimpy swimsuit. The calendar is sold to the public to raise money for a children's charity.

   You think the calendar is unprofessional and in very poor taste. When you tell your colleague that you find the calendar offensive, she laughs and says, "It's for a very good cause. Why don't you get a life?"

   Does this constitute harassment?

4. As a paralegal, how can you promote equity and diversity in your workplace?

CHAPTER 3

The Client

LEARNING OBJECTIVES

After reading this chapter, you will understand:

- How to identify a client.
- The paralegal–client relationship.
- A paralegal's duties to a prospective client.
- The retainer agreement.
- The non-engagement letter.
- Joint retainer clients.
- Clients who are organizations.
- Clients under disability.
- The limited scope retainer.
- Phantom clients.
- Verification of client identity.

WHO IS A CLIENT? (GUIDELINE 5)

To decide whether another person is your client, you must consider some or all of the following:

1. the general definition of "client";

2. the definition of "client" in rule 1.02 of the Paralegal Rules of Conduct;

3. the nature of your dealings with the person;

4. whether the person has provided satisfactory evidence as to her identity in accordance with By-law 7.1; and

5. whether there is or was a contractual relationship with the person, and the terms of that relationship.

Any person who seeks your professional advice or services is a **client**, to whom you owe certain duties, regardless of whether or not that person actually retains you to provide legal services. To be **retained** means to be hired to represent a person in a legal matter.

Any person who discloses confidential information to you is a client, to whom you owe certain duties. Here again, it does not matter whether the person actually retains you to represent him.

Any person who is a client of the paralegal firm of which you are a partner or an employee is a client, regardless of whether you actually handle that person's work (rule 1.02). In a busy firm with many clients and/or a high client turnover, you may have no knowledge of a client's existence or the fact that your firm ever represented him. Nevertheless, a paralegal–client relationship exists between you and that client, and you owe him certain duties, including the duty of confidentiality and the duty to avoid conflicts of interest.

PROSPECTIVE CLIENTS

A **prospective client** is a person who contacts you to discuss a legal matter but has not yet hired you to represent her in that matter. In some cases, the client's initial contact with your firm may consist of nothing more than a brief telephone conversation with your receptionist, a voicemail message, or an email. The initial contact may or may not result in a consultation with you about the client's legal problem and her objectives. Regardless of the brevity or casual nature of the client's initial contact with your firm, a professional relationship is established between the client and your firm during the initial contact. This professional relationship is called the **paralegal–client relationship**. The paralegal–client relationship exists whether or not a consultation with you or another paralegal in your firm follows the initial contact, and whether or not the prospective client decides to hire you or another paralegal in your firm. The paralegal–client relationship gives rise to at least two important duties: the duty of confidentiality and the duty to avoid conflicts of interest.

Records should be kept of all initial contacts and of all consultations with persons seeking legal services, regardless of whether or not a retainer is entered into. These procedures will help you comply with your professional obligations to all of your clients, including clients you have never met or spoken with.

Confidential information is any information acquired in the course of the paralegal–client relationship touching on the business and affairs of a client. You have a duty to hold all such information disclosed to you by the prospective client in strictest confidence and not to disclose it to any other person unless you are authorized to do so by the client or required to do so by law (rule 3.03(1)). The duty applies to you and to any other members of your firm, including support staff and students.

Conflicts of interest were discussed briefly in Chapter 2 (page 22). Rule 3.04(1) defines a conflict of interest as an interest, financial or otherwise,

(a) that would be likely to have an adverse effect on a paralegal's judgment on behalf of, or loyalty to, a client or prospective client; or

(b) that a paralegal might be prompted to give preference to over the interests of a client or a prospective client.

Both the duty of confidentiality and the duty to avoid conflicts of interest flow from the relationship of trust and confidence that must exist between the paralegal and the client. Where there is a paralegal–client relationship, the duty of confidentiality and the duty to avoid conflicts continue indefinitely, whether or not the client actually retains you as his legal representative.

To avoid conflicts of interest, you must establish and maintain a **conflict-checking system** containing a list of all clients (including telephone contacts and other prospective clients) and related parties, if any. You should search for conflicts before the initial consultation with a prospective client. That way, if a conflict or potential conflict exists, you can refer the prospective client to another paralegal or a lawyer, and the conflict may not affect your firm's representation of any existing clients. You should search for conflicts again after the initial consultation, when you have more information about opposing parties. You should also do a conflict search any time a new party is added in a proceeding.

THE PARALEGAL–CLIENT RETAINER

As discussed, the paralegal–client relationship begins during the initial consultation with a prospective client. Thereafter, you owe certain duties to the prospective client, even if the client does not hire you. Those duties continue indefinitely.

The **paralegal–client retainer** (also called a **retainer**) is established when the client agrees to hire the paralegal and the paralegal agrees to provide legal services to the client. It is the contractual relationship between the client and the paralegal. As with all contracts, best practice requires that the terms of the retainer be established in writing. The written confirmation of the retainer should contain terms identifying who the client is and the person who will provide instructions to the paralegal in the client matter.

When you have completed the services contracted for, the paralegal–client retainer ends for that client matter. However, your duties to the client continue indefinitely.

BOX 3.1

What Is a Retainer?

In a legal services context, the word "retainer" is used to mean several different things.

- A paralegal–client retainer (also called a retainer) is the agreement between a client and a paralegal that the paralegal shall provide legal services to the client in a particular matter. A retainer is the contractual relationship between a client and a paralegal.

- A retainer agreement is a written contract between the paralegal and the client that sets out the terms of the contractual relationship, including the scope of the legal services to be provided in the client matter and the likely cost of those services, along with disbursements and GST, to the client.

- A **money retainer** is money paid by the client to the paralegal for future legal services. A money retainer for future legal services belongs to the client, and must be held in trust for the client until legal services have been provided and billed to the client. ◇

Declining to Provide Legal Services

You are not obliged to accept every retainer. After the initial contact or consultation, you may decide not to provide legal services to the client or the client may decide not to retain you. You must confirm the **non-engagement** (that is, the failure to enter into a contract or agreement to provide legal services) in writing to the client with a **non-engagement letter**.

The non-engagement letter should contain the following:

- the date of the initial consultation;

- clear confirmation that you have not been retained and will not be providing further legal services for the matter discussed in the consultation;

- the reason(s) why you will not be providing legal services in the matter (for example, unauthorized area of law, conflict of interest, unavailability, client's inability to pay retainer);

- any upcoming limitation periods or procedural deadlines (in the case of a limitation period that is about to expire, you should urge the client to take immediate action);

- a recommendation that the client seek other legal representation; and

- a list of any documents or other client property that have been returned to the client.

You must ensure that the client receives the non-engagement letter. If it will be sent by registered mail, you or your staff must obtain a current mailing address for the client at or before the initial consultation.

You should keep a copy of the non-engagement letter for your records. The client's information should be entered in your conflict-checking system. Your duties to the client of confidentiality and avoidance of conflicts of interest continue indefinitely.

For sample non-engagement letters, see Appendixes 4.2 and 4.3.

Written Confirmation of the Paralegal–Client Retainer

Your paralegal firm should consider preparing a written confirmation of the paralegal–client retainer in every new client matter that is accepted by your firm. The written confirmation should be prepared at the outset of the paralegal–client relationship. A written confirmation should be prepared whether the client matter involves a $60.00 parking ticket, an unpaid debt of $1,500.00, or a fine of up to $100,000.00 upon conviction.

At the outset of the paralegal–client retainer, you should discuss with the client two essential terms of the retainer:

- the **scope of the retainer** (that is, the nature and extent of the legal services to be provided), and

- the likely cost of those services.

Other terms that you should consider discussing with the client are:

- who the client is,

- the person who will provide instructions in the client matter,

- your billing practices (that is, how frequently the client will be billed for fees and disbursements),

- whether and how often a money retainer may be required from the client, and

- how client settlement funds are to be handled.

Fees are what you charge the client for legal services you have provided to the client. Legal services may include legal advice, correspondence, research, drafting pleadings and other documents, and time spent in court. **Disbursements** are expenses related to the client matter, which are paid by you on behalf of the client and for which you are entitled to be reimbursed.

You must ensure that the client understands the scope of the legal services to be provided; how fees, disbursements, and GST will be charged; and any other terms of the paralegal–client retainer. The terms of the retainer should be confirmed in writing to the client.

Depending on the nature of the client matter, confirmation in writing may be done by:

- a retainer agreement signed by the paralegal and the client;

- an engagement letter delivered by the paralegal to the client; or

- a confirming memorandum delivered to the client by mail, email, or fax.

If the client has agreed that any outstanding fees or disbursements may be paid from client settlement funds received in trust, that arrangement should be confirmed in writing.

The Retainer Agreement

The retainer agreement is a contract that sets out the terms upon which the client hires the paralegal and agrees to pay for the paralegal's services, and the terms upon which the paralegal agrees to provide those services to the client. The purpose of the retainer agreement is to promote certainty in paralegal–client relations. The retainer agreement with the client should always be in writing, and should be signed by both the paralegal and the client.

The contents of the retainer agreement will vary, depending on the preferences of individual paralegals and the type of law involved. At a minimum, the retainer agreement should include the following:

- the name and address of the paralegal firm;

- the name and address of the client;

- the nature and scope of the work to be performed, including key steps in the process;

- an estimate of the time it will take to complete key steps, if appropriate;

- an estimate of the approximate cost of the legal services to be provided, with a careful statement of any assumptions upon which that estimate is based;

- a request for any additional information or documents that you require from the client;

- if the client is an organization, the individual(s) in the organization who are authorized to give you instructions on the organization's behalf;

- client instructions regarding handling of settlement funds, if appropriate;

- the name and hourly rate of the paralegal responsible for the file;

- the names and hourly rates of other paralegals, staff, or students who may assist with the file;

- if you are charging a fixed fee for the service, the agreed-upon amount;

- the amount of the money retainer, with confirmation that the money will be placed in trust;

- if and when further money retainers may be required;

- the firm's billing policies, and the consequences of late payment;

- events that will terminate the retainer; and

- a stipulation that any changes to the agreement shall be in writing.

If a money retainer was received at the initial consultation, the retainer agreement should acknowledge receipt, and confirm that the retainer has been deposited to your trust account. The **trust account** is a bank account in which client money is held.

An engagement letter and a confirming memo will contain many of the same terms, as appropriate. However, they are not signed by the client.

You will find a sample retainer agreement in Appendix 3.1.

LIMITED SCOPE RETAINERS

A **limited scope retainer** is a retainer where the client hires you to perform one specific task, such as drafting a demand letter. The retainer agreement or engagement letter should state the precise limits of the task to be performed. As with any other client, a client with a limited scope retainer is owed the duties of competence, confidentiality, and avoidance of conflicts of interest. The client's name, along with that of any related persons, should be entered in your conflict-checking system.

Joint Retainer Clients (Rules 3.04(8) to (14))

A **joint retainer** is an arrangement where a paralegal agrees to represent two or more clients in the same matter. The clients in a joint retainer are called **joint clients**. Before agreeing to a joint retainer, you must clearly identify the clients to whom you will be providing legal services in order to ensure that you can fulfill your duties to them, including the duty to avoid conflicts of interest. You must also advise them that (rule 3.04(8)):

1. you have been asked to provide legal services to both or all of them;

2. no information provided by one client can be treated as confidential as far as the other joint clients are concerned; and

3. if a conflict develops that cannot be resolved, you cannot continue to act for both or all clients, and may have to withdraw completely.

If one of the joint retainer clients is a client with whom you have a continuing relationship and for whom you have acted regularly, you must advise the other joint retainer client(s) of the continuing relationship and recommend that the other client(s) obtain independent legal advice with respect to the joint retainer (rule 3.04(9)). **Independent legal advice** is impartial, confidential advice obtained from competent counsel with no personal interest in the matter.

If you have advised all joint retainer clients in accordance with rules 3.04(8) and (9) and they are in agreement that you should act for them, you shall obtain their consent in writing to that effect (rule 3.04(10)). If there are any issues of inequality of knowledge, sophistication, or authority among the joint retainer clients, you should recommend that they obtain independent legal advice before signing the consent.

BOX 3.2

Consent (Rule 1.02)

Rule 1.02(1) defines "consent" as:

(a) a consent in writing, provided that where more than one person consents, each may sign a separate document recording his or her consent, or

(b) an oral (spoken) consent, provided that each person giving the oral consent receives a separate letter recording his or her consent.

With joint retainers, you are required to obtain the consent of all joint clients in writing. ◇

Even if all joint retainer clients have indicated that they will consent to the joint retainer, you should refuse to act for more than one client if it is likely that the interests or rights of the joint retainer clients will diverge, or that they will disagree on one or more issues at some point (rule 3.04(11)). This is subject to rule 3.04(14), which states that in the joint retainer consent, the joint retainer clients may agree that if a contentious issue arises, you may continue to advise one of them about the contentious issue, and shall refer the others to another licensee or licensees.

If neither the joint retainer consent nor the joint retainer agreement contains a rule 3.04(14) consent provision, then the joint retainer agreement should contain a term stating that, if a conflict arises after the joint retainer and cannot be resolved, you shall immediately advise the joint retainer clients of the contentious issue and withdraw your services.

Before accepting the retainer, you should discuss whether one, some, or all of the joint retainer clients will be giving you instructions in the matter. **Instructions** are directions or authorizations from a client to a paralegal with respect to a particular course of action to be taken in a matter. You should not agree to accept the joint retainer unless you are satisfied that the arrangement with respect to obtaining instructions is workable. The retainer agreement should identify the joint client(s) from whom you are to receive instructions.

Client Under Disability (Rules 3.02(7), (8); Guideline 7)

A **client under disability** is an individual who lacks legal capacity to perform certain acts—for example, to understand legal advice and give instructions based on that understanding, and to enter into binding contracts.

If your client is a person whose ability to make decisions is impaired because he is a minor or is mentally or otherwise disabled, you shall maintain a normal professional relationship with him to the extent that it is reasonably possible to do so (rule 3.02(7)). If the disability is such that the client no longer has the capacity to manage his affairs, you must take any steps that are appropriate to have a lawfully authorized representative appointed (rule 3.02(8)), keeping in mind your duty of confidentiality to the client.

When representing a client under disability, you must be sensitive to the client's individual needs and be aware of your duty to accommodate him.

MINORS

A **minor** (in Ontario, any person under 18 years of age) is a person who, because of age, lacks legal capacity to give instructions or enter into binding contractual relationships. The Rules of the Small Claims Court permit minors to sue for amounts not exceeding $500 (rule 4.01(2)).

In all other matters, minors must be represented by a litigation guardian. A **litigation guardian** is a person who makes decisions for a person under disability in a court proceeding. In the proceeding, the litigation guardian must have no interest that is adverse to the interests of the person under disability. A person who acts as a litigation guardian has a duty to attend diligently to the interests of the person under disability and take all steps reasonably necessary for the protection of those interests.

In a matter involving a minor, you must confirm with the litigation guardian or other authorized representative whether you are retained to represent the minor or to represent both the minor and the litigation guardian. If you are representing both the minor and the authorized representative, you must comply with the rules on joint retainers. You must obtain a joint retainer consent to represent both the minor and the authorized representative. The person(s) from whom you will receive instructions must be stated in the joint retainer agreement.

MENTAL INCAPACITY

There are varying degrees of mental incapacity. If a prospective client's conduct during the initial consultation causes concern, you should consider declining to represent the client. You must confirm the non-engagement in writing to the client with a non-engagement letter. Your duties of confidentiality and avoidance of conflicts of interest continue indefinitely.

You may decide to represent a client who is mentally incapable because you are satisfied that the client has a valid legal issue and is competent to give you instructions. If you decide to accept the retainer, you should ensure that you document in writing all communications between you and the client.

During the course of the retainer, you may begin to have concerns about the client's ability to understand legal advice and give instructions. You must take steps to have an authorized representative, such as a litigation guardian, appointed. If the required steps fall outside of permissible paralegal practice, you must refer the client to a licensee who is authorized to take those steps.

Where litigation is pending or already proceeding, an individual who has been declared mentally incapable must be represented by a litigation guardian. See rules 1.02(1) and 4.01 of the Rules of the Small Claims Court.

If you are representing both the client under disability and the authorized representative, you must comply with the rules on joint retainers. You must obtain a joint retainer consent to represent both the person under disability and the authorized representative. The person(s) from whom you will receive instructions must be stated in the joint retainer agreement.

Acting for an Organization

If your client is an organization, you should determine which individuals within the organization may properly give you instructions on the client organization's behalf (guideline 5). These individuals may be directors, officers, employees, or agents of the organization. This should be done at the commencement of the paralegal–client retainer, and should be confirmed in the written confirmation of the retainer. You should also confirm in the written confirmation of the retainer that you are acting for the organization, and not for the individuals who have been designated to give you instructions on its behalf.

If you are retained to act for both an organization and one or more of its officers, employees, or agents in the same matter, you must comply with the rules on joint retainers. Be alert for conflicts of interest that may arise in this situation.

PHANTOM CLIENTS

Phantom clients are not specifically addressed in the Rules, but they are discussed in the Guidelines. A **phantom client** is a person who believes that you are representing him, even though you have not been formally retained and may be completely unaware that the phantom client considers you his legal representative (guideline 5). Depending on what happened during your encounter with the phantom client, a paralegal–client relationship—with its attendant duties—may exist between you and that individual.

Phantom clients cannot be avoided, but they can be managed. Do not engage in casual social conversation with others about their legal problems. After a consultation with a person, confirm in writing the status of the paralegal–client relationship, by way of a retainer agreement, engagement letter, or non-engagement letter. If third-party members are present at a client consultation, inform them that you represent the client only, not them. Encourage your clients not to discuss legal advice with third parties.

The following are some situations that may create phantom clients.

1. *Telephone contact*

Ms. W calls your office and speaks to your legal assistant about a *Human Rights Code* complaint. Your legal assistant takes down Ms. W's name, telephone number, and some details about the matter. Later you call Ms. W and leave a message on her voicemail. She does not return your call, and you never hear from her again.

Question: Is Ms. W your client?

Discussion: The paralegal–client relationship begins when a prospective client first contacts your office seeking legal services. Although you were not retained, you owe Ms. W the same duties that you owe to any prospective client—that is, the duties of confidentiality and avoidance of conflicts of interest, both of which continue indefinitely. You should enter Ms. W's name, and the names of any related parties if that information was given to your legal assistant, into your conflict-checking system.

Paralegal practice tip: You, your fellow paralegals, and your staff and students should maintain detailed records of all telephone conversations, including the date of the call, the caller's name in full, current telephone number, and details of the call.

2. *No formal retainer*

Mr. X meets with you at your office to consult with you about a careless driving charge. Based on the information he provides, you recommend that he consider pleading to a lesser charge. He becomes agitated, and insists that he wants to have a trial and prove his innocence. You advise him of your fee for that service, and tell him you will require a money retainer by certified cheque within two weeks.

You do not hear from Mr. X for several months. Then one day, he phones you, very angry. He tells you that he has been convicted of the careless driving charge and now faces licence suspension. "You were supposed to stay on top of all this!" he yells. "Instead, you didn't even show up for the trial! I'm going to report you to the Law Society!"

Question: Is Mr. X your client?

Discussion: Although you were not retained, a paralegal–client relationship with Mr. X may have been formed during the initial consultation about the careless driving charge. You owe Mr. X the same duties that you owe to any prospective client—that is, the duties of confidentiality and avoidance of conflicts of interest, both of which continue indefinitely. Mr. X's name should be entered in your conflict-checking system.

Question: How could you have avoided the misunderstanding about the retainer?

Discussion: You should have diarized for the two-week deadline for receiving the money retainer. When it expired, you should have sent a non-engagement letter to Mr. X, confirming that you were not retained because he failed to provide the money retainer requested. The non-engagement letter should recommend that Mr. X seek the services of another paralegal or a lawyer. You must keep a copy of the non-engagement letter for your records.

Paralegal practice tip: Whenever you have a consultation with a prospective client, obtain the client's name, current mailing address, and a telephone number where he can be reached. If you decline the retainer, you will need this information for the non-engagement letter. You should send a non-engagement letter every time you decline a retainer.

For any retainer after December 31, 2008, you must comply with the client identification and verification requirements set out in Part III of By-law 7.1.

3. *Casual conversation*

Two of your neighbours and acquaintances, Plaintiff and Defendant, are involved in Small Claims Court litigation. One morning at a local supermarket, Plaintiff approaches you in the produce section, where you are selecting a head of lettuce. The two of you begin to chat, and she shares confidential information with you about her action against Defendant. You listen, but do not comment.

Question: Is Plaintiff your client?

Discussion: Probably not. However, she has shared confidential information with you. This gives rise to duties similar to those that arise where a paralegal–client relationship exists. You have a duty to keep the information confidential. You should ensure that Plaintiff's and Defendant's names are entered into your conflict-checking system, along with any other relevant information that Plaintiff shared with you. If Defendant contacts you to seek legal assistance in this matter, you may have a conflict of interest and should probably decline to act against Plaintiff. If Defendant contacts you to seek legal assistance in a related matter, you must carefully consider whether you have a conflict because of the confidential information provided to you by Plaintiff.

4. *Friends and family members*

Sometimes a friend or family member will attend the initial consultation with the prospective client. He or she will often know as much about the situation as the prospective client, and may take a very active role at the consultation, commenting or elaborating on what the client tells you, asking you questions, and so on.

Question: What's the risk?

Discussion: If the friend or family member has a legal interest in the matter, they may form the impression that you will be acting for them also. If they have no legal interest in the matter, they may continue to play a role that is inappropriate for a non-client.

You should clearly identify who is the client, what the client's matter is, and that it is the client who will be providing instructions. This should be confirmed in the retainer agreement or engagement letter.

You should inform the friend or family member that you represent the client only.

You should encourage the client to not share your legal advice with third parties.

BOX 3.3

Who Is the Client?

Scenario

Mr. Yi and his daughter, Violet, come to your office to discuss a landlord–tenant problem. Violet is the person who phoned to set up the appointment. At the outset of the interview, Violet explains to you that her father speaks Cantonese, but very little English, and that she is there to act as his spokesperson and translator. You neither speak nor understand Cantonese.

While Mr. Yi sits quietly, saying very little, Violet explains the situation to you in English, pausing now and then to ask her father a question or explain something in Cantonese. He replies in Cantonese. She explains that Mr. Yi rents the legal basement apartment in his house to a tenant who has been there for two years. Mr. Yi is a widower and lives alone on the main floor of the house. There is no written tenancy agreement. Mr. Yi never had any problem collecting the rent until two months ago, when the tenant lost her job. Violet says that they want you to commence an application to evict the tenant.

Who is your client?

Discussion

This is a landlord–tenant matter. Mr. Yi owns the house. The tenant has possession of the rented premises, and until recently Mr. Yi has collected the rent, so a landlord–tenant relationship exists between Mr. Yi and the tenant. Mr. Yi, the landlord, is your client in the application to terminate the tenancy.

What about Violet? Based on the information provided, she does not live with her father and has nothing to do with the tenancy. She is a stranger to the tenancy agreement. However, she is the person who sought your legal services, she acts as spokesperson for her father throughout the interview, and she is the one instructing you to take steps to evict the tenant.

Violet is a problem. Is Violet is going to continue to be the person providing instructions on behalf of her father in this matter? How will you, as a non-Cantonese speaker, know if Violet's instructions over the course of the matter accurately reflect the wishes of your client, Mr. Yi?

If Violet is going to continue to give instructions on behalf of her father in this matter, she will, from time to time, require you to disclose confidential information about her father's matter to her. This situation does not fall within any of the grounds for justified or permitted disclosure of confidential information set out in rules 3.03(4) to (8). If Mr. Yi authorizes disclosure of confidential information to Violet, how will you, as a non-Cantonese speaker, know if Mr. Yi's consent is informed?

You should consider declining to represent Mr. Yi. You should also consider referring Mr. Yi to a Cantonese-speaking paralegal who is competent in landlord–tenant matters and can take instructions directly from Mr. Yi, if you know of such a person. If this is the course you adopt, you must send a non-engagement letter explaining why you cannot represent him to Mr. Yi by registered mail without delay, so that he can seek other legal assistance. Enter Violet's and Mr. Yi's names in your conflict-checking database. Your duties of confidentiality and avoidance of conflicts of interest continue indefinitely. ◇

CLIENT IDENTIFICATION AND VERIFICATION (BY-LAW 7.1)

Amendments to By-law 7.1 with respect to client identification and verification came into effect in Ontario on December 31, 2008. They are part of a Canada-wide initiative by provincial law societies to fight fraud and money laundering.

By-law 7.1, Part III applies to retainers in matters for new or existing clients entered into on or after December 31, 2008 (s. 21).

Unless otherwise noted, all references to section numbers in the following discussion refer to By-law 7.1, Part III.

Compliance with the By-law 7.1 Client Identification and Verification Requirements

Section 22(1) requires a licensee to comply with the client identification and verification requirements set out in s. 23 whenever he is retained to provide legal services to a new or existing client on or after December 31, 2008.

You do not have to identify or verify clients on matters that were in existence prior to December 31, 2008. However, if you are retained in a new or related matter for any of those clients on or after December 31, 2008, you must comply with the client identification and verification requirements in Part III.

LICENSEES WHO ARE EXEMPT FROM THE S. 23 CLIENT IDENTIFICATION AND VERIFICATION REQUIREMENTS

You are not required to comply with the s. 23 client identification and verification requirements if (s. 22(2)):

(a) you provide legal services to your employer (for example, as in-house counsel);

(b) you are acting as agent for another licensee or paralegal who has already identified the client;

(c) you are acting for a client who was referred to you by another paralegal or a lawyer who has already identified the client; or

(d) you are acting as duty counsel or providing summary legal services under the *Legal Aid Services Act* or providing legal services through a duty counsel program of a non-profit organization, unless a financial transaction is involved.

With respect to (b) and (c) above, you should require the paralegal or lawyer for whom you are acting as an agent, or the paralegal or lawyer who made the referral, to confirm that they have already identified the client in compliance with the requirements of the by-law.

WHAT IS THE DIFFERENCE BETWEEN CLIENT IDENTIFICATION AND CLIENT VERIFICATION?

Client identification refers to information you obtain from the client regarding who the client is and what the client does. **Client verification** refers to information you must obtain in order to confirm that the client is who he says he is.

Licensees must obtain and record client identification information in accordance with the criteria set out in s. 23(1) for the client in every new client matter opened on or after December 31, 2008. This includes existing clients who retain you in new or related matters on or after December 31, 2008.

If you engage in or give instructions for the receiving, paying, or transferring of funds, then you must obtain the additional client identification information set out in s. 23(2) and you must comply with the client verification requirements set out in s. 23(4) (s. 22(1)(b)).

Funds include cash, currency, securities, negotiable instruments, or other financial instruments that indicate a person's title or interest in them (s. 20). A **negotiable instrument** is an unconditional order or promise to pay an amount of money, which can be transferred—for example, cheques or banknotes (paper money).

EXEMPTIONS FOR CERTAIN TYPES OF FUNDS (S. 22(3))

You do not have to comply with the s. 23(2) client identification requirements and the s. 23(4) client verification requirements if the funds you are handling fall within one of the following exemptions (the list is not exhaustive) (s. 22(3)):

(a) funds paid to or received from a financial institution such as a bank, credit union, trust company, and so on; a public body such as a government ministry or a municipality; or a reporting issuer (public company) or subsidiary of a reporting issuer;

(b) funds received from the trust account of another paralegal or a lawyer;

(c) funds received from a peace officer, law enforcement agency, or other public official acting in an official capacity;

(d) funds paid or received pursuant to a court order;

(e) funds paid for a fine or penalty;

(f) funds paid or received in settlement of legal or administrative proceedings;

(g) funds paid or received for professional fees, disbursements, expenses, or bail;

(h) funds paid, received, or transferred by electronic funds transfer.

CLIENTS WHO ARE EXEMPT FROM CLIENT IDENTIFICATION AND VERIFICATION

You are not required to comply with the Part III client identification and verification requirements if your client is (s. 22(4)):

1. a financial institution,

2. a public body, or

3. a reporting issuer.

> ### BOX 3.4
>
> ## Reminder: Public and Private Companies
>
> A **public company** (referred to as a "reporting issuer" in By-law 7.1, Part III) is a corporation whose shares are for sale to the general public. Public companies are subject to rigorous disclosure requirements under securities legislation.
>
> A **private company** (also called a closely held company) is a corporation whose shares are not publicly traded. Its incorporating documents (1) restrict the right to sell shares, (2) limit the number of its shareholders (excluding employees) to 50, and (3) prohibit public trading of its shares or securities. ◇

THE CRITERIA FOR CLIENT IDENTIFICATION AND VERIFICATION

The criteria for identifying and verifying clients are set out in Table 3.1. Verification of identity forms for individuals, organizations, third-party beneficiaries, and principals are available at the Law Society website. You will find samples, adapted for use in paralegal firms, in Appendixes 3.2 and 3.3.

CLIENT VERIFICATION, NON-FACE-TO-FACE (S. 23(8))

You may use this form of client verification if you engage in or give instructions for the receiving, paying, or transferring of non-exempt funds on behalf of an individual client who is elsewhere in Canada, so that you are unable to receive instructions from the client face-to-face (s. 23(8)). To comply with the s. 23(4) verification requirements, you must obtain an attestation from a commissioner of oaths or a guarantor certifying that he has verified the client's identity by looking at the appropriate independent source documents (s. 23(8)). Section 23(9) provides a list of professionals who may be used as guarantors, including dentists, lawyers, physicians, and accountants. You must exercise due diligence in confirming that the attestor is a member of one of these professions. **Due diligence** means exercising the prudence and vigilance that a reasonable and prudent paralegal would exercise in similar circumstances.

The attestation must be printed on a legible photocopy of the document. It must include the name, occupation, address, and signature of the attestor, and the type and number of the document seen by the attestor (s. 23(10)). A sample attestation form for use by paralegal firms is available at the Law Society website. You will find the text of a sample attestation in Appendix 3.4.

CLIENT VERIFICATION, USE OF AGENT (S. 23(11))

You may use this form of client verification if you engage in or give instructions for the receiving, paying, or transferring of non-exempt funds on behalf of a client who is outside of Canada, or as an alternative to the s. 23(8) procedure for verifying the identity of an individual client who is elsewhere in Canada.

If the agent acting on your behalf is not an employee of your firm or a paralegal who provides legal services through your firm, you shall enter into a written agreement with the agent specifying the steps that the agent will be taking on your behalf to comply with the verification requirements (s. 23(11)). The agent may provide the information to you in the form of an attestation. See Appendix 3.4 for a sample attestation.

Table 3.1   By-law 7.1 Criteria for Client Identification and Verification

Client Identification Requirements

You shall obtain the following information about the client when you are retained to provide legal services to the client.

Whether the client is an individual or an organization, if the client is acting for or representing a third party, you shall obtain the following information for the third party also.

Individual	Organization*
Full name	Full name
Business address and business telephone number, if applicable	Business address and business telephone number
Home address and home telephone number	The organization's incorporation or business identification number, if applicable
	The place of issue of its incorporation or business identification number, if applicable
Occupation(s)—does not have to be employment	The general nature of the type of business or activity engaged in by the client
If the client refuses to provide this information, you must inform the client that you will be in breach of By-law 7.1 if you do not obtain this information and will be obliged to decline the retainer	The name, position, and contact information for the person(s) authorized to provide instructions in the matter

Additional Client Identification Requirements When Handling Non-Exempt Funds

Individual	Organization*
None	The name and occupation(s) of each director of the organization (other than an organization that is a securities dealer)
	The name, address, and occupation(s) of each person who owns 25% or more of the organization or of the shares of the organization
	You must make reasonable efforts to obtain the above information. Asking your client may be sufficient, or you may consult the corporate minute books if available or an online corporate registry service

Client Verification Requirements When Handling Non-Exempt Funds

Individual	Organization*
Verification shall take place immediately after you first engage in or give instructions for the receiving, paying, or transferring of funds	Verification shall take place no later than 60 days after you first engage in or give instructions for the receiving, paying, or transferring of funds

You shall take reasonable steps to verify the identity of the client using what you reasonably consider to be reliable, independent source documents, data, or information.

You should take reasonable steps to comply with the verification requirement as early as possible in the retainer.

You shall verify the identity of an individual who is authorized to give instructions on behalf of a client who is an organization.

Whether the client is an individual or an organization, if the client is acting for or representing a third party, you shall verify the identity of the third party also.

You shall complete and sign a verification of identity form for each individual, organization, third-party beneficiary, or principal, with photocopies of the documentation relied upon attached.

Table 3.1 Continued

Examples of Independent Source Documents

An original, government-issued identification that is valid and has not expired, and that you reasonably believe to be independent and reliable, such as: ◆ a driver's licence ◆ a birth certificate ◆ a passport ◆ a provincial or territorial health card (if such use is not prohibited by law)	If the client is a private company or society created under legislative authority: ◆ a certificate of corporate status ◆ an annual filing ◆ a similar record obtained from a public body confirming the organization's existence If the client is a trust, partnership, or other organization that is not registered in any government registry, a constating document confirming the organization's existence, such as: ◆ a trust agreement ◆ a partnership agreement ◆ articles of association ◆ other similar records confirming the organization's existence as an organization

You shall retain a record of the information that you obtain and copies of all documents used to verify client identification for the longer of:

◆ the duration of the paralegal–client relationship, and for as long as is necessary to complete the work for which you were retained; and

◆ six years following the completion of the work for which you were retained.

* An organization can be a private company, partnership, fund, trust, co-operative, or unincorporated association.

PREVIOUS CLIENT VERIFICATION (S. 23(12))

For an individual client, a licensee complies with the s. 23(4) verification requirement if she has already verified the individual client's identity and recognizes the individual (s. 23(12)(a)).

For a client that is an organization, a licensee complies with the s. 23(2) identification requirements and the s. 23(4) verification requirements if she has already complied with those requirements with respect to the organization (s. 23(12)(b)).

DOCUMENTATION (SS. 23(13), (14))

You must obtain copies of every document used to verify the identity of a client, a third-party beneficiary, or a principal, including copies of documents used by agents for client verification under s. 23(11) (s. 23(13)).

You must keep records of all information obtained for purposes of client identification and verification, including copies of supporting documents, attestations, and so on, for the longer of (s. 23(14)):

(a)   the duration of the paralegal–client relationship, and for as long as is necessary to provide service to the client; and

(b)   at least six years following completion of the work for which you were retained.

CRIMINAL ACTIVITY (S. 24)

In the course of complying with the s. 23 client identification and verification requirements, you may begin to reasonably suspect that you are or will be assisting the client in dishonesty, fraud, crime, or illegal conduct. If that happens, you shall immediately cease to engage in any activities that would assist the client in dishonesty, fraud, crime, or illegal conduct (s. 24(a)), and, if necessary, withdraw from providing legal services to the client (s. 24(b)).

CHAPTER SUMMARY

During the initial contact or consultation with a client—including prospective clients who may decide not to hire you—a paralegal–client relationship is established between you and the client. This relationship gives rise to at least two important duties, which continue indefinitely: the duty of confidentiality and the duty to avoid conflicts of interest.

The paralegal–client retainer is the contractual relationship between you and the client. It is established when the client agrees to hire you and you agree to provide legal services to the client. The terms of the retainer should always be established in writing by way of a retainer agreement or engagement letter. After the initial consultation, you may decide not to provide legal services to the client, or the client may decide not to retain you. You must confirm the non-engagement in writing to the client with a non-engagement letter.

When you have completed the services provided for in the retainer agreement, the paralegal–client retainer ends for that client matter. However, your duties to the client continue indefinitely.

You should maintain a conflict-checking system, and the names of all clients and prospective clients, along with any related parties, should be entered into it.

A joint retainer is an arrangement where a paralegal agrees to represent two or more clients in the same matter. Before agreeing to a joint retainer, you must clearly identify your prospective clients to ensure that you can fulfill your duties to them, including the duty to avoid conflicts of interest.

Clients under disability are individuals who, due to minority or mental incapacity, have no legal capacity to enter into binding contracts (including retainer agreements) or to understand legal advice and give instructions. They must be represented by a litigation guardian or other client representative.

If your client is an organization you should determine, and confirm in the retainer agreement, which individuals within the organization may properly give you instructions on the client organization's behalf. You should also confirm that you are acting for the organization, and not for the individuals who have been designated to give you instructions on its behalf.

A phantom client is a person who believes that you are representing him, even though you have not been formally retained and may be completely unaware that he considers you his legal representative. Depending on what happened during your encounter with the phantom client, a paralegal–client relationship may exist between you and that individual.

Effective December 31, 2008, licensees must comply with the client identification and verification requirements set out in By-law 7.1, Part III, unless they fall within the stated exemptions.

APPENDIX 3.1
Sample Retainer Agreement in a Collection File

[letterhead]

Retainer Agreement
General

[date]

[client name and address]

Dear [client name]:

Re: [description of matter]

1. Description of Services

You have asked us, and we have agreed, to act for you in the matter described below. On [date], we [met/spoke] to discuss the scope of our firm's intended representation. We covered this subject in some detail and considered the nature of our fee arrangement. The purpose of this letter is to summarize and confirm the terms of your engagement of us.

You retain us to represent you in connection with [description of matter]. We anticipate that our representation will involve taking the following steps on your behalf:

(a) [describe]

(b) [describe]

(c) [describe]

At this time we have not been retained to represent you generally or in connection with any other matter. We will not be performing the following services:

(d) [describe]

(e) [describe]

(f) [describe]

[Optional] Your desired outcome and time frame for resolution of this matter is as follows:

[describe]

[Optional] We will work with you toward your desired outcome. However, all legal actions are subject to many possible variables, including the demeanour and recollection of witnesses, the availability of substantiating documents and other evidence, and the evidence marshalled by the other side—all of which affect the decision of a judge or jury. Accordingly, we cannot guarantee that your desired result will in fact be achieved. For us to work toward your desired outcome, it will be necessary for you to abide by the terms described in this letter.

2. Paralegals

We expect that most of the work will be performed or supervised by myself (a partner in this firm), assisted by [name], an [associate/student] in this firm. However, we reserve the right to assign other paralegals in our firm to perform legal services if in our judgment that becomes necessary or desirable.

3. Fees

(a) Our fee will be based principally on the time spent by us on your behalf. Records of all time will be kept and accounts will then be prepared and sent to you periodically.

Our hourly rates range from $[amount] for students to $[amount] for my associate to $[amount] for me.

While we expect that our fee will be calculated on the basis of our regular hourly rates, we reserve the right to charge more in appropriate cases, such as pressing circumstances, the requirement for work outside normal business hours, exceptionally successful or efficient representation, or special demands on us.

You will be charged GST on fees and GST on some disbursements.

(b) [Optional] Based on our consideration of the materials and information you have provided to us, and assuming that there are no further developments or information that would cause us to vary our preliminary opinion and that nothing out of the ordinary is encountered in the course of completing this matter, we estimate that our fee, excluding disbursements, will be approximately $[amount]. We are not guaranteeing that we can accomplish the work for that sum, but are representing to you that in our judgment that amount appears reasonable under the circumstances.

4. Expenses and Allocated Charges (also called disbursements)

You will be responsible for reimbursing us for expenses (also called disbursements) we incur on your behalf and for office charges allocated to your file. These include long distance calls, faxes, postage, deliveries, travel expenses, photocopying, and government filing and search charges; the fees of agents who conduct investigations, searches, and registrations; and all other reasonable out-of-pocket expenses and office charges. We do not charge for staff overtime on evenings or weekends in order to meet time deadlines.

5. Interest

Payment is due on all of our accounts when rendered. If any account is not paid within 30 days, interest will be charged on the outstanding balance at a rate of [rate]% per annum from the date of the account, until paid.

... / 3

6. Retainer

Before we begin work on your behalf, we require a retainer in the amount of $[amount]. The retainer will be placed in our trust account and will serve as a source of payment for all or part of our account or accounts when rendered. You will be asked to replenish the retainer from time to time. Any unused portion will be returned to you upon the completion or termination of our services.

7. Termination of Legal Services

You have the right to terminate our services to you upon written notice to us.

Subject to our obligations to you to maintain proper standards of professional conduct, we reserve the right to terminate our services to you for good reasons, which include but are not limited to:

(a)   if you fail to cooperate with us in any reasonable request;

(b)   if our continuing to act would be unethical or impractical;

(c)   if our retainer has not been paid; or

(d)   if you fail to pay our accounts when rendered.

If you terminate our services or we withdraw, you will be responsible only for our fees and expenses up until the time we stop acting for you.

If you terminate our services or we withdraw, the following documents and information will be returned to you:

[list documents and information]

Agreement

You may want to have this agreement reviewed by another paralegal or a lawyer.

If you want us to proceed on the terms described above, please sign the enclosed copy of this letter in the space provided and return it to us, together with a retainer in the sum of $[amount], in the enclosed self-addressed envelope. If you decide that you do not want us to proceed on your behalf in this matter, please inform us promptly.

Yours truly,

[paralegal firm name]

[signature]

[signatory name]

Paralegal

I have read and understand the retainer agreement, and agree to its terms.

_____   _____

Client's signature   Date

[Adapted from the precedent retainer agreement at www.lawpro.ca.]

APPENDIX 3.2
Verification of Identity (Individual)

[PARALEGAL FIRM NAME]

Paralegals

VERIFICATION OF IDENTITY

(For use where the client or third party is an individual)

Name: _____

Address (home): _____

Telephone number (home): _____

Address (business): _____

Telephone number (business): _____

Occupation(s): _____

Original Document Reviewed—Copy Attached

_____ Driver's Licence

_____ Birth Certificate

_____ Passport

_____ Other (specify type): _____

Meeting date identity verified: _____

Identity verified by: _____

Date file reviewed by paralegal: _____

Name of paralegal: _____

APPENDIX 3.3
Verification of Identity (Organization)

[PARALEGAL FIRM NAME]

Paralegals

VERIFICATION OF IDENTITY

(For use where the client or third party is an organization)

Name: _____

Address (business): _____

Telephone number (business): _____

Incorporation or Business Identification Number: _____

Place of issue of number: _____

Type of business or activity: _____

Person Authorized to Instruct

Name: _____

Position: _____

Telephone number: _____

Original Document Reviewed—Copy Attached

_____ Driver's Licence

_____ Birth Certificate

_____ Passport

_____ Other (specify type): _____

Names and occupation(s) of directors:

[list]

Names, addresses and occupation(s) of owners or shareholders owning a 25% interest or more of the organization or shares in the organization:

[list]

Original Document Reviewed—Copy Attached

_____ Certificate of Corporate Status

_____ Annual Filings of the Organization (specify type): _____

_____ Partnership Agreement

_____ Trust Agreement

_____ Articles of Association

_____ Other (specify type): _____

Meeting date identity verified: _____

Identity verified by: _____

Date file reviewed by paralegal: _____

Name of paralegal: _____

APPENDIX 3.4
Attestation for Verification of Identity When the Client or Third Party Is Present in Canada and Is Not Instructing the Paralegal Face-to-Face

INSTRUCTIONS

The Attestor should photocopy the identity document being used to verify identity and ensure that it is legible, unexpired, and shows the name of the person whose identity is being verified, the number of the document, the name of the issuing authority, the date of issue, and a photograph of the person.

The Attestor will *print* the following attestation on the photocopy and date and sign the attestation.

> I, the Attestor named below, hereby certify to [name of paralegal receiving the attestation] that I met with [name of person] on [date] and verified this person's identity by examining the original of this person's identity document, of which a photocopy is contained on this page. The photograph in the identity document is a true likeness of the said person, and to the best of my knowledge and belief the identity document that I examined is valid and unexpired.
>
> Attested to by mc at _____, on _____ ___, 20__.

Signature of Attestor: _____

Printed Name of Attestor: _____

Title or Profession of Attestor: _____

Address of Attestor for Service: _____

_____

Telephone Number of Attestor: _____

KEY TERMS

client	joint retainer
retained	joint clients
prospective client	independent legal advice
paralegal–client relationship	instructions
confidential information	client under disability
conflict-checking system	minor
paralegal–client retainer	litigation guardian
retainer	phantom client
money retainer	client identification
non-engagement	client verification
non-engagement letter	funds
scope of the retainer	negotiable instrument
fees	public company
disbursements	private company
trust account	due diligence
limited scope retainer	

REFERENCES

Law Society of Upper Canada (LSUC), By-Laws (Toronto: LSUC, 2005); available online at http://www.lsuc.on.ca/regulation/a/by-laws.

Law Society of Upper Canada (LSUC), Paralegal Professional Conduct Guidelines (Toronto: LSUC, 2008) ("the Guidelines"); available online at http://www.lsuc.on.ca/paralegals/a/paralegal-professional-conduct-guidelines.

Law Society of Upper Canada (LSUC), Paralegal Rules of Conduct (Toronto: LSUC, 2007, as amended) ("the Rules"); available online at http://www.lsuc.on.ca/paralegals/a/paralegal-rules-of-conduct.

Rules of the Small Claims Court, O. Reg. 258/98.

REVIEW QUESTIONS

1. Define the following words and phrases. Provide the source of your definition, including the section or rule number.

   a. client;

   b. client identification;

   c. client under disability;

   d. client verification;

   e. confidential information;

   f. conflict-checking system;

   g. conflict of interest;

   h. engagement letter;

   i. funds;

   j. instructions;

   k. litigation guardian;

   l. non-engagement;

   m. non-engagement letter;

   n. paralegal–client relationship;

   o. paralegal–client retainer;

   p. phantom client;

   q. private company;

   r. public company;

   s. retainer agreement;

   t. scope of the retainer.

2. Mr. A calls your office and speaks to your legal assistant about a *Highway Traffic Act* matter. The trial is scheduled for next Wednesday. Your assistant takes down Mr. A's name, telephone number, and some details about the matter, including the trial date. He tells Mr. A that you will call him.

   Later the same day, you call Mr. A back. He does not answer the phone, and he does not have voicemail.

   On Wednesday morning, you receive a phone call from Mr. A. He is at court. "Where are you?" he says. "Today's the trial. Your secretary said you'd be here."

   a. Is Mr. A your client?

   b. Are you required to represent Mr. A at the trial of the *Highway Traffic Act* matter?

3. Your client is a small private company specializing in property management of multi-unit residential buildings, owned by a husband and wife. You handle their Landlord and Tenant Board matters. You have always taken instructions from the wife, but the husband has become more active in the business and recently has begun instructing you as well. His management style is very different from his wife's, and sometimes the instructions he gives you are different from those you have already received from his wife. What should you do?

4. You are contacted by Mrs. Q. She wants you to represent her 15-year-old son, P, in a Small Claims Court action for a slip and fall. You have never acted for Mrs. Q or P before. What should you do?

CHAPTER 4

Duty to Clients

LEARNING OBJECTIVES

After reading this chapter, you will understand:

- The role of the paralegal as fiduciary.
- The required standard of competence.
- The elements of competence.
- Communicating effectively with clients.
- Management of client expectations.
- The duty to be honest and candid when advising clients.
- The duty of confidentiality.
- Justified or permitted disclosure.
- The duty to avoid conflicts of interest.
- Preservation of client property.
- Withdrawal from representation.

THE PARALEGAL AS FIDUCIARY

The paralegal–client relationship is governed by a set of overlapping obligations and responsibilities (see Figure 4.1).

FIGURE 4.1 The Paralegal–Client Relationship

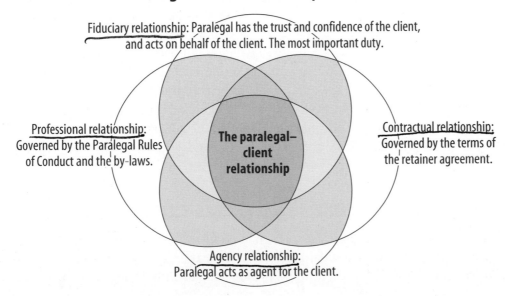

Many of a paralegal's duties and obligations to a client arise out of the fiduciary relationship between the paralegal and the client. A **fiduciary relationship** is a relationship of absolute trust and confidence between two persons, in which one person (the **fiduciary**) is required to act with scrupulous good faith, honesty, and candour for the benefit of the other person. In the paralegal–client relationship, the paralegal is the fiduciary. The paralegal must put the client's interests ahead of her own in all dealings with the client. The client is entitled to place absolute confidence, reliance, and trust in the paralegal.

The fiduciary relationship between the paralegal and the client gives rise to a special standard of care, or ethical duty, based in the law of trusts. The paralegal must comply with this special standard of care for the benefit of the client. The standard of care imposes the duties of honesty and candour, confidentiality, avoidance of conflicts of interest, and accounting for client property. These duties characterize the paralegal–client relationship and are codified in the Paralegal Rules of Conduct.

COMPETENCE (RULE 3.01; GUIDELINE 6)

General

The *Law Society Act* (s. 41) states that a licensee fails to meet standards of professional competence if there are deficiencies in any of the following:

- the licensee's knowledge, skill, or judgment;

- the licensee's attention to the interests of clients;

- the records, systems, or procedures of the licensee's professional business; or

- other aspects of the licensee's professional business; and

the deficiencies give rise to a reasonable apprehension that the quality of service to clients may be adversely affected.

Like all professionals, paralegals are required to be knowledgeable about the areas in which they provide legal services. A client hires a paralegal because the paralegal has knowledge and skills the client does not have. A paralegal who holds herself out as having certain kinds of expertise must ensure that she does in fact possess that expertise and can apply it for the benefit of her clients.

Paralegals who fail to meet standards of professional competence when providing legal services to the public may cause harm to their clients, and to their business partners and associates. They may also bring the paralegal profession and the justice system into disrepute.

The Competent Paralegal (Rules 3.01(1), (2), (3))

Rule 3.01(1) imposes a general obligation to perform any legal services undertaken on a client's behalf to the standard of a competent paralegal. You shall not undertake to represent a client in a matter unless you are familiar with the legal principles and procedures governing the applicable area of law, or are confident that you can become familiar with those legal principles and procedures in a timely and cost-effective manner.

If at any stage of the matter you discover that you are not competent to complete the tasks for which you were retained, you shall (rule 3.01(3)):

1. decline to act; or

2. obtain the client's consent to retain, consult, or collaborate with another licensee who is competent to perform the task and is licensed to do so.

When you are first approached by a client about a particular matter, you shall carefully consider whether you are competent to provide the legal services required. When assessing your own competence, keep in mind that a lack of competence on your part may do the client a disservice, bring discredit to the paralegal profession, and bring the administration of justice into disrepute. The best time to turn your mind to this is before accepting the retainer, at which time you may decline to act if you are not satisfied that you possess the required knowledge and skills. If you decline to act, you should consider referring the client to another paralegal or a lawyer with the required expertise. You should also consider sending a non-engagement letter to the client confirming that you have not accepted the retainer and stating your reasons.

Sometimes a matter takes a direction that could not be anticipated when you accepted the retainer. If you are no longer competent to act for a client because of unforeseen developments in an ongoing matter, you may consider withdrawing from representation. Subject to restrictions upon withdrawal in criminal and quasi-criminal cases and the direction of a tribunal, lack of competence is a ground for mandatory withdrawal of legal representation (rule 3.08(5)(e)).

If you have already agreed to the retainer, you may continue to represent the client if (1) you advise the client that you are not competent to perform a particular task, and (2) you obtain the client's consent to obtain expert advice or assistance from another licensee who is competent and licensed to perform the task.

Regardless of expertise, no paralegal licensee should provide legal services to a client in an unauthorized area of law. Clients with such matters should be directed to the Lawyer Referral Service (1-900-565-4577) or referred to a lawyer.

Who Is Competent? (Rule 3.01(4))

A **competent paralegal** is a paralegal who has and applies the relevant skills, attributes, and values appropriate to each matter undertaken on behalf of a client, including (1) knowledge; (2) client service and communication; (3) practice management; (4) skills and judgment; and (5) continuing education or professional development.

KNOWLEDGE

A competent paralegal is required to know general legal principles and procedures, and the substantive law and procedures with respect to the legal services the paralegal provides (rule 3.01(4)(a)). **Substantive law** is the statutory law and jurisprudence

---

BOX 4.1

Should You Accept the Retainer?

Scenario

You are a licensed paralegal specializing in *Highway Traffic Act* matters. You also do some residential tenancies work.

You have been approached by a residential tenant who has applied to the Landlord and Tenant Board for an abatement (reduction) of rent on grounds of non-repair of the premises by the landlord. The matter went to voluntary mediation but did not settle. A hearing date has been set for two weeks' time. The tenant has come to you because she does not feel comfortable about going to a hearing without representation.

The residential tenancies matters that you have handled have all been landlord applications for termination for non-payment of rent. Should you accept the retainer?

Discussion

This application is at an advanced procedural stage, with a hearing in two weeks' time. The principles governing landlord applications for termination for non-payment of rent are different from those governing a tenant application for a rent abatement. It appears that you do not have the knowledge and skills required to represent this client at the hearing, and you have very little time to acquire them. You probably are not competent to handle the matter, and should decline the retainer.

Practice Management Tip

You should send the client a non-engagement letter confirming that you are declining the retainer. You should urge the client to seek other legal representation. You should consider referring the client to another paralegal or a lawyer with expertise in the area, if you know of such a person.

You possess confidential information about this client. The client's name and the name of the respondent landlord should be entered into your conflict-checking system. The duty of confidentiality and the duty to avoid conflicts of interest continue indefinitely. ◇

---

that creates, defines, and interprets the rights and obligations of those who are subject to it. **Procedural law** sets out the methods or procedures for enforcement of those rights or redress for a wrong or harm.

In addition to knowing the law, the competent paralegal shall (rule 3.01(4)(b)):

- investigate facts,

- identify issues,

- ascertain client objectives,

- consider all possible options, and

- advise the client upon appropriate courses of action.

You should consider the client's circumstances when advising him as to the next steps that are most likely to meet his goals, at the same time advising him of the likely risks and costs associated with pursuing those outcomes. If some or all of the client's objectives are not achievable, the client should be advised of that.

This process of evaluating facts and issues with reference to client goals and expectations should happen at every stage of the proceeding, as your knowledge of the facts, issues, and possible outcomes evolves.

CLIENT SERVICE AND COMMUNICATION

A competent paralegal is a paralegal who communicates effectively with clients. Effective, timely communication promotes good client relations, and protects you in the event of a breakdown in the paralegal–client relationship.

Effective communication includes:

1. effective listening, to determine what the issues are and what the client wants or expects;

2. advising the client as to the merits (if any) of his case, appropriate courses of action, and possible outcomes and their cost;

3. keeping the client fully informed of all steps (other than routine matters) being taken in the matter and their cost; and

4. obtaining and confirming client instructions when necessary.

A written confirmation of the terms of the paralegal–client retainer, by way of a retainer agreement or engagement letter, is an excellent communication tool for managing client expectations about what the paralegal will do and at what cost from the outset of the paralegal–client relationship.

You should be cautious about giving unqualified assurances at the commencement of the paralegal–client relationship, when, in spite of your and the client's best efforts, you may not have complete information. Any predictions about outcomes that you make at the commencement of the paralegal–client relationship (for example, in a retainer agreement) should clearly state the facts, circumstances, and assumptions on which you are relying.

During the course of the retainer, as your knowledge of the facts, issues, and possible outcomes evolves, you may find that you can no longer meet the client's goals. Or, your client's expectations may change over time, so that the retainer agreement no longer addresses the client's goals. In either of these cases, you must advise the client of the situation and obtain the client's instructions. You should confirm the client's instructions and the particulars of any new agreement in writing.

The economics of a small paralegal practice may not always be conducive to effective client communication. If you operate a busy legal services practice that depends on competitive fees and high volume to generate profit, you may be disinclined to confirm every client retainer in writing, or keep the client informed of steps being taken in the matter. It may not seem cost-effective to report the outcome to the client in writing. However, it is sound practice management to do these things. Not doing them may adversely affect the quality of your service to clients, cause damage to the paralegal–client relationship, and bring the paralegal profession into disrepute.

> **BOX 4.2**

Reminder: Write It Down!

One of the most important things to remember when communicating with clients is: *always write it down*. And when you have written it down, *put it in the client file*. This rule applies whether you are using a pen and paper, or keyboarding. During the initial consultation, you should listen carefully to what the client is saying and take detailed notes. You should keep a written record of every telephone conversation. If you are communicating by email, all email to and from your client should be stored in a special folder. Copies of all notes and correspondence should be kept in an appropriate subfile in the client file.

Paralegal Practice Tip: Initial Client Consultation

During the initial consultation, you should take detailed notes of what the client says and of what you say to the client. You may wish to use a standard checklist, covering topics such as the following:

- how the client heard about you (for marketing purposes);
- how the client's identification was verified;
- whether the client's matter falls within authorized areas of paralegal practice;
- whether the client's matter falls within your areas of professional competence;
- whether a conflict check has been performed, and its results (ideally, the conflict check should take place before the initial consultation);
- approaching procedural deadlines or limitation periods;
- the client's expectations; and
- whether those expectations are reasonable in the circumstances.

Whether or not the initial client consultation results in a retainer, you should open a new file in the matter. The conflict check and your notes of the consultation should be put in the file. The file should have a unique file number assigned to it, so that you can track it in your file management system and in your conflict-checking system.

Listen carefully   Take detailed notes   File everything

◇

PRACTICE MANAGEMENT

Guideline 6 states that practice management includes ensuring that you have enough staff to assist you in meeting your professional obligations, including your obligation to maintain books and records in compliance with By-law 9. It also includes managing client information and expectations, managing your staff and field placement students, time management, and financial management. You cannot provide quality legal services to your clients if you do not have effective practice management tools and procedures in place.

Guideline 6 recommends the following practice management tools:

- a policies and procedures manual for staff;
- a conflict-checking system;
- a tickler or reminder system;

- docketing your time; and

- filing, organizational, and storage systems for management of client information.

Appropriate technology can also be very helpful in managing a busy legal services practice efficiently and cost-effectively.

Practice management will be discussed in Chapter 7.

APPLYING SKILLS AND JUDGMENT

When beginning a new client matter, a competent paralegal uses his knowledge of general legal principles and procedures and of substantive law and procedures to (1) gather, review, and consider all necessary and available information; and (2) make appropriate recommendations to the client as to courses of action appropriate to the client's goals and circumstances.

Having obtained the client's instructions, a competent paralegal then uses his judgment and the appropriate skills to implement the chosen course(s) of action. Appropriate skills include (rule 3.01(4)):

- legal research,

- analysis,

- applying legal principles to the relevant facts,

- writing and drafting,

- negotiation,

- alternative dispute resolution,

- advocacy, and

- problem-solving.

In addition to applying his skills, the competent paralegal must also apply his **professional judgment** to client matters, as well as to his other activities as a paralegal. In this context, judgment means the capacity to assess situations or circumstances carefully and to make sensible decisions.

Where client matters are concerned, this includes (guideline 6):

- being able to understand how legal principles apply to the issues and relevant facts,

- giving careful consideration to the client matters the paralegal handles,

- understanding and applying any relevant rules or by-laws, and

- making decisions that are reasonable and sensible in view of the client's circumstances.

Where a competent paralegal's professional conduct is concerned, he must:

- know and understand the Rules,

- understand why each Rule is important, and

- use the Rules to guide his conduct.

The Rules cannot address every situation. Rule 3.01 requires competent paralegals to comply with both the letter and the spirit of the Rules. Complying with the letter of a rule means complying with its literal meaning—the words on the page—but not necessarily with the intent or principle behind the rule. Complying with the spirit of a rule means that you conduct yourself in accordance with the intent or principle behind the rule, even though that intent or principle may not be expressly stated in the rule. Rule 1.03, Standards of Paralegals, contains a list of principles to be considered when interpreting and applying the Rules.

CONTINUING LEGAL EDUCATION AND PROFESSIONAL DEVELOPMENT

A competent paralegal is a paralegal who pursues appropriate training and development to maintain and enhance his knowledge and skills (rule 3.01(4)(j)) and adapts to changing requirements, standards, techniques, and practices (rule 3.01(4)(k)). Maintaining competence is an ongoing professional commitment that requires a paralegal to constantly assess his knowledge and skills (guideline 6).

The professional obligation to remain competent is ongoing. To remain competent, you must keep abreast of changes in the law and in legal practice. You must be adaptable to change, and you must be prepared for lifelong learning. You must assess your knowledge and skills on a regular basis to see if there are areas that require improvement. If there are, you should seek appropriate training and development.

The Law Society has established minimum expectations for professional development and continuing legal education (CLE). Professional development and continuing legal education are not mandatory. However, paralegal licensees are required to report the self-study and CLE they undertake each year in the Paralegal Annual Report (PAR).

Professional development consists of self-study and participation in CLE activities and programs. Self-study activities include online CLE, and reading or conducting file-specific or work-related research from law reports, legal journals, case law, statutes and regulations, relevant interdisciplinary materials, CLE materials, online sources, and texts.

The professional development minimum expectation for self-study is 50 hours of self-study annually (about one hour of reading work-related materials or file-related research per week). The minimum expectation for CLE is 12 hours of continuing legal education annually (two full-day or three half-day programs per year).

Meeting the minimum expectations for professional development is not mandatory. However, if there are reasonable grounds for believing a paralegal is failing or has failed to meet standards of professional competence as defined in s. 41 of the *Law Society Act*, and a practice review is ordered or a competence hearing authorized, the paralegal's participation or lack of participation in CLE and self-study may be relevant.

For more information on professional development and CLE, go to the "Practice Resources" section at the Law Society website (www.lsuc.on.ca).

FAILURE TO BE COMPETENT

Guideline 6 points out that the standard set by rule 3.01 is one of competence, not perfection. An error or omission may give a client grounds to commence an action against you for damages for negligence or breach of contract. This does not necessarily mean that you have not complied with the standard of competence required by rule 3.01.

Conversely, the fact that you have never been sued by a client does not mean that you are competent. You may conduct your practice in such a way that you are routinely in breach of rule 3.01. Examples of non-compliant conduct include poor client communication, acceptance of client matters for which you lack appropriate knowledge and skills, exercising poor judgment in client matters, and advising clients inappropriately. Your non-compliance may be unintentional. Absent a client complaint, a failure to report, or a practice review, your non-compliance may never come to the attention of the Law Society. Nevertheless, you may be in breach of your professional obligations, and if you are, you bring the paralegal profession into disrepute. This is why it is essential that all paralegals read, understand, and comply with the Rules, the Guidelines, and the by-laws.

ADVISING CLIENTS (RULE 3.02; GUIDELINE 7)

General (Rules 3.02(1), (2))

HONESTY AND CANDOUR

A paralegal must be honest and candid when advising a client. This is true whether the client is seeking to retain you in a matter or is a casual client seeking quick advice.

In this context, being **candid** means being forthright and sincere, and looking at both sides of each issue without bias. You must advise the client honestly and candidly of the applicable law, the client's options, possible outcomes, and possible risks. Your advice should enable the client to make informed decisions and give appropriate instructions in the matter.

You should always ensure that clients, including prospective clients, understand that you are a paralegal, not a lawyer.

You must never undertake or provide advice regarding a matter that is outside the scope of permissible practice for paralegals.

When advising a client, you must never knowingly assist in or encourage any dishonesty, fraud, crime, or illegal conduct. You must not instruct a client on how to violate the law and avoid punishment.

BAD NEWS

Clients like to hear good news. If they intend to sue someone in Small Claims Court for an unpaid debt, they want to hear that they have a good case and will get their money back. If they are trying to evict a tenant from rental housing, they want to hear that they will get an eviction order. If they are fighting a speeding ticket, they want to hear that the case will be thrown out due to a deficiency on the face of the charging document.

Your duty to be honest and candid applies when the news is good and when it is bad. The downside of being honest and candid about bad news is that, if the client is not happy with what he hears, he may seek legal assistance elsewhere. In a competitive market, it can be difficult to let any client walk out the door, however unreasonable his expectations. Nonetheless, your professional duty requires you to give honest, candid advice as to the merits of the matter and whether the client's objectives are achievable.

In situations where you decline to accept a retainer or a client declines to retain you after the initial consultation, you should send the client a non-engagement letter, confirming that you will not be acting in the matter.

THE RETAINER

When advising the client, you should establish the scope of the retainer—that is, what legal services will be provided and at what cost, specific client goals, and any other relevant conditions. You should discuss these terms with the client and obtain the client's agreement to them. You should confirm the terms in writing by way of a retainer agreement or engagement letter.

Generally, you do not have to seek client instructions for decisions that require the exercise of your professional judgment as to how the matter should proceed. However, you should explain the circumstances in which you may not be able to accept or act on the client's instructions—for instance, if following them would cause you to violate the Rules.

You should also explain to both clients and prospective clients that you are a paralegal, not a lawyer.

BOX 4.3

When Should I Ask My Client for Instructions?

Clients hire you because you have professional knowledge and competence that they do not, and they pay you for that knowledge and competence.

For example, if you are representing a plaintiff in a Small Claims Court proceeding, you are expected to apply your knowledge and skills to advancing the matter through the various procedural stages without seeking the client's instructions at every stage. Doing so would be a waste of your time and the client's money. However, you should keep the client informed of the progress of the matter.

What if the defendant makes an offer to settle? You should inform your client of the terms of the offer. Keeping in mind your duty to promote compromise and settlement, you should advise him whether you think the offer is reasonable or unreasonable, and why. Depending on the circumstances, you may wish to advise your client to make a counter-offer.

The final decision about accepting the offer, rejecting the offer, or making a counter-offer must be the client's, unless you have a written agreement or written instructions to the contrary. You cannot accept or reject the offer, or make a counter-offer, without first obtaining the client's instructions to do so.

In a provincial offences or criminal matter, you should never enter into an agreement with a prosecutor about a guilty plea without first advising your client about the prospects for an acquittal and the consequences of the guilty plea, ensuring that the client understands the elements of the offence, and obtaining the client's voluntary instructions to agree to the guilty plea. ◇

Client Dishonesty or Fraud (Rules 3.02(3), (4))

When advising a client, you must never knowingly assist in or encourage any dishonesty, fraud, crime, or illegal conduct. You must not instruct a client on how to violate the law and avoid punishment (rule 3.02(3)).

You must take all reasonable measures to avoid becoming the tool or dupe of an unscrupulous client or that person's associates (rule 3.02(4)). Guideline 7 recommends making reasonable inquiries to obtain information about the client and the purpose of the retainer, and keeping written notes of the results of those inquiries. Reasonable measures also include complying with the client verification requirements set out in Part III of By-law 7.1 (discussed in Chapter 3) and complying with By-law 9.

By-law 9, Part III, which governs cash transactions, prohibits licensees from accepting or receiving cash from a person in respect of any one client file in an aggregate amount of 7,500 or more Canadian dollars (s. 4(1)). If the cash is in a foreign currency, the value of the foreign currency when converted to Canadian dollars shall not exceed that amount. By-law 9, s. 19 sets out additional bookkeeping requirements for cash receipts.

If you are employed or retained by an organization to act in a matter and you know that the organization intends to act dishonestly, fraudulently, criminally, or illegally, then in addition to your obligations under rules 3.02(3) and (4), you must (rule 4.1):

- advise the person from whom you take instructions that the proposed conduct would be dishonest, fraudulent, criminal, or illegal;

- if that person refuses to take any action to prevent the proposed wrongful conduct, advise the organization's chief legal officer and/or the chief executive officer that the proposed conduct would be dishonest, fraudulent, criminal, or illegal;

- if those individuals refuse to take any action to prevent the proposed wrongful conduct, take the matter to the next level in the organization's reporting structure, continuing up through reporting levels until you find someone who agrees to prevent the conduct; or

- if the organization, in spite of your advice, intends to pursue the proposed course of conduct, withdraw from representation in accordance with rule 3.08.

If you are employed or retained by an organization to act in a matter and you know that the organization has acted or is acting dishonestly, fraudulently, criminally, or illegally, then in addition to your obligations under rules 3.02(3) and (4), you must (rule 4.2):

- advise the person from whom you take instructions, as well as the chief legal officer and/or the chief executive officer, that the conduct was or is dishonest, fraudulent, criminal, or illegal;

- if those individuals refuse to take any action to stop the wrongful conduct, take the matter to the next level in the organization's reporting structure, continuing up through reporting levels until you find someone who agrees to put a stop to the conduct; or

- if the organization, in spite of your advice, continues with the wrongful conduct, withdraw from representation in accordance with rule 3.08.

Withdrawal from representation (rule 3.08) is discussed at pages 111 to 116 in this chapter.

Settlement (Rules 3.02(5), (6))

Rule 3.02 requires a paralegal to advise and encourage a client to compromise or settle a dispute whenever it is possible to do so on a reasonable basis. As well, a paralegal must discourage a client from commencing ill-advised legal proceedings.

For every dispute, you shall consider the use of alternative dispute resolution. **Alternative dispute resolution** is resolution of a dispute through negotiation, mediation, arbitration, or similar means, instead of litigation. If appropriate, you shall inform the client of any available alternative dispute resolution options and, if the client instructs you to do so, take steps to pursue them.

ILL-ADVISED LITIGATION

The best possible outcome for your client is not always achieved by a court or tribunal proceeding. In some cases, it may be advisable to take no legal action at all. Some clients believe that a sense of grievance—of having been wronged by others—automatically entitles them to some sort of remedy at law. If there is no legal basis for a dispute, you must advise the client of this at the outset.

If the client matter has serious weaknesses, you must discuss those weaknesses (as well as any strengths) candidly with the client, and advise the client of the possible consequences of commencing litigation.

In the end, it is the client's decision whether or not to commence a legal proceeding. All you can do is give the client honest, candid advice about the merits of the matter and potential outcomes. If, having heard your opinion, the client decides to commence a proceeding that you believe to be without merit, you may wish to consider declining the retainer. If the client's motive for commencing the litigation is to harass or maliciously injure another party, you must decline the retainer (rule 3.08(5)(c)).

COMPROMISE AND SETTLEMENT

You must advise and encourage a client to compromise or settle a dispute whenever it is possible to do so on a reasonable basis (rule 3.02(5)).

The costs of legal proceedings are not just monetary. There is also a certain amount of wear and tear on the parties and on others associated with the matter. Litigation tends to keep alive grievances and ill-feeling that might otherwise dissipate over time. It can be very stressful, and it is often time-consuming. **Compromise and settlement** means that a party to a dispute agrees to waive some part of what is owing or make other concessions in order to resolve a matter without the additional costs, delay, and uncertainty of continuing a legal proceeding.

You should seek your client's instructions to make an offer to settle to the other party as soon as reasonably possible in the proceeding. Before making an offer to settle, you should discuss possible terms with your client and obtain his informed

Difficult Clients

Dealing with difficult clients can be very challenging. Difficult clients are often extremely demanding and very hard to satisfy. They may ignore or misinterpret your advice. They require much more time, effort, and attention than your other clients.

You should consider avoiding difficult clients altogether, if possible. If it is not possible, then you must implement strategies for managing the paralegal–client relationship.

The first step in managing a difficult client is to recognize one when you see one. To determine whether a particular client is or may be difficult, consider whether the client:

1. has come to you at the last minute, when a major deadline requiring a lot of work (such as a procedural deadline or a limitation period) is approaching;

2. has already hired and fired a number of paralegals;

3. has unrealistic expectations about the progress of the matter and its outcomes;

4. makes constant demands on you and your staff; and/or

5. questions and/or disregards your legal advice.

With a difficult client, you should consider confirming your discussions in writing at every stage of the paralegal–client relationship. If the client continues to be uncooperative or provides inappropriate instructions, you should consider taking steps to withdraw from representation.

Keep in mind that, when withdrawing from representation, you must try to minimize expense and avoid prejudice to the client, and to do all that can reasonably be done to facilitate the orderly transfer of the matter to another licensee (rules 3.08(10) and (11)).

For more information on difficult clients, see "Difficult Clients" in the Knowledge Tree in the "Practice Resources" section at the Law Society website, where you will also find a very useful article on this topic by Carole Curtis. ◈

instructions as to what those terms should be. You should confirm his instructions in writing.

Before accepting an offer to settle from another party, you should review the offer with your client. If you think the offer is reasonable and the client should accept the offer, you should discuss your reasons with the client and ensure that he understands them. You must obtain his informed instructions before accepting the offer, and you should confirm those instructions in writing.

If you receive an offer to settle from another party and you think your client should make a counter-offer, you should discuss your reasons with the client and ensure that he understands them. Before making the counter-offer, you must obtain the client's instructions to do so. You should confirm those instructions in writing.

When making an offer to settle or a counter-offer, you should include a term stating a date and time when the offer or counter-offer expires.

Negotiating settlement with self-represented parties presents unique challenges. The self-represented party must understand that you are acting exclusively in the interests of your own client. Unsophisticated individuals will sometimes mistake politeness and professionalism for sympathy with their own case. You must be very careful not to encourage this misconception or say anything to a self-represented opposing party that could be mistaken for legal advice.

Some tribunals offer alternative dispute resolution services. For example, the Landlord and Tenant Board offers voluntary mediation. In Statutory Accident Benefits Schedule claims under the *Insurance Act*, mediation is a mandatory first step in dispute resolution.

Client Under Disability (Rules 3.02(7), (8); Guideline 7)

A client under disability is an individual who lacks legal capacity to perform certain acts—for example, to understand legal advice and give instructions based on that understanding, and to enter into binding contracts.

If your client is a person whose ability to make decisions is impaired because he is a minor, is mentally disabled, or for some other reason, you shall maintain a normal professional relationship with the client to the extent that it is reasonably possible (rule 3.02(7)). If the disability is such that the client no longer has legal capacity to manage his or her legal affairs, you must take any steps that are appropriate to have a lawfully authorized representative appointed (rule 3.02(8)), keeping in mind your duty of confidentiality to the client.

When representing a client under disability, you must be sensitive to the client's individual needs and be aware of your duty to accommodate him.

Medical–Legal Reports (Rules 3.02(9), (10), (11))

In the course of providing legal services to a client, you may be required to obtain a medical–legal report from a physician or health professional containing that person's opinion or findings on the client's mental and/or physical health or other matters. Before ordering the report, you should obtain the client's instructions to do so, along with a written release signed by the client.

Guideline 7 recommends that you speak to the physician or health professional after he or she has been hired but before the report has been written, to find out if the report will advance the client's cause. If you are satisfied that the findings will not advance the client's cause, and subject to any legal requirements, you may decide not to obtain a written copy of the report.

If the medical–legal report contains a provision that the report shall not be shown to the client, your duty of honesty and candour to your client requires you to return the report immediately to the physician or health professional, without making a copy, unless you have specific instructions from your client to accept the report on that basis.

It is advisable to have a full and frank discussion with the physician or health-care professional before the report is prepared, so that you can inform him or her of your obligation to disclose its contents to your client.

If the report contains opinions or findings that, if disclosed, might cause harm to the client, you must try to persuade the client not to read the report. If the client insists, you must produce the report. You must also recommend that the client attend at the office of the physician or health professional who prepared the report, and review the report there. This will allow the client to ask questions about the opinions and findings in the report, and to benefit from the expertise of the physician or health professional in understanding the significance of the conclusions stated in the report.

Errors and Omissions (Rules 3.02(12), (13))

An **error** is an action by a legal representative that may result in harm to a client. An **omission** is a failure to act by a legal representative that may result in harm to a client.

You are responsible for your own errors and omissions in matters for which you are responsible, and for those of any persons acting under your supervision in matters for which you are responsible.

Paralegals are required to carry errors and omissions insurance as set out in By-law 6, Part II, s. 12(1). When dealing with errors or omissions, you must ensure that you comply with your duties to the client. At the same time, the insurer's rights must be preserved.

Before reporting an error or omission, you must:

1. be satisfied that the error or omission is or may be damaging to the client, and

2. be satisfied that the error or omission cannot be easily corrected.

If those preconditions are met, then you shall:

(a) promptly inform the client of the error or omission, being careful not to prejudice any rights of indemnity that the client or you may have under the errors and omissions insurance policy or otherwise;

(b) recommend that the client obtain legal advice elsewhere concerning any rights the client may have arising from the error or omission; and

(c) advise the client that in the circumstances you may no longer be able to act for the client.

As well, you must give prompt notice to your errors and omissions insurer of the circumstances giving rise to a possible claim, so that the client's protection from that source will not be prejudiced. When giving notice to the insurer, you must be careful to observe your duty of confidentiality to the client.

Official Language Rights (Rule 3.02(14))

French and English are the two official languages of Canada. When advising French-speaking clients, you shall, where appropriate, inform them of their language rights, including their right to be represented by a paralegal who is competent to provide legal services in the French language.

Guideline 7 recommends that you refer to the following, where appropriate, when advising the client:

- s. 19(1) of the *Constitution Act, 1982*, on the use of French or English in any court established by Parliament;

- s. 530 of the *Criminal Code*, on an accused's right to a trial before a court that speaks the official language of Canada that is the language of the accused;

- s. 126 of the *Courts of Justice Act*, which requires that a proceeding in which the client is a party be conducted as a bilingual (English and French) proceeding; and

- s. 5(1) of the *French Language Services Act*, for services available in French from Ontario government agencies and legislative institutions.

Claims Under the Statutory Accident Benefits Schedule (Rule 3.02(15))

A paralegal who is acting as an adviser, consultant, or representative to a person making a claim under the Statutory Accident Benefits Schedule to the *Insurance Act* shall comply with the Act, the regulations to the Act, and the Code of Conduct for Statutory Accident Benefits Representatives.

CONFIDENTIALITY (RULE 3.03; GUIDELINE 8)

Confidential Information (Rules 3.03(1), (2), (3))

THE DUTY

A paralegal shall, at all times, hold in strict confidence all information concerning the business and affairs of a client acquired in the course of their professional relationship and shall not disclose any such information unless expressly or impliedly authorized by the client or required by law to do so.

The **duty of confidentiality** means that you shall not share client information with anyone unless authorized to do so by the client or required to do so by law. The duty begins at the commencement of the paralegal–client relationship and continues indefinitely, regardless of whether differences have arisen between the paralegal and the client.

The paralegal shall ensure that the client's papers and other property are kept out of sight and out of reach of those not entitled to see them.

Guideline 8 provides the following context for the duty of confidentiality:

1. A paralegal cannot render effective professional service to a client, unless there is full and unreserved communication between them. The client must feel completely secure that all matters discussed with the paralegal will be held in strict confidence. The client is entitled to proceed on this basis, without any express request or stipulation.

2. A paralegal's duty of loyalty to a client prohibits the paralegal from using any client information for a purpose other than serving the client in accordance with the terms of the retainer. A paralegal cannot disclose client information to serve another client or for his or her own benefit.

The duty of confidentiality arises out of the fiduciary relationship between the paralegal and the client. As a fiduciary, the paralegal is required to act with scrupulous good faith, honesty, and candour for the benefit of the client. The paralegal must put the client's interests ahead of her own in all dealings with the client. The client is entitled to place absolute confidence, reliance, and trust in the paralegal. For that relationship of absolute trust to exist, the client must have complete confidence that information shared with the paralegal will not be passed on to others, except with the client's authorization or as required by law. The client must also have complete confidence that information shared with the paralegal will not be used for a purpose other than serving the client.

THE SCOPE OF THE DUTY

The duty of confidentiality applies to all information of any kind that you acquire from or on behalf of a client during the paralegal–client relationship, including the client's identity and the fact that the client has consulted or retained you. It also applies to information that is not relevant to the specific matter for which you have been retained, and to information about the client that others may already have.

The duty of confidentiality is owed to all clients of your paralegal firm by all paralegals in the firm, including associates, as well as anyone in your employment or under your supervision, including students.

Any time you hire new staff or accept a new field placement student, you should consider requiring them to review rule 3.03 and any applicable guidelines, and to swear an oath of confidentiality. The oath should be placed in their personnel file. If you have a confidentiality policy in your firm, it should state the possible sanctions for breach by staff or students of the duty of confidentiality.

You must never use confidential information for your own benefit, whether personal or financial, even if doing so does not harm your client. You must never use such information for the benefit of a third party. You must never use confidential information to the client's disadvantage.

DURATION OF THE DUTY OF CONFIDENTIALITY

The duty of confidentiality arises when the paralegal–client relationship begins. It applies to prospective clients, who may or may not retain you, and to clients who have retained you in a matter or a number of matters.

The duty of confidentiality continues indefinitely. This means that it continues:

- regardless of the brevity of the initial paralegal–client contact;

- regardless of whether or not the paralegal was actually retained by the client;

- after the professional relationship has ended, and regardless of the circumstances in which it ended;

- after the paralegal–client retainer has ended; and

- after the client's death.

The obligation to hold client information in strict confidence for an indefinite period applies to paralegals, employees, and field placement students. It continues whether or not a person is still employed by the firm where the confidential information was obtained.

> ### BOX 4.5
>
> ## What Not to Do: Use of Precedent Documents
>
> ### Scenario
>
> You are a student in a Paralegal program at an Ontario college. You are completing your field placement requirement in the collections department at a law firm. You have been given a lot of interesting work to do in collections, and you have kept copies of many of the documents you worked on to use as precedents.
>
> You are discussing field placements with some classmates one day. They are impressed by your enthusiasm, and ask if they can take a look at your precedent binder.
>
> You bring the binder to class the following week to show your classmates. The binder contains demand letters, reporting letters, Small Claims Court pleadings, and enforcement documents. Your classmates look through these documents with interest. They are particularly impressed by some of the corporate clients you have done work for.
>
> Have you breached the duty of confidentiality?
>
> ### Discussion
>
> As a paralegal student on placement, you owe the same duty of confidentiality to firm clients as do lawyers, paralegals, and employees of the firm. This is the case whether or not you took an oath of confidentiality. The duty of confidentiality extends beyond the details of individual cases, to the identity of your clients.
>
> You must seek the permission of your placement supervisor to retain client documents to use as precedents. If that permission is granted, you must be careful to remove names and all other identifiers from your documents. You should review your precedent documents with your field placement supervisor before leaving your placement, to ensure that all confidential information has been removed. You should keep your precedents to yourself. This includes pleadings, even though they are public documents available to anyone who requests access to the court file. Remember, just because client information is public does not mean that you are entitled to disclose it. Those seeking the information can get it from other sources. ◇

GOSSIP

You should never discuss a client or anything connected with a client matter with anyone not entitled to the information. Persons who are not entitled to client information include friends, spouses, partners, and members of your family. You should not share client information with them, even if the client is not named or identified and the discussion is couched in general terms. You should not talk about client matters in circumstances where third parties may overhear what you are saying. Friends, family members, and strangers who may overhear your conversation have no obligation to keep the information confidential. If they repeat the information to others, this could prejudice your client. Even if no prejudice to your client results, such conduct is a breach of the duty of confidentiality.

You should never discuss client matters in public areas of the paralegal firm, where you may be overheard by non-members of the firm.

What Not to Do: Gossip About Clients

Scenario

You are a paralegal student completing your field placement requirement in a paralegal firm. At the end of the last week of your placement, you arrange to meet with some other students from your program at a local restaurant for drinks and dinner, to celebrate the end of your placement. Over the course of the evening, you discuss a couple of your client files in general terms, without mentioning client names. People at adjoining tables can hear some of your remarks, but you think it is okay to talk about the files because the placement is over and no one will be able to figure out who you are talking about anyway.

Have you breached the duty of confidentiality?

Discussion

Yes. You shall not disclose client information to others, even in general terms, in any circumstances. Your duty to hold client information obtained during your field placement in strict confidence continues indefinitely. It does not end with the field placement. Finally, you should never gossip about clients, past or present, whether or not you are still working at the firm whose clients you are discussing.

Question: What would be the consequences for you if one of the people who overheard you gossiping at the restaurant was your placement supervisor? ◇

LITERARY WORKS

You are not permitted to use confidential information about a client for your own benefit, for the benefit of third parties, or to the disadvantage of the client. This restriction continues indefinitely. It applies whether you are writing a murder mystery, appearing on a television show to discuss your famous cases, or blogging on the Internet.

If you intend to use confidential information about a client in a publication of any kind, you must first obtain the client's authorization, if the client is alive. If the client is dead, you should seek authorization from the client's estate.

OFFICE PROCEDURES

A paralegal shall assume complete professional responsibility for all business entrusted to him or her (rule 8.01(1)). Among other things, this means that you are ultimately responsible for ensuring compliance with the duty of confidentiality in your firm. You should establish office procedures to ensure that client confidentiality is protected. Guideline 8 recommends the following:

- recording the identity and particulars of every client and potential client;

- screening for conflicts of interest when a potential client first contacts the firm, and prior to disclosure of confidential information by the client to the paralegal;

- establishing forms of acceptable communication between the paralegal and the client;

- taking steps to secure confidential information transmitted in an electronic form;
- ensuring that all staff and students understand their obligation to hold client information in strict confidence;
- keeping file cabinets away from areas to which members of the public have access;
- locking file cabinets when no one is in the office;
- placing computer monitors so that they cannot be viewed by members of the public;
- keeping client files out of sight;
- limiting staff access to client files to those who are working on them;
- shredding confidential information before discarding;
- ensuring that closed files are stored in a secure facility; and
- limiting access to confidential information by outside service providers.

An office policies and procedures manual is a useful management tool for improving staff efficiency and ensuring that staff, including field placement students, follow appropriate file management and other procedures to ensure client confidentiality. Office procedures are discussed in more detail in Chapter 7.

EXCEPTIONS TO RULE 3.03: CONFIDENTIALITY

Rule 3.03(1) provides exceptions to the general duty to hold all information concerning the business and affairs of a client in strict confidence. You may disclose client information if you are (1) expressly or impliedly authorized by the client to do so, or (2) required by law to do so.

Disclosure with Client Authority (Rule 3.03(1))

You may disclose confidential client information if the client consents to the disclosure. Client consent may be express or implied. **Express (or explicit) consent** means that the client provides you with spoken or written authorization to disclose particular information to specified third parties. **Implied consent** is not spoken or written down, but is implied by the paralegal–client relationship.

Office Procedures

Scenario

You are a paralegal licensee. You run a small but profitable practice and have one employee, an office assistant named Dana.

Dana's workspace is set up in the reception area. A counter separates her workspace from the reception area. Because your practice is a busy one, Dana's workspace is often covered with client files. Anyone standing at the counter can see the labels on the files, and the contents of any files that are open. People waiting in the reception area can overhear Dana's telephone conversations with clients.

For ready access, Dana keeps active files that she is not working on in a small, locked filing cabinet in her workspace in the reception area. Before she leaves at the end of the day, she is careful to refile any loose documents in the correct client files. She leaves the files she is working on in a neat pile by her computer monitor.

Question: Do your office procedures preserve client confidentiality? If not, what can be done to remedy this?

Discussion: You have set up your office space so that Dana answers client calls and works on client files in a public area. Client files should be kept out of sight of the public. They should be worked on in a private area, where others cannot see them. Client calls should be redirected from the reception area to offices or private areas where others cannot overhear them.

Dana keeps active files in her work area in the reception area. She keeps active files that she is not working on in a locked filing cabinet in her workspace. She leaves active files that she is working on stacked by her computer monitor, which is in a public area.

File cabinets should be kept away from areas in the firm to which the public has access. All files should be returned to file cabinets, in a storage area apart from the public areas, at the end of each working day. If the storage area is a separate room, the door should be locked. If the storage area is private but not in a separate room, the file cabinets should be locked.

It is not clear whether Dana's computer monitor is visible to the public. If it is, it should be moved to a location where it is not visible to the public, and you should consider installing a filter.

Question: Who is responsible for the breach of confidentiality?

Discussion: Rule 8.01(1) states that a paralegal shall assume complete professional responsibility for all business entrusted to him or her. This means that you are responsible for any breaches of client confidentiality that occur in your practice.

You are responsible for ensuring that all staff and students understand their obligation to hold client information in strict confidence. You are also responsible for implementing policies and procedures that make it possible for staff to do so. Even if Dana is aware of her obligation to hold client information in strict confidence, your office setup makes it difficult or impossible for her to comply. You are responsible for that non-compliance. ◈

EXPRESS CONSENT

Guideline 8 recommends that you consider the following issues when disclosing confidential information with the express authorization (spoken or written) of the client:

- Does the client understand her right to confidentiality?

- Does the client understand the possible consequences of the disclosure?

- Does the client show a clear, informed, and voluntary intention to waive the right to confidentiality?

- Is it advisable in the circumstances to obtain the client's authorization to disclose in writing?

If you decide that a written authorization is advisable, you must draft it carefully. You should explain its terms to the client. Any restrictions on disclosure should be clearly stated. The authorization should also state to whom you may disclose the information, and for what period of time, if that is appropriate.

You will find a sample client authorization for disclosure in Appendix 4.1.

IMPLIED CONSENT

Unless the client directs otherwise, you have implied consent to disclose confidential information to other paralegals and employees (including field placement students) who are working on the client file. You must ensure that anyone to whom confidential client information is disclosed understands his duty to hold that information in strict confidence.

You have implied consent to reveal certain client information if the nature of the client matter requires that disclosure. For example, in Small Claims Court proceedings, client information that would otherwise be confidential may be disclosed in pleadings and other court documents.

Disclosure Without Client Authority: Justified or Permitted Disclosure (Rules 3.03(4) to (8))

Justified disclosure occurs in situations where a paralegal must reveal confidential information without the client's authority. Justified disclosure is mandatory.

Permitted disclosure occurs in situations where a paralegal may reveal confidential information without the client's authority. Permitted disclosure is discretionary on the part of the paralegal.

In either set of circumstances, a paralegal shall not disclose more confidential information than is necessary (rule 3.03(8)).

Guideline 8 points out that this rule does not permit you to reveal confidential information about past criminal conduct.

JUSTIFIED DISCLOSURE (RULES 3.03(4), (8))

A paralegal must disclose confidential information when required by law or by order of a court or tribunal to do so.

When you are ordered by a court or tribunal to disclose confidential information, you should first satisfy yourself that the court or tribunal has jurisdiction to make the order. If you are not competent to determine this issue yourself, you should seek legal assistance.

If you are satisfied that the order is valid, you should advise your client of the terms of the order and of the obligation to comply with its terms.

You must not disclose more information than is required by the court or tribunal order.

PERMITTED DISCLOSURE (RULES 3.03(5) TO (8))

Permitted disclosure is at the discretion of the paralegal. Disclosure of confidential information without client authority is permitted in the following circumstances:

- if you believe upon reasonable grounds that there is an imminent risk to an identifiable person or group of death or serious bodily harm, including serious psychological harm that substantially interferes with health or well-being;

- to defend against allegations that you or your employees are guilty of a criminal offence involving a client's affairs;

- to defend against allegations that you or your employees are civilly liable with respect to a matter involving a client's affairs;

- to defend against allegations that you or your employees are guilty of malpractice or misconduct; and/or

- to establish or collect your fees.

You shall not disclose more confidential information than is necessary in any of the above situations (rule 3.03(8)).

Imminent Risk (Rules 3.03(5), (8))

You may reveal confidential information without client authority pursuant to rule 3.03(5) if:

- you believe upon reasonable grounds that there is an imminent risk to an identifiable person or group of death;

- you believe upon reasonable grounds that there is imminent risk to an identifiable person or group of serious bodily harm; and/or

- you believe upon reasonable grounds that there is imminent risk to an identifiable person or group of serious psychological harm that substantially interferes with health or well-being.

Guideline 8 points out that this rule does not permit you to reveal confidential information about past criminal conduct, or in order to prevent future illegal or criminal conduct that does not involve death, serious bodily harm, or serious psychological harm.

To determine whether this ground for permitted disclosure applies, you must evaluate the following factors.

Future Harm and Imminent Risk

The harm must be something that will occur in the future. If a client confesses to a harm committed in the past, you must keep the disclosure confidential.

"Imminent" means something that is pending—that is about to happen very soon. The client must threaten to commit the harm in the immediate future.

The threat must be unconditional. There must be no mention of intervening events or preconditions to causing the harm.

Death or Serious Bodily Harm

The imminent risk to the victim or victims must be death or serious bodily harm. Serious bodily harm includes serious psychological harm that substantially interferes with health or well-being—in other words, psychological damage that seriously undermines physical health.

Identifiable Person or Group

The client must threaten serious harm to a particular human being or group of human beings, and she must be specific when identifying them. Institutions and corporations are excluded from this category.

Reasonable Grounds

The test for reasonable grounds is both objective and subjective. Having heard the unconditional threat to cause death or serious bodily harm, you must decide whether the client might reasonably be expected to carry out the threat. You must consider what you know of the client, her means and capacity for committing the harm threatened, and any other relevant circumstances. This is the objective standard.

You must also personally believe, based on what you know of the client and the circumstances, that she will carry out the threat. This is the subjective standard.

Necessary to Prevent Death or Harm

Disclosure of confidential information without the client's authority is permitted only if all of the above conditions are satisfied and you are convinced that the disclosure is necessary to prevent the death or harm threatened by the client—in other words, the information necessary to prevent the harm is not available from any other source.

Rule 3.03(5) contemplates application to a court for an order permitting necessary disclosure where practicable.

Defending Civil Liability or Allegations of Misconduct (Rules 3.03(6), (8))

You may reveal confidential information without client authority to defend against allegations that you or your employees are:

- guilty of a criminal offence involving a client's affairs;
- civilly liable with respect to a matter involving a client's affairs; or
- guilty of malpractice or misconduct.

BOX 4.8

Reminder: Always Write It Down

If you find yourself in a situation to which rule 3.03(5) may apply, you should consider taking several steps. First, if it is feasible in the circumstances, you should discuss your concerns with your client, and try to suggest solutions. If your client is unreceptive, you should carefully consider what you know of your client, and the likelihood that he will cause harm or death to himself or to others. Remember, if the threat of harm or death is to others, they must be identifiable. If you are satisfied that your belief that harm or death will occur is reasonable, and that the harm or death is imminent, you should reveal only enough information to prevent it from occurring.

You should keep detailed notes of the circumstances that gave rise to your concerns, of any conversations with your client about your concerns, and of subsequent steps taken by you and your reasons for taking those steps. Your notes will help you respond to any future complaints or actions against you. ◇

When responding to allegations of criminal wrongdoing or civil liability, you are permitted to disclose only as much confidential information as is necessary to defend yourself against the allegations (rule 3.03(8)).

Establishing or Collecting Fees (Rules 3.03(7), (8))

A paralegal may disclose confidential information in order to establish or collect her fees.

You shall not disclose more confidential information than is necessary to establish a fee or collect an unpaid fee. If you use a collection agency to collect your unpaid accounts, you must limit the information you provide to the collection agency to what is necessary to collect your fees. Information that is not required for the collection process should be blocked out or deleted on any documents forwarded to the collection agency (guideline 8).

Other Obligations Relating to Confidential Disclosure

SECURITY OF COURT FACILITIES (RULES 3.03 AND 6.01(3))

A paralegal who has reasonable grounds to believe that a dangerous situation is likely to develop at a court facility shall inform the local police force and give particulars. This professional obligation is mandatory.

If the paralegal's reasonable belief is based on confidential information, the paralegal must consider her obligations under rule 3.03. Guideline 8 recommends that a paralegal who discloses confidential information to prevent a dangerous situation from developing at a court facility should consider providing this information to the court facility anonymously, or through another paralegal or a lawyer.

DUTY TO REPORT MISCONDUCT (RULES 3.03 AND 9.01(2))

If a paralegal learns of certain types of misconduct by another licensee, the paralegal shall report the misconduct to the Law Society unless doing so would be unlawful or would involve a breach of confidentiality between the paralegal and the paralegal's client. This professional obligation is mandatory.

If the paralegal learns of the misconduct of another licensee from a client, the paralegal must obtain the client's consent to disclose information about the client to the Law Society. You should consider obtaining the client's consent in writing.

If the client will not consent to disclosure of any information about herself to the Law Society, the paralegal must report the misconduct to the Law Society in a way that does not disclose any client information.

Rules 6.01(3) and 9.01(2) are discussed in more detail in Chapter 6.

PERSONAL INFORMATION PROTECTION AND ELECTRONIC DOCUMENTS ACT (PIPEDA)

The *Personal Information Protection and Electronic Documents Act* (PIPEDA) applies to the collection, use, or disclosure of personal information by organizations in the course of any commercial activity within a province (s. 4(1)). Organizations and/or activities in provinces that have adopted substantially similar privacy legislation may be exempted from PIPEDA by the federal government. Because there is no substantially similar privacy legislation that applies to commercial activity in the province, PIPEDA applies to commercial activity in Ontario.

PIPEDA sets up procedures for the collection, use, and disclosure of personal information. These procedures are intended to give individuals control over how their personal information is handled in the private sector. An organization is responsible for the protection of personal information and the fair handling of it at all times, both within the organization and in dealings with third parties.

In the course of providing legal services to the public, you collect, use, and disclose personal information about clients. That information is already protected by your professional and ethical duty to hold client information in strict confidence, and not to disclose it except with the client's authorization or as required by law. However, because paralegal firms are engaged in commercial activity in Ontario, PIPEDA applies to the provision of legal services. You must implement a privacy policy and procedures in compliance with PIPEDA requirements.

A fact sheet prepared by the Office of the Privacy Commissioner of Canada (available at http://www.privcom.gc.ca) outlines the Act's requirements. You must:

- obtain the consent of people whose personal information you collect, use, or disclose, except in a few specific and limited circumstances;

- use or disclose people's personal information only for the purpose for which they gave consent;

- even with consent, limit collection, use, and disclosure of personal information to purposes that a reasonable person would consider appropriate under the circumstances;

- permit individuals to see the personal information that your business holds about them, and to correct any inaccuracies; and

- advise people whose personal information you collect of procedures to follow if they believe their rights have been violated.

PIPEDA does not apply to an employee's name, title, business address, or telephone number, or other employee information gathered by organizations engaged in commercial activity in the private sector. However, you may wish to consider reviewing your privacy practices in employment, and including employees in your privacy policy.

CONFLICTS OF INTEREST (RULE 3.04; GUIDELINE 9)

General

A conflict of interest is any circumstance that may negatively affect a paralegal's ability to fulfill her ethical and professional obligations to the client. Conflicts of interest may arise at any time in a client matter, as the matter evolves, as new parties are added, and as new circumstances or information come to light.

Rule 3.04(1) defines "conflict of interest" or "conflicting interest" as an interest, financial or otherwise,

(a) that would be likely to have an adverse effect on a paralegal's judgment on behalf of, or loyalty to, a client or prospective client; or

(b) that a paralegal might be prompted to give preference to over the interests of a client or a prospective client.

A paralegal shall not advise or represent more than one side in a dispute (rule 3.04(2)). A **dispute** is an argument or disagreement between two or more persons in which the interest of one side is adverse to the interest of the other side. A paralegal cannot act for opposite sides, because to do so would adversely influence the paralegal's judgment and loyalty to the client.

A paralegal shall not act or continue to act in a matter when there is, or is likely to be, a conflicting interest unless, after disclosure adequate to make an informed decision, the client or prospective client consents (rule 3.04(3)).

CONFLICTS OF INTEREST ARISING FROM PERSONAL RELATIONSHIPS (RULE 3.04(1))

There is nothing in the Rules prohibiting a paralegal from providing legal services to family members or friends. However, you have the same duty to avoid conflicts of interest when representing friends and family members as you do when representing other clients. If there is anything in your personal relationship with a friend or a family member who is a prospective client that may affect adversely your judgment on behalf of or loyalty to that person, you should consider declining the retainer.

If a paralegal has a sexual or intimate relationship with a client, this may conflict with the paralegal's duty to provide objective, disinterested professional advice to the client, because the paralegal's personal feelings may cloud his or her judgment. Guideline 9 recommends that, before agreeing or continuing to act for a person with whom a paralegal has had a sexual or intimate relationship, the paralegal should consider the following factors:

- the vulnerability of the client, both emotional and economic;

- the fact that the paralegal–client relationship may create a power imbalance either in favour of the paralegal or the client;

- whether the personal relationship may jeopardize the client's right to have all information concerning the client's business and affairs held in strict confidence (for example, the question of whether certain information was acquired in the course of the paralegal–client relationship or in the course of the personal relationship may become an issue);

- whether the personal relationship may require the paralegal to act as a witness in the proceeding; and

- whether the personal relationship may interfere with the paralegal's fidiciary obligations to the client, including the paralegal's ability to exercise independent professional judgment and to fulfill obligations owed as an officer of the court and to the administration of justice.

Generally, there is no conflict of interest if another paralegal at the firm who does not have a personal or intimate relationship with the client handles the client's matter.

CONFLICTS OF INTEREST ARISING FROM OUTSIDE INTERESTS (RULES 3.04(1) AND 2.01(3), (4))

A paralegal who engages in another profession, business, occupation, or other outside interest, or who holds public office at the same time as he or she is providing legal services, shall not allow the outside interest or public office to jeopardize her integrity, independence, or competence, or to impair the exercise of her independent judgment on behalf of a client (rules 2.01(3), (4)).

Guideline 9 states that the term "outside interest" covers the widest possible range of activities, including activities that may overlap or be connected with the provision of legal services, such as acting as a director of a corporation or writing on legal subjects. It also covers activities in areas loosely connected or unconnected to the provision of legal services, such as business, politics, or the performing arts. The question of whether and to what extent it is proper for the paralegal to engage in the outside interest will be subject to any applicable by-laws or rule of the Law Society.

When acting in her outside role, a paralegal must continue to fulfill her obligations under the Rules. She must refrain from acting in a manner that would bring her or the paralegal profession into disrepute. Her conduct must be characterized by integrity and civility. She must continue to provide legal services to her clients to an acceptable standard of professional competence. She must avoid conflicts of interest and maintain confidentiality.

BOX 4.9

Personal Relationships

Scenario

Six months ago, you broke off a relationship with a man with whom you were sexually involved for over two years. You were never really committed to the relationship, and toward the end you became very impatient with his inability to make decisions and what you perceived as his manipulative behaviour and emotional dependency on you. When he began to pressure you to marry him, you ended the relationship.

For about two months after you stopped seeing him, he phoned and emailed you frequently, promising to change whatever was wrong and asking to see you. When you stopped responding to his calls and emails, they tapered off and finally ceased.

One day, your former partner contacts you at your firm. He assures you that his reasons for wanting to see you are purely professional—to consult with you about some problems he is having with his landlord.

You suspect that this is just his latest ploy for getting back into your life. You would prefer to have nothing more to do with him.

Are you obliged to represent this client?

Discussion

The Rules do not prohibit you from representing friends, family members, and persons with whom you have conducted an intimate relationship. However, you have a general right to decline to provide legal representation, and a professional obligation to avoid existing and potential conflicts of interest.

Referring to guideline 9, you should consider the vulnerability of the client, both emotional and economic, arising out of your past relationship and its breakdown; the fact that the paralegal–client relationship may create a power imbalance in your favour; and the possibility that your personal feelings of distaste and distrust may interfere with your ability to exercise independent professional judgment for the benefit of the client. Even if you are satisfied that there are no conflicts of interest at this time, it may be prudent in the circumstances to decline the retainer. You should confirm your decision in a non-engagement letter. The non-engagement letter must recommend that the client seek legal assistance from another paralegal or a lawyer. ◇

It is the paralegal's responsibility to determine whether involvement in the outside interest may impair her ability to act in the best interest of her clients, either because of an existing or potential conflict of interest or for some other reason. Where a conflict of interest exists, the paralegal must comply with rule 3.04.

If a paralegal holding public office continues to provide legal services to clients, he must guard against conflicts between his duties as a public official and his professional responsibilities to his clients. If there is a possibility of a conflict of interest, the Guidelines recommend that the paralegal avoid it by removing himself from any discussion and voting in a public capacity or by withdrawing from representation of the client.

The Duty to Avoid Conflicts of Interest: Prospective and Current Clients (Rules 3.04(1), (2), (3))

Because conflicts of interest may result in harm to the client, paralegals have an obligation to prospective clients, current clients, and former clients to avoid conflicts of interest and potential conflicts of interest.

CONFLICT-CHECKING SYSTEM

How do you find out whether or not there may be a conflict of interest in a particular client matter? To assist in avoiding conflicts of interest, paralegals should consider maintaining a searchable database of information about prospective, current, and former clients, as well as information about related persons and conflicting or adverse parties. The database should include fields for the following information (the list is not exhaustive):

- client's name, and aliases and former names, if applicable;

- client contact information;

- date the file was opened;

- client file name and active file code;

- subject matter of the file;

- date the file was closed, and closed file code; and

- names and contact information of related persons, and of conflicting or adverse parties (if available), cross-referenced to the client file.

The database may be maintained in a paper or electronic format. Some legal software applications automatically enter client and other data into a conflicts database as new electronic files are opened.

As part of your conflict-checking system, you should have standard office procedures in place for conducting conflict searches at critical points in the paralegal–client relationship. Your first search should take place after the initial contact with a prospective client. You should search for conflicts again when you have more information about the client, and related or adverse parties. If a retainer is entered into, you should conduct a conflict search any time a new party is added in a proceeding. If a conflict arises after you are retained, you may be required to withdraw from representing the client.

CLIENT CONSENT

The existence of a conflict or potential conflict does not always mean that you cannot represent the client. Rule 3.04(3) permits you to act or continue to act if the client consents to your doing so.

Consent—Prospective Client

If practicable, whenever a prospective client contacts your firm, certain information (such as the client's name, including any aliases, and contact information) should

> ## BOX 4.10
>
> ### Conflicts of Interest: Who Is the Client?
>
> Any person who is a client of the paralegal firm of which you are a partner or an employee is a client, regardless of whether you actually handle that person's work (rule 1.02). In a busy firm with many clients and/or a high client turnover, you may have no knowledge of a client's existence or that your firm ever represented him. Nevertheless, a paralegal–client relationship exists between you and that client and entails various duties, including the duty of confidentiality and the duty to avoid conflicts of interest.
>
> Since every client of a paralegal firm is also the client of every other paralegal in the firm, if one paralegal has a conflict of interest in a matter, then all paralegals in the firm have a conflict of interest in that matter (guideline 9).
>
> This means that when you check for conflicts, you must review the names of all current and former clients of the firm, not just the clients you personally represented or represent. ◇

be obtained from the client and entered immediately into your conflict-checking system. A conflicts search should be carried out before there is any further contact with the prospective client. The results of the search should be reviewed by the paralegal.

If the search reveals a conflict or potential conflict, you must consider whether you should accept the retainer or decline to represent the prospective client. Rule 3.04(3) permits you to accept the retainer if the prospective client consents. To comply with rule 3.04(3), you must first disclose the conflict or potential conflict to the client. You must provide sufficient detail about the conflict to enable the client to make an informed decision about whether retaining you is in her best interests in the circumstances. This is called **informed consent**. Guideline 9 recommends that you give the prospective client some time to consider the disclosure and ask for further clarification.

If there are other persons who are involved in or connected with the client matter, you may have a duty to avoid conflicts of interest with respect to those persons as well. Examples of such individuals are members of the client's family, the client's spouse, and the client's business associates or employees. You must obtain informed consent from those persons as well (rule 3.04(4)).

If, having reviewed the information provided, the prospective client consents to your representation, you may accept the client retainer. The prospective client's consent, and the consents of any client associates, should be in writing.

Conflict of Interest—Client Declines Retainer

If, having reviewed the information provided, the prospective client declines to retain you, that decision should be confirmed in a non-engagement letter. The non-engagement letter must recommend that the client obtain independent legal representation from a competent paralegal or lawyer with no personal interest in the matter. **Independent legal representation** is legal advice and assistance from a competent paralegal or lawyer with no personal interest in the matter. See Appendix 4.2 for a sample non-engagement letter to a prospective client who has declined to retain you based on a conflict of interest.

Conflict of Interest—Paralegal Declines Retainer

There may be situations where you cannot provide full disclosure about the conflict of interest without revealing confidential information about another client or clients. When that happens, you must advise the prospective client that there is a conflict of interest and that you cannot accept the retainer (guideline 9). You should confirm your decision in writing in a non-engagement letter. The non-engagement letter must recommend that the client obtain independent legal representation from a competent paralegal or lawyer with no personal interest in the matter.

Guideline 9 recommends that you consider whether to accept or decline a prospective client's retainer any time you become aware of a conflict or potential conflict. You should do this even if you have the client's consent and if, in your opinion, the retainer would not breach the Rules. When considering whether to accept the client matter, you should take into account the delay, expense, and inconvenience that will arise for the client and/or for you, should you be required to withdraw at a later stage in the proceeding.

Guideline 9 also notes that, in some cases, even though the client has indicated that he wants to retain you, the only way to deal with the conflict is to decline the retainer. If you decide to decline the retainer, you should confirm your decision in writing in a non-engagement letter. The non-engagement letter must recommend that the client obtain independent legal representation from a competent paralegal or lawyer with no personal interest in the matter. See Appendix 4.3 for a sample non-engagement letter to a prospective client based on a conflict of interest.

Consent—Existing Client

Existing client matters should be checked for conflicts at critical points throughout the paralegal–client retainer. You should conduct a conflict search any time a new party is added in a proceeding or new information about the client matter comes to light. If a conflict arises after you are retained, you may be required to withdraw from representing the client.

If a conflict search reveals a conflict or potential conflict in an existing client matter, you must consider whether or not to continue to act in the matter. Rule 3.04(3) permits you to continue to act if the client gives you informed consent based on disclosure of all information regarding the conflict that the client requires to make a decision. The client should be given some time to consider the disclosure and ask for further clarification.

If there are other persons who are involved in or connected with the client matter, you may have a duty to avoid conflicts of interest with respect to those persons as well. You must obtain informed consent from them.

If, having reviewed the information provided, the client and any client associates consent to your continuing representation, you may continue to act in the client matter. The client's consent, and the consents of any client associates, should be in writing.

Conflict of Interest—Client Terminates Retainer

If, having reviewed the information provided, the client decides to terminate the retainer, you should confirm the termination of the retainer in writing. If the client requests that the matter be transferred to another paralegal or a lawyer, you should obtain a direction, in writing and signed by the client, for release of the client's file to the successor licensee. If the client collects the file herself, you should obtain an acknowledgment in writing and signed by the client confirming that she has received the file.

Conflict of Interest—Paralegal Withdraws From Representation

There may be situations where you cannot provide full disclosure about the conflict of interest without revealing confidential information about another client or clients. When that happens, you must advise the client that there is a conflict of interest and that you must withdraw from representation. You should confirm your decision in writing to the client.

Any time you become aware of a conflict or potential conflict, you should consider whether or not to continue to act in the client matter. You should do this even if you have the client's consent to continue to act and are satisfied that your continued involvement would not put you in breach of the Rules. When coming to a decision about whether to continue to act in the matter, you should take into account the delay, expense, and inconvenience that will arise for the client and/or for you, should you be required to withdraw at a later stage in the proceeding.

Sometimes the only way to deal with the conflict in an ongoing client matter is to withdraw from representation, even though the client may want you to continue to act in the matter. When withdrawing your services, you must comply with rule 3.08. You shall not withdraw from representation unless you are satisfied that there is good cause. You must give the client notice that is appropriate in the circumstances, try to minimize expense and avoid prejudice to the client, and do all that reasonably can be done to facilitate the orderly transfer of the client matter to a successor licensee.

INDEPENDENT LEGAL ADVICE

In certain situations, the client's consent will not be sufficient to allow you to accept the retainer or continue your representation in the matter. This will happen when the conflict is such that the client cannot possibly assess all of its possible implications without impartial, confidential, professional assistance. It may also happen where the client is unsophisticated or vulnerable.

In these situations, the client must receive independent legal advice before the paralegal accepts or continues to act in the matter. Independent legal advice is impartial, confidential advice obtained from a competent paralegal or lawyer with no personal interest in the matter. It helps ensure that a client's consent is informed and uncoerced. The paralegal should not accept or continue with the client matter until the client has had the benefit of independent legal advice.

Acting Against Clients or Former Clients (Rules 3.04(2) to (7))

SAME OR RELATED MATTERS (RULES 3.04(2), (4)(a), (b))

Rule 3.04(2) states that a paralegal shall not advise or represent more than one side of a dispute.

Same Matter (Rule 3.04(4)(a))

If you have acted for a client in a matter you shall not, after that, act in the same matter against the client. You shall not act in the same matter against any persons involved or associated with the client in that matter.

You are prohibited from doing so because you possess confidential information about the client and/or the client's associates that is relevant to issues in the matter. Your duty to the client and the client's associates requires you to hold that information in strict confidence. Your duty as legal representative to an adverse party in the same proceeding would require you to disclose that information, to the possible detriment of your client and the client's associates. The two duties conflict.

Related Matter (Rule 3.04(4)(b))

A related matter is a matter involving issues that are similar or related to the issues in the original client matter. If you have acted for a client in a matter you shall not, after that, act against the client in a matter related to the client matter. You shall not act in a matter related to the client matter against any persons involved or associated with the client in the client matter.

You are prohibited from doing so because you possess confidential information about the client and/or the client's associates from the original client matter that is relevant to issues in the related matter. Your duty to the client and the client's associates requires you to hold that information in strict confidence. Your duty as legal representative to an adverse party in the related matter would require you to disclose that information, to the possible detriment of the client and/or the client's associates. The two duties conflict.

Acting against a client or a client's associates in the same or a related matter also raises issues about your loyalty to your clients.

NEW MATTERS (RULES 3.04(3), (4)(c), (5), (6), (7))

You may act against a client or former client in a fresh, independent, and unrelated matter if previously obtained confidential information is irrelevant to any issue in the new matter (rule 3.04(7)).

You are prohibited from acting against a client or former client in a new matter if you obtained any confidential information that is relevant to the new matter from the former retainer. You are prohibited from acting against any persons involved or associated with the client in the other retainer if you obtained any confidential information that is relevant to the new matter from the other client retainer (rule 3.04(4)(c)).

If a partner or paralegal employee in a paralegal firm has obtained confidential information from a former client that is relevant in a new matter, no partner or paralegal employee in the firm may act against the former client in the new matter (rule 3.04(6)).

EXCEPTIONS

Rule 3.04(4) states that, *unless the client and those involved or associated with the client consent*, a paralegal who has acted for a client in a matter shall not thereafter act against the client or against persons who were involved or associated with the client in that matter:

(a) in the same matter;

(b) in any related matter; or

(c) subject to rule 3.04(6), in a new matter if the paralegal has obtained relevant confidential information from the other retainer.

Both the current or former client and any persons associated with the current or former client must give informed consent to the paralegal acting against them and using any confidential information in his possession against them. A paralegal who is contemplating acting against a client or a client's associates in the same or a related matter should carefully consider rule 1.03 and rule 3.04(2).

Rule 3.04(5) sets out exceptions to rules 3.04(4)(c) and (6). If a paralegal has acted for a client and obtained confidential information relevant to a matter, the paralegal's partner or employee may act against that client in a subsequent matter if:

(a) the former client and any persons involved or associated with the former client in the original matter consent to the paralegal's partner or employee acting in the new matter and using that information against the former client and/or any persons involved or associated with the former client in the original matter; or

(b) the paralegal's firm establishes that it is appropriate to continue to act in the new matter in all of the circumstances, including:

    (i) the availability to the client of suitable alternative representation in the new matter,

    (ii) the measures being taken to ensure that no disclosure of the former client's confidential information to the partner or employee with carriage of the new matter will occur,

    (iii) the extent of the prejudice to any party,

    (iv) the good faith of the parties, and

    (v) any issues affecting the public interest.

Guideline 9 suggests that, even where the Rules do not prohibit a paralegal from acting against a client or former client, you should consider whether to accept the retainer or continue acting. Acting against a client or former client raises issues of your loyalty to your clients. It may damage the paralegal–client relationship. It may also result in court proceedings against you, and/or a complaint to the Law Society.

Joint Retainers (Rules 3.04(8) to (18))

GENERAL

A joint retainer is created when a paralegal is hired to represent more than one client in a matter or transaction. The clients in a joint retainer are called joint clients.

You owe the duty of loyalty to all joint clients equally. When the interests of all joint clients coincide, you can be loyal and devoted to the interests of all clients equally. If the interests of joint clients diverge as the matter progresses, you may find yourself in a position of conflict. The divergent interests of the joint clients may require different levels of care and attention, in which case you cannot comply with your duty to be devoted and loyal to the interests of all joint clients equally.

DISCLOSURE AND CLIENT CONSENT (RULES 3.04(8) TO (11))

Before agreeing to act for joint clients in a matter or transaction, you shall advise the joint clients that (rule 3.04(8)):

(a) you have been asked to act for both or all of them, and must serve the interests of all of them equally;

(b) no information received from one joint client in connection with the matter can be treated as confidential so far as any other joint clients are concerned—in other words, all information will be shared equally among all joint clients; and

(c) if a conflict develops that cannot be resolved, you cannot continue to act for both or all joint clients and may have to withdraw completely.

Additional disclosure is required if you have a continuing relationship with a client for whom you act regularly, before you agree to a joint retainer in which you act for the continuing client and another client in a matter or transaction. A **continuing relationship** is a paralegal–client relationship where you act for the same client in several different matters or transactions over a period of time. A **continuing client** is a client for whom you act in several different matters or transactions over a period of time.

When one of the clients in a proposed joint retainer is a continuing client, you must advise the new client(s) of the continuing relationship, and recommend that the new client(s) obtain independent legal advice about the joint retainer (rule 3.04(9)).

If you have advised the clients as set out above and they are content that you shall act for them, you shall obtain their consent (rule 3.04(10)). Client consents should always be in writing.

Even if all concerned parties have consented to the joint retainer, you shall avoid acting for joint clients if it is likely that a contentious issue will arise between them, or that their interests, rights, or obligations will diverge as the matter progresses (rule 3.04(11)).

Rules 3.04(12) to (14) set out procedures to be followed in the event that a conflict develops between joint clients. These are summarized in Figure 4.2.

FIGURE 4.2   Joint Retainer: Contentious Issue (Rules 3.04(12) to (14))

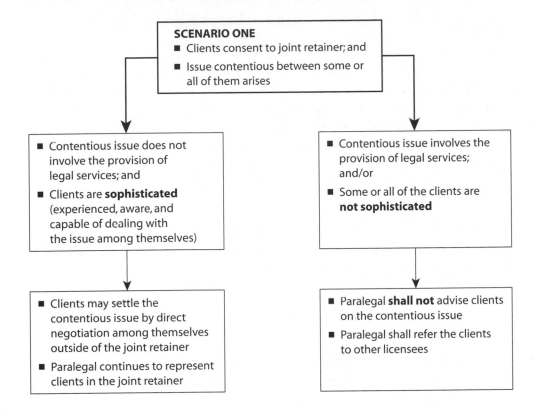

SCENARIO ONE
- Clients consent to joint retainer; and
- Issue contentious between some or all of them arises

- Contentious issue does not involve the provision of legal services; and
- Clients are **sophisticated** (experienced, aware, and capable of dealing with the issue among themselves)

- Contentious issue involves the provision of legal services; and/or
- Some or all of the clients are **not sophisticated**

- Clients may settle the contentious issue by direct negotiation among themselves outside of the joint retainer
- Paralegal continues to represent clients in the joint retainer

- Paralegal **shall not** advise clients on the contentious issue
- Paralegal shall refer the clients to other licensees

SCENARIO TWO
- Clients consent to joint retainer; and
- Clients agree that if a contentious issue arises the paralegal may continue to advise one of them; and
- Issue contentious between some or all of them arises

- Paralegal may advise the client named in the agreement about the contentious issue
- Paralegal shall refer other client(s) to other licensee(s)

> **BOX 4.11**
>
> ## Independent Legal Advice—Unsophisticated and Vulnerable Clients
>
> Sometimes the client's consent will not be sufficient to allow you to accept the retainer or continue your representation in a matter. This might happen when the conflict is such that the client cannot assess all of its possible implications without impartial, confidential, professional assistance. It may also happen where the client is unsophisticated or vulnerable. In these situations, you should recommend that the client obtain independent legal advice before a retainer is entered into.
>
> In a joint retainer, issues of ability to process information, unequal bargaining power, and coercion arise when one of the joint clients is unsophisticated and/or vulnerable and the others are not. Guideline 9 recommends that you consider rules 3.02(7) and (8), which deal with clients under disability, in cases where one of the joint clients is unsophisticated or vulnerable. In addition, you should consider recommending independent legal advice to the unsophisticated or vulnerable joint client. Independent legal advice will help ensure that the vulnerable client's consent to the joint retainer is informed, genuine, and uncoerced. ◇

UNREPRESENTED PARTIES (RULES 3.04(2), (8) TO (14) AND 4.05)

When providing legal services, you may find yourself dealing with opposing parties or other individuals with an interest in the matter who are not represented by a paralegal or a lawyer. A conflict of interest may arise if the unrepresented person comes to believe that you are protecting his or her interests.

Rule 4.05 states that, when dealing on a client's behalf with an unrepresented person, you shall:

(a) urge the unrepresented person to obtain independent legal representation from a competent paralegal or lawyer with no personal interest in the matter;

(b) take care to see that the unrepresented person is not proceeding under the impression that you will protect his interests; and

(c) make it clear to the unrepresented person that you are acting exclusively in the interests of the client, and that your comments may be partisan.

Making it clear to the unrepresented person that you are acting exclusively in the interests of your own client may require more than simply saying this to the unrepresented person. It may be prudent to send the unrepresented person a letter stating the information above.

You may be able to act for unrepresented persons who have an interest in the matter, such as co-accuseds, but you must consider rules 3.04(8) to (14) governing joint retainers.

MULTI-DISCIPLINE PRACTICE (BY-LAW 7, PART III; RULES 3.04(15) AND 8.01)

A **multi-discipline practice** (MDP) is a business arrangement that permits paralegal licensees to enter into a partnership or association that is not a corporation with non-licensees to provide to clients the services of a non-licensee who practises a profession, trade, or occupation that supports or supplements the provision of legal services (By-law 7, s. 18(1)). The paralegal licensee must have effective control over the provision of services by non-professionals to clients of the multi-discipline practice (By-law 7, s. 18(2)2).

A paralegal in a multi-discipline practice is required to assume complete professional responsibility for all business entrusted to him or her (rule 8.01(1)). In accordance with By-Law 7.1 and rule 8.01(5), a paralegal in a multi-discipline practice shall ensure that non-licensee partners and associates comply with the Rules and all ethical principles that govern paralegals in the discharge of their professional obligations. These professional and ethical duties include the duty to hold all client information in strict confidence and the duty to avoid conflicts of interest.

A paralegal in a multi-discipline practice must ensure that the client understands that legal services are provided by the paralegal, and supplemented by the non-legal professional services of non-paralegal partners and associates. A paralegal in a multi-discipline practice must also ensure that non-paralegal partners and associates comply with the rules regarding the avoidance of conflicts of interest when providing non-legal professional services within the paralegal practice, and when carrying on business or fulfilling professional undertakings outside of the paralegal practice.

AFFILIATIONS (BY-LAW 7, PART IV; RULES 3.04(16), (17), (18) AND 8.01)

A paralegal services firm may form an affiliation with a non-legal entity whose members practise a profession, trade, or occupation that supports or supplements the paralegal's provision of legal services ("affiliated entity"). An **affiliation** is considered to have formed when the paralegal on a regular basis joins with the **affiliated entity** in the delivery and promotion of their services to the public (By-law 7, s. 31(2)).

A conflict of interest may arise when a paralegal's interest in an affiliated entity, or the interest of his partners or associates, conflicts with the paralegal's duties to a client. Where legal services are provided jointly to a client by the paralegal firm and the affiliated entity, the paralegal must check for and deal with any conflicts as if the paralegal practice and the affiliated entity were a single entity (rule 3.04(18)).

Before accepting a retainer to provide legal services to a client jointly with non-legal services of an affiliated entity, you shall disclose to the client (rule 3.04(16)):

(a) any possible loss of confidentiality because of the involvement of the affiliated entity, including circumstances where a non-licensee or staff of the affiliated entity provide services in your office;

(b) your role in providing legal and non-legal services, or both;

(c) any financial, economic, or other arrangements between you and the affiliated entity that may affect the independence of your representation of the client, including whether you share in the revenue, profits, or cash flow of the affiliated entity; and

(d) any agreements between you and the affiliated entity that may affect the independence of your representation of the client, including any agreements with respect to referral of clients between you and the affiliated entity.

After making the above disclosure to the client, you shall obtain the client's consent in writing before accepting the retainer (rule 3.04(17)).

Transfers Between Paralegal Firms (Rule 3.05)

When a paralegal changes firms, a conflict of interest may arise because the transferring paralegal possesses relevant confidential information about a client from the former firm, and the paralegal's new firm represents a client in the same or a related matter whose interests conflict with those of the transferring paralegal's former client. The danger is that the confidential information about the former client may be revealed to the paralegal's colleagues in the new firm and used against the former client.

BOX 4.12

What Is "Confidential Information" for Purposes of Rule 3.05?

The duty of confidentiality requires a paralegal to hold in strict confidence all information concerning the business and affairs of the client acquired in the course of the professional relationship, without regard to the nature or source of the information or the fact that others may share the knowledge.

Rule 2.05 of the Rules of Professional Conduct deals with transfers between firms by lawyers. It is the equivalent of rule 3.05 of the Paralegal Rules of Conduct.

For purposes of transfers between law firms by lawyers, rule 2.05 restricts "confidential information" to information obtained from a client that is not generally known to the public.

The commentary to rule 2.05 states that the duties imposed by the rule concerning confidential information should be distinguished from the general ethical duty to hold in strict confidence all information concerning the business and affairs of the client acquired in the course of the professional relationship.

Rule 3.05 of the Paralegal Rules distinguishes between "confidential information"—that is, client information that, if disclosed to a paralegal in the new paralegal firm, might prejudice the client (rule 3.05(2))—and "relevant information"—that is, client information that, if disclosed, would not prejudice the client (rule 3.05(4)). An example of relevant information might be the client's name, if it has already been disclosed on public documents such as pleadings. ◇

Rule 3.05 applies where a paralegal transfers to a new paralegal firm and either the transferring paralegal or the new firm is aware at the time of the transfer, or later discovers, that (rule 3.05(1)):

(a)   the new paralegal firm represents a client in a matter that is the same as or related to a matter in which the former paralegal firm represents its client ("former client");

(b)   the interests of those clients in that matter conflict; and

(c) the transferring paralegal actually possesses relevant information respecting that matter.

If the transferring paralegal possesses confidential information respecting a former client that may prejudice the former client if disclosed to a paralegal in the new paralegal firm, the new paralegal firm shall cease representation of its client unless (rule 3.05(2)):

1. the former client consents to the new paralegal firm's continued representation, or

2. the new paralegal firm establishes that it is in the interests of justice that it continue to represent the client.

In deciding whether or not it is appropriate to continue to act for a client, the new paralegal firm shall consider all of the circumstances, including (rule 3.05(3)):

(a) the adequacy and timing of the measures taken to ensure that no disclosure of the former client's confidential information to any paralegal of the new paralegal firm will occur;

(b) the availability of suitable alternative representation;

(c) the measures taken to ensure that no disclosure of the former client's confidential information to any paralegal in the new paralegal firm will occur;

(d) the extent of any prejudice to any party;

(e) the good faith of the parties; and

(f) issues affecting the public interest.

If a transferring paralegal possesses relevant information respecting a former client but that information is not confidential information as defined in rule 3.05(2), the paralegal shall execute an affidavit or solemn declaration to that effect, and the new paralegal firm shall (rule 3.05(4)):

(a) notify its client and the former client, or the former client's licensee representative, of the relevant circumstances and its intended action under this rule; and

(b) deliver to its client and the former client or the former client's licensee representative a copy of the transferring paralegal's affidavit or solemn declaration.

A transferring paralegal who possesses confidential information about a former client under rule 3.05(2), or relevant (but not confidential) information under rule 3.05(4), shall not

(a) participate in any manner in the new paralegal firm's representation of the client in that matter, or

(b) disclose any confidential information respecting the former client,

unless the former client consents (rule 3.05(5)).

No paralegal in the new paralegal firm shall discuss the new paralegal firm's representation of its client or the former paralegal firm's representation of the former client with a transferring paralegal described in rule 3.05(2) or 3.05(4), unless the former client consents (rule 3.05(6)).

Anyone with an interest in a matter referred to in rule 3.05, or who represents a party in a matter referred to in rule 3.05, may apply to a tribunal of competent jurisdiction for a determination of any aspect of the rule.

Guideline 9 recommends that a paralegal should carefully review the Rules when transferring to a new office or when a new paralegal is about to join the paralegal firm.

Doing Business with a Client (Rule 3.06)

INVESTMENT BY A CLIENT WHERE A PARALEGAL HAS AN INTEREST (RULES 3.06(1) TO (4))

Guideline 9 cautions paralegals about entering with a client into any business arrangement that is unrelated to the provision of paralegal services. Since the paralegal is the client's current or former adviser, such an arrangement may result in a conflict of interest on the part of the paralegal. For example, a conflict might arise if the business arrangement prompts the paralegal—knowingly or unknowingly—to prefer her own financial interests over those of the client, or if the business interest adversely affects the paralegal's judgment on behalf of, or loyalty to, the client.

Rule 3.06(1) applies to an investment by a client in a business where a paralegal has an interest in either or both of the following situations:

- a client intends to enter into a business transaction with a paralegal who is representing the client; and/or

- a client intends to enter into a business transaction with a corporation or other business entity in which the paralegal has an interest and whose securities are not publicly traded (in other words, a privately controlled business).

No issues of conflict arise if the paralegal and the client happen to own stock in the same publicly traded company.

Where a client intends to enter into a business transaction to which rule 3.06(1) applies, the paralegal, before accepting the retainer:

(a) shall disclose and explain the nature of any existing conflict to the client, or, if there is a potential conflict, how and why it might develop later;

(b) shall recommend that the client seek independent legal representation, and, if the client chooses not to seek independent legal representation, shall require that the client receive independent legal advice; and

(c) if the client asks the paralegal to act, shall obtain the client's written consent.

In this situation, it may be advisable to decline the retainer even if you have complied with rule 3.06(1) and obtained the client's consent. You should critically evaluate all of the circumstances, keeping in mind that if you accept the retainer,

Reminder: What Is the Difference Between Independent Legal Advice and Independent Legal Representation?

In certain situations, the client cannot make an informed decision about a conflict of interest based on disclosure from the paralegal alone. This will happen when the client cannot possibly assess all of the possible implications of the conflicting interest without impartial, confidential, professional assistance. It may also happen where the client is unsophisticated or vulnerable.

In these situations, the client must receive independent legal advice before the paralegal accepts or continues to act in the matter. Independent legal advice is impartial, confidential advice obtained from a competent paralegal or lawyer with no personal interest in the matter. It helps ensure that a client's consent is informed and uncoerced.

In other situations, the conflict is such that the paralegal cannot accept the retainer or cannot continue to act. In those situations, the paralegal shall recommend that the client obtain independent legal representation—that is, legal advice and assistance from a competent paralegal or lawyer with no personal interest in the matter. ◇

your first duty will be to your client. If you have any concerns about being able to put the client's interests first, you should decline the retainer. You should consider sending the client a non-engagement letter confirming that you have declined the retainer.

Non-Monetary Payment for Legal Services (Rules 3.06(2), (3))

What if a client wants to retain you in a matter but does not want to pay you with money? Instead, she tells you that she intends to pay for your legal services by transferring to you a share, participation, or other interest in property or in an enterprise.

Before you accept the retainer, you shall recommend that the client receive independent legal advice from a competent paralegal or lawyer with no personal interest in the matter (rule 3.06(2)). Making the recommendation to the client is mandatory. However, the client may then make up her own mind about whether she wishes to seek independent legal advice or not. It is advisable to make the recommendation in writing.

Rule 3.06(2) does not apply if the client proposes to pay you by transferring to you a non-material interest in a publicly traded enterprise (rule 3.06(3)). A non-material interest is an interest that does not affect control or management of the publicly traded enterprise.

Declining the Retainer (Rule 3.06(4))

If a client intends to enter into a business arrangement with you, and you choose not to make disclosure of a conflicting interest or cannot disclose a conflicting interest without breaching a confidence, you shall decline the retainer. You should consider sending the client a non-engagement letter confirming that you have declined the retainer.

BORROWING FROM CLIENTS

A paralegal shall not borrow money from a client except where the client is:

(a) a lending institution, financial institution, insurance company, trust corporation, or any similar institution whose business includes lending money to members of the public; or

(b) a "related person" as defined by the *Income Tax Act* (Canada) (in which case the paralegal bears the onus of proving that the client's interests were fully protected by the nature of the case and by independent legal advice or independent legal representation).

BOX 4.14

Who Are Related Persons as Defined by the Income Tax Act (Canada)?

Definition of "related persons"

251.(2) For the purpose of this Act, "related persons," or persons related to each other, are

(a) individuals connected by blood relationship, marriage or common-law partnership or adoption;

(b) a corporation and

(i) a person who controls the corporation, if it is controlled by one person,

(ii) a person who is a member of a related group that controls the corporation, or

(iii) any person related to a person described in subparagraph 251(2)(b)(i) or 251(2)(b)(ii); and

(c) any two corporations

(i) if they are controlled by the same person or group of persons,

(ii) if each of the corporations is controlled by one person and the person who controls one of the corporations is related to the person who controls the other corporation,

(iii) if one of the corporations is controlled by one person and that person is related to any member of a related group that controls the other corporation,

(iv) if one of the corporations is controlled by one person and that person is related to each member of an unrelated group that controls the other corporation,

(v) if any member of a related group that controls one of the corporations is related to each member of an unrelated group that controls the other corporation, or

(vi) if each member of an unrelated group that controls one of the corporations is related to at least one member of an unrelated group that controls the other corporation. ◇

GUARANTEES BY PARALEGAL (RULES 3.06(6), (7))

A **guarantee** is an agreement to make oneself liable or responsible to a lender for the payment of a debt if the debtor defaults in payment. A paralegal may give a personal guarantee for a debt if the following conditions are met:

1. the lender is a lending institution, financial institution, insurance company, trust company, or any similar corporation whose business includes lending money to members of the public, and the lender is directly or indirectly providing funds solely for the use of the paralegal or the paralegal's spouse, parent or child;

2. the transaction is for the benefit of a non-profit or charitable institution and the paralegal, as a member or supporter of the non-profit or charitable institution, is asked, as an individual or with other members or supporters of the institution, to provide a guarantee; or

3. the paralegal has entered into a business venture with a client, and the lender requires personal guarantees from all participants in the venture in the ordinary course of doing business and,

    (i) the paralegal has complied with the requirements of the Rules regarding avoidance of conflicts, and

    (ii) the lender and the participants in the business venture who are or were clients of the paralegal, have received independent legal representation.

In any other circumstances, the paralegal shall not guarantee personally or otherwise provide security for any debts where a client is a borrower or a lender (rule 3.06(6)).

BOX 4.15

What Is a Guarantee?

A guarantee is an agreement to make oneself liable or responsible to a lender for the payment of a debt if the debtor defaults in payment. The lender is the person or institution lending the money to the debtor. The debtor is the person who owes the money. The person making the guarantee to pay the debt if the debtor fails to pay is called a guarantor.

In other words, the guarantor undertakes to pay the lender personally if the debtor fails to pay the debt.

It is in the guarantor's best interest that the debtor pay the debt, so that the guarantor does not have to pay it. If the debtor fails to pay the debt, the guarantor's interest and the debtor's interest may become adverse. The guarantor is bound by the promise to pay in the event of default by the debtor, but would prefer that the debtor pay the debt. The debtor, if unable to pay the debt for whatever reason, is relying upon the guarantor to honour the promise to pay. The lender does not care who pays the debt, so long as it is paid. ◇

Client Property (Rule 3.07; Guideline 10)

PARALEGAL AS FIDUCIARY WITH RESPECT TO CLIENT PROPERTY (RULE 3.07(1))

A paralegal is a fiduciary with respect to any property of the client that comes into the paralegal's possession. The paralegal shall care for a client's property as a careful and prudent owner would when dealing with similar property. The paralegal must comply with the rules and the law about the preservation of property entrusted to a fiduciary.

BOX 4.16

Reminder: What Is a Fiduciary?

A fiduciary relationship is a relationship of absolute trust and confidence between two persons, in which one person (the fiduciary) is required to act with scrupulous good faith, honesty, and candour for the benefit of the other person. In the paralegal–client relationship, the paralegal is the fiduciary. The paralegal must put the client's interests ahead of her own in all dealings with the client. The client is entitled to place absolute confidence, reliance, and trust in the paralegal. ◇

Guideline 9 defines **client property** as a wide range of items, including money, other valuables, physical items, and information. Documents that are given to the paralegal at the beginning of the paralegal–client retainer, as well as those that are prepared by or given to the paralegal in the course of the retainer, also belong to the client.

As a fiduciary, the paralegal holds client property, including client money, in trust for the client.

DEALING WITH CLIENT PROPERTY (RULES 3.07(2) TO (6); BY-LAW 9, S. 18.9)

A paralegal shall notify the client promptly when the paralegal receives money or other property that belongs to the client, unless the client is aware that the money or other property has been received by the paralegal (rule 3.07(2)). The paralegal should consider notifying the client in writing.

A paralegal shall clearly label and identify the client's property and place it in safekeeping. While in safekeeping, the client's property must be distinguishable from the paralegal's own property (rule 3.07(3)). For example, you would not store client property in the same safe deposit box that you use for your own valuables.

A paralegal shall maintain a valuable property record in accordance with By-law 9, s. 18(9). The **valuable property record** is a record of all property, other than money, held in trust for clients. It should contain, at a minimum, the following information for each item held in trust (*Paralegal Bookkeeping Guide*, at 29):

- a description of the property;

- the date when the paralegal took possession of the property;

- the person who had possession of the property immediately before the paralegal took possession of it;

- the value of the property;

- the client for whom the property is held in trust;

- the date on which the property is given away; and

- the name of the person to whom possession of the property is given.

The trust is terminated when the property is delivered or transferred to the person for whose benefit it was held, or to another person on the written direction of the person for whose benefit the property was held.

The following properties should be included in the valuable property record:

- instruments registered in the paralegal's name in trust;

- stocks, bonds, or other securities in bearer form (that is, payable to the person having possession of them);

- jewellery, paints, furs, collector's items, or any variety of saleable valuables; and

- any property that a paralegal can convert, on her own authority, to cash.

Term deposits, deposit slips, savings accounts, or similar deposit accounts maintained for individual clients at chartered banks or registered trust companies are not included in the valuable property record. These are trust monies and must be recorded in the financial accounting records in accordance with By-law 9.

BOX 4.17

Valuable Property Record

Pending the outcome of a Small Claims Court action against him for return of property, your client, Felix Krull, is ordered by the court to deliver to you to hold in safekeeping a laptop computer and digital camera, ownership of which is in dispute in the proceeding. Mr. Krull hands the laptop computer and digital camera over to you on January 5, 20—. On March 3, 20—, the matter settles on terms that the digital camera is to be delivered to the plaintiff, Andrew Ekpunobe; your client is to keep the laptop. In accordance with the Minutes of Settlement, and pursuant to a written direction from Mr. Krull, on March 7, 20— the digital camera is delivered to Andrew Ekpunobe and the laptop is delivered to Mr. Krull.

At the end of these transactions, the valuable property record would look like this:

Schwarz and Berryman PC
Paralegals
Valuable Property Record

Client	Description of property	Date received	Received from	Value	Delivered to	Date of delivery
KRULL, Felix	Sony laptop	Jan 05, 20—	KRULL, Felix	$2,300.00	KRULL, Felix	Mar 07, 20—
KRULL, Felix	Canon digital camera	Jan 05, 20—	KRULL, Felix	$1,279.00	EKPUNOBE, Andrew	Mar 07, 20—

A paralegal shall account promptly for any property owned by a client that is in the paralegal's custody (rule 3.07(5)). Upon request, the paralegal shall deliver it to the order of the client—that is, as directed by the client. It is advisable to obtain the client's direction in writing.

If you are not sure who is the proper person to receive a client's property, you shall apply to a tribunal of competent jurisdiction for direction (rule 3.07(6)).

THE CLIENT FILE (RULE 3.07)

As of January 2009, the jurisprudence on what the client does or does not own in the client file applies to lawyers and their clients. However, this jurisprudence may be applied to define the paralegal's role with respect to client files (guideline 10).

Based on that assumption, the paralegal's duty to preserve client property also applies to the documents that a client delivers to you at the beginning of the paralegal–client relationship, and to those that you create or collect for the client's benefit during the relationship. For example, documentary disclosure from an adverse party in a proceeding would be the client's property.

Accordingly, the following documents are the property of the client (guideline 10):

- originals of all documents prepared for the client;

- all copies of documents where the client has paid for the copies;

- copies of correspondence between the paralegal and third parties;

- originals of correspondence from the paralegal to the client;

- copies of case law;

- briefs (that is, summaries of the facts in cases and the applicable legal principles, with argument as to how the law applies to the facts to support a party's position in the matter);

- memoranda of law, where the client paid for preparation of the memoranda;

- notes or memoranda of meetings with opposing parties or their representatives, court or tribunal conferences, interviews with clients, and so on;

- trial preparation documents;

- copies of vouchers and receipts for disbursements made on the client's behalf;

- experts' reports; and

- photographs, and electronic media such as computer discs.

When the paralegal–client retainer is terminated before the client matter is concluded, you must deliver the above documents to the client. You should have the client sign an acknowledgment of receipt of the documents. If the client instructs you to release the documents to a successor licensee, you should obtain a written direction confirming those instructions, signed by the client.

When you close the file in a client matter that is concluded, you shall return the above documents to the client. You should have the client sign an acknowledgment indicating receipt of the documents. The acknowledgment may be filed in the client's closed file.

Documents belonging to the paralegal, such as notes or memoranda of meetings or telephone conversations with the client, would not have to be provided to the client.

Guideline 10 recommends that you make, at your own cost, copies of all client documents, and keep them to defend against future complaints or claims against you. The copies should be filed in the client's closed file.

WITHDRAWAL FROM REPRESENTATION (RULE 3.08; GUIDELINE 11)

As a general rule, when you have been retained to represent a client in a matter, you are required to represent the client until the matter is concluded. For example, if you have been retained to represent a defendant in a provincial offences prosecution, you must continue to represent the client until the matter is concluded, by way of a plea to a lesser offence or an acquittal or conviction at trial.

The client may terminate the paralegal–client relationship at any time, for any reason.

A paralegal shall not withdraw from representation of a client before the matter in which he was retained is concluded, except for good cause and upon notice to the client appropriate in the circumstances (rule 3.08(1)).

Whether or not you have good cause for withdrawal will depend on many factors, including (guideline 11):

- the nature of the matter and the stage you are at in the matter,

- the relationship with the client,

- your expertise and experience, and

- any harm or prejudice to the client that may result from the withdrawal of services.

The above factors may also be determinative of what is appropriate notice in the circumstances. Generally, you should try to safeguard the client from prejudice or harm. If you are at a critical procedural stage in a matter, such that prejudice or harm to the client would be unavoidable if you were to withdraw your services, then you should continue your representation of the client.

Guideline 11 suggests that you consider including information in the retainer agreement or engagement letter advising the client of situations in which you may or must withdraw from representation, which documents she is entitled to have returned to her when the relationship ends or the matter is concluded, and which documents will belong to and be kept by you when the relationship ends or the matter is concluded. Refer to the discussion of rule 3.07 above.

Types of Withdrawal

OPTIONAL WITHDRAWAL (RULES 3.08(1) TO (4))

In certain situations outlined in rule 3.08, you may choose to withdraw from representation, but you are not obligated to withdraw.

SERIOUS LOSS OF CONFIDENCE (RULES 3.08(2), (3))

A paralegal may withdraw if there has been a serious loss of confidence between the paralegal and the client (rule 3.08(2)). The rules of the tribunal may require that you apply to the tribunal for direction. In criminal and quasi-criminal matters, withdrawal on grounds of serious loss of confidence is subject to the restrictions set out in rules 3.08(7), (8), and (9).

A **serious loss of confidence** means that the paralegal and the client can no longer trust and rely on each other, making it impossible to have a normal paralegal–client relationship (guideline 11). This might occur where the client (rule 3.08(3)):

- deceives you or lies to you, or

- refuses to accept and act upon advice from you on an important point.

Subject to the direction of the tribunal, you may withdraw in either of the above situations. When withdrawing from representation, you shall try to minimize expense and avoid prejudice to the client (rule 3.08(10)).

Whether your withdrawal causes prejudice or harm to the client often depends on the complexity of the matter and what stage the proceeding is at. A client may be prejudiced by withdrawal of representation in the following circumstances (commentary to rule 2.09(1) of the Rules of Professional Conduct for lawyers):

- the client does not have sufficient time to retain a successor paralegal or lawyer, with the result that the client may have to represent herself at a critical point in the proceeding;

- the successor paralegal or lawyer will have to do the same work or some part of it again, thus causing additional expense for the client; or

- the successor paralegal or lawyer does not have time to prepare properly to represent the client.

Whatever the circumstances, you shall not threaten to withdraw from representation in order to force the client to make a hasty decision on a difficult question (rule 3.08(4)).

MANDATORY WITHDRAWAL (RULES 3.08(1), (5))

In certain situations, you are required to withdraw from representation, even if you wish to continue the retainer or the client wants you to continue as her legal representative (rule 3.08(5)):

(a) You shall withdraw from representation if the client terminates the retainer. You should confirm the termination in writing.

(b) You shall withdraw from representation if the client instructs you to do something inconsistent with your duty to the tribunal and, after you have given the client an explanation, the client persists in such instructions.

When acting as an advocate, your duty to the tribunal takes precedence over the client's self-interest.

(c) You shall withdraw from representation if the client is guilty of dishonourable conduct in the proceedings or is taking a certain position solely to harass or maliciously injure another. You shall not knowingly assist or permit the client to do anything that you consider dishonest or dishonourable, or abuse the process of the tribunal by going forward with a proceeding that is clearly motivated by malice on the part of the client and is brought solely for the purpose of injuring the other party. See also rule 4.01(5).

(d) You shall withdraw from representation if it becomes clear that your continued representation will lead to a breach of the Rules.

(e) You shall withdraw from representation if you are not competent to handle the matter.

Depending on the circumstances, failure to withdraw pursuant to rule 3.06(5) may be subject to disciplinary action.

NON-PAYMENT OF FEES (RULES 3.08(1), (6))

Unless serious prejudice to the client would result, a paralegal may withdraw from representation if, after reasonable notice, the client fails to provide funds on account of disbursements or fees. Withdrawal for non-payment of fees is subject to rules 3.08(7), (8), and (9), and the direction of the tribunal.

If the client would suffer serious prejudice or harm by reason of your withdrawal for non-payment of fees, you must continue to represent the client to the best of your ability, even if your fees remain unpaid.

Where no harm to the client will occur as a result of your withdrawal, you must first notify the client in writing that you require funds on account, and that failure to receive those funds by a stated deadline will result in your withdrawal from representation. You must give the client reasonable time to pay the funds.

Quasi-Criminal and Criminal Cases (Rules 3.08(1), (7), (8), (9))

When representing a client in a quasi-criminal or criminal matter, there are special rules for withdrawal from representation that apply whether withdrawal is optional, mandatory, or due to non-payment of fees. These rules apply to summary conviction matters and to *Provincial Offences Act* prosecutions.

PERMITTED WITHDRAWAL (RULE 3.08(7))

A paralegal who has agreed to act in a quasi-criminal or criminal case may withdraw for good cause if the interval between the withdrawal and the trial of the case is sufficient to

- enable the client to obtain alternate representation, and
- give the successor licensee adequate time to prepare for the trial.

BOX 4.18

Withdrawal from Representation

Scenario

You are representing Jane Doe in an application by her residential landlord for early termination of her tenancy on grounds that she has substantially interfered with the reasonable enjoyment of the residential complex by other tenants. According to the landlord's application, Jane's two sons, who are 11 and 13, are left unsupervised on a regular basis. They play loud music, slam doors, have violent fights, and make a lot of noise at all hours of the day and night, disturbing the tenants in the neighbouring apartments. Witnesses have seen the 11-year-old throwing things, including a glass bottle, off the balcony of their apartment, which is on the tenth floor. There is a pedestrian walkway and a playground below their balcony.

The matter went to voluntary mediation, but there was no settlement.

You have spoken to the paralegal for the landlord, and she has advised you that if the matter goes to a hearing, the landlord will call the building manager and four tenants as witnesses. She has given you copies of the complaint letters and the building manager's complaints log. Two of the tenants are threatening to leave the building if the matter is not resolved.

Jane has admitted to you that she is not home a lot, because she has to work two jobs to support her sons and herself.

The hearing date is set for May 15. It is now April 30. The landlord has just sent you a written offer to settle, stipulating that Jane will have 60 days to find another place to live, failing which the landlord may apply for an order to evict her forthwith.

You have carefully considered the matter, and you believe that, if the matter goes to a hearing, Jane may be unsuccessful and there will be an order for immediate eviction. You have advised Jane that you think it would be prudent to accept the landlord's offer. Jane thinks this is outrageous. She wants to have a hearing and assert her rights. She is convinced that the landlord cannot just kick her out, when she has lived in the building for five years and there have been no complaints until six months ago. "Who are you working for?" she shouts at you. "Me or the landlord?"

At the beginning of April, you sent Jane an interim invoice for $800.00. She has not paid it.

You do not think that Jane is making good decisions right now. You do not believe that going to a hearing is in her best interests. You would like to give Jane notice that you are withdrawing from representation. You think that it will be a wake-up call for her to start listening to your advice.

Question: Are you entitled to withdraw your services based on Jane's refusal to listen to your advice?

Discussion: You may not withdraw from representation except for good cause and upon notice that is appropriate in the circumstances. Jane's refusal to listen to your advice, which was given by you after careful consideration of the matter, may be grounds for withdrawal based on a serious loss of confidence. She has refused to accept and act upon your advice on a significant point—that is, whether to agree to the landlord's settlement proposal.

Question: Can you withdraw based on serious loss of confidence without causing prejudice or harm to Jane?

Discussion: Probably not. The hearing date is two weeks away. If you withdraw, Jane will have very little time to find another legal representative, and her new representative (if she can find one) will have very little time to prepare for the hearing.

Question: Can you withdraw based on non-payment of fees?

Discussion: Probably not. Here again, if you withdraw at this stage, you cannot be assured that Jane will be able to find someone else to represent her at the hearing in two weeks' time. Accordingly, you may be required to continue to represent Jane to the best of your ability, even if she is proving to be a difficult client and your fees remain unpaid.

Question: Can you give Jane notice that you are withdrawing from representation as a wake-up call for her to start listening to your advice about accepting the landlord's settlement offer?

Discussion: No. You cannot use the threat of withdrawal to force a client to make a hasty decision on a difficult question—in this case, about accepting the landlord's settlement offer. ◇

If the above conditions are met, a paralegal may withdraw from representation pursuant to rule 3.08(7) if he does all of the following:

(a) advises the client, preferably in writing, that the paralegal is withdrawing and the reason for the withdrawal;

(b) accounts to the client for any monies received on account of fees and disbursements;

(c) notifies the prosecution in writing that the paralegal is no longer acting; and

(d) in a case where the paralegal's name appears in the court records as acting for the accused, notifies the clerk or registrar of the appropriate court in writing that the paralegal is no longer acting.

Although the Rules do not require you to apply to the tribunal to be removed as the client's paralegal, the rules or practice directions of the court may require that you do so. When withdrawing from representation, you should ensure that you follow the correct procedures for the tribunal in which the matter is being heard.

When advising the prosecution of the withdrawal or applying to the tribunal for direction, you shall not disclose the reasons for the withdrawal, unless the Rules permit such disclosure (guideline 11).

NON-PAYMENT OF FEES—QUASI-CRIMINAL AND CRIMINAL CASES (RULE 3.08(8))

A paralegal who has agreed to act in a quasi-criminal or criminal case may not withdraw because of non-payment of fees if:

- the date set for trial is not far enough removed to enable the client to obtain the services of another licensee, or

- the date set for trial is not far enough removed to enable the successor licensee to prepare adequately for trial, and

- an adjournment of the trial date cannot be obtained without adversely affecting the client's interests.

ADJOURNMENT OF THE TRIAL DATE—QUASI-CRIMINAL AND CRIMINAL CASES (RULE 3.08(9))

Unless instructed otherwise by the client, the paralegal shall attempt to have the trial date adjourned if the following conditions are met:

- the paralegal has good cause to withdraw for a reason other than non-payment of fees; and

- there is not sufficient time between a notice to the client of the paralegal's intention to withdraw and the trial date to enable the client to obtain the services of another licensee and to enable the successor licensee to prepare adequately for trial.

In this situation, the paralegal may withdraw from the case only with permission of the court before which the case is to be tried.

Manner of Withdrawal (Rules 3.08(10), (11))

When you withdraw from representation, you shall try to minimize expense and avoid prejudice to the client, and you shall do all that can reasonably be done to facilitate the orderly transfer of the matter to the successor licensee (rule 3.08(10)).

Upon discharge or withdrawal, a paralegal shall (rule 3.08(11)):

(a) deliver to the client or as directed by the client all papers and property to which the client is entitled;

(b) give the client all information that may be required in connection with the case or matter;

(c) account for all funds of the client held at the time of the discharge or withdrawal, and all funds previously dealt with, including refunding any monies not earned during the representation;

(d) promptly render an account for outstanding fees and disbursements; and

(e) cooperate with the successor licensee so as to minimize expense and avoid prejudice to the client.

When delivering the client's file to the client, you should have the client sign an acknowledgment of receipt of the file. If the client instructs you to release the file to a successor licensee, you should obtain a written direction confirming those instructions, signed by the client.

Duties of Successor Paralegal (Rule 3.08(12))

Before agreeing to represent a client of a predecessor licensee, a successor paralegal shall be satisfied that the predecessor licensee has withdrawn or has been discharged by the client. The successor paralegal may contact the predecessor licensee to confirm this and advise the predecessor licensee that she has been retained.

It is appropriate for a successor licensee to urge the client to settle or take reasonable steps toward settling an outstanding account with the predecessor licensee, especially if the predecessor licensee withdrew for good cause or was capriciously dismissed. If a trial or hearing is imminent or if the client would be otherwise prejudiced, the existence of an outstanding account should not be allowed to interfere with the successor licensee acting for the client (commentary to rule 2.09(10) of the Rules of Professional Conduct for lawyers).

BOX 4.19

Restrictions on Disclosure of Client Information

When you withdraw, you are subject to restrictions on disclosure of client information. You shall not disclose the reasons for the withdrawal to a successor paralegal. When advising the prosecution of the withdrawal in a criminal or quasi-criminal case, you shall not disclose the reasons for the withdrawal, unless the Rules permit such disclosure. When applying to a tribunal for direction with respect to the withdrawal, you shall not disclose the reasons for the withdrawal, unless the Rules permit such disclosure. ◇

Termination by Client—Written Confirmation (Guideline 11)

If the client terminates the retainer while the client matter is ongoing, you should confirm, in writing, the termination of the retainer. If the client requests that his file be returned to him personally, you should obtain a written acknowledgment, signed by the client, confirming that he has received the file. If the client requests that his file be transferred to a successor licensee, you should obtain a written direction confirming those instructions, signed by the client.

CHAPTER SUMMARY

The fiduciary relationship between the paralegal and the client gives rise to a special standard of care, which imposes the following duties on the paralegal: honesty and candour, confidentiality, avoidance of conflicts of interest, and accounting for client property. These duties are codified in the Rules.

A paralegal shall perform any services undertaken on a client's behalf to the standard of a competent paralegal. A competent paralegal is a paralegal who has and applies the relevant skills, attributes, and values appropriate to each client matter. These include (1) knowledge; (2) client service and communication; (3) practice management; (4) skills and judgment; and (5) continuing education or professional development.

A paralegal must be honest and candid when advising all clients. You must advise the client honestly and candidly of the applicable law, the client's options, possible outcomes, and possible risks. Your advice should enable the client to make informed decisions and give appropriate instructions in the matter.

You should always ensure that clients, including prospective clients, understand that you are a paralegal, not a lawyer. You must never undertake or provide advice about a matter that is outside of the scope of permissible practice for paralegals.

When advising a client, you must never knowingly assist in or encourage any dishonesty, fraud, crime, or illegal conduct. You must not instruct a client on how to violate the law and avoid punishment.

A paralegal shall, at all times, hold in strict confidence all information concerning the business and affairs of a client acquired in the course of their professional relationship, and shall not disclose any such information unless expressly or impliedly authorized by the client or required by law to do so. The duty of confidentiality begins at the commencement of the paralegal–client relationship and continues indefinitely.

A paralegal shall not advise or represent more than one side of a dispute. A paralegal shall not act or continue to act in a matter when there is or is likely to be a conflicting interest unless, after disclosure adequate to make an informed decision, the client or prospective client consents. To help avoid conflicts of interest, a paralegal should consider maintaining a conflict-checking system and should carefully consider his obligations under rule 3.04.

When a paralegal changes firms, a conflict of interest may arise. Rule 3.05 sets out procedures to be followed by paralegals who are transferring to a new firm and by new paralegals who are preparing to join a firm.

A paralegal should be cautious about entering with a client into any business arrangement that is unrelated to the provision of paralegal services, as this may cause a conflict of interest for the paralegal.

A paralegal is a fiduciary with respect to any client property that comes into her possession, and shall care for that property as a careful and prudent owner would when dealing with similar property. The paralegal must comply with the rules and the law about the preservation of property entrusted to a fiduciary, including maintaining a valuable property record in accordance with By-law 9.

The client may terminate the paralegal–client relationship at any time, for any reason. A paralegal shall not withdraw from representation of a client before the matter in which the paralegal was retained is concluded except for good cause and upon notice to the client appropriate in the circumstances.

Good cause for withdrawal will depend on many factors, including: the nature of the matter and the stage you are at in the matter; the relationship with the client; your expertise and experience; and any harm or prejudice to the client that may result from the withdrawal of services. These factors may also determine what appropriate notice is in the circumstances. Generally, you should try to safeguard the client from prejudice or harm. If you are at a critical procedural stage in a matter, then you should continue your representation of the client.

In certain situations, a paralegal is required to withdraw from representation, even if the paralegal or the client wishes to continue with the retainer.

APPENDIX 4.1
Client Disclosure Authorization

AUTHORIZATION

I, [name of client], do hereby authorize [name of paralegal licensee] of [name of paralegal firm] to release to [name(s) of authorized recipient(s)] or their legal representatives of record the following documents or other information:

[particulars of permitted disclosure]

I have been advised of and understand the purpose and consequences of this disclosure.

Date: _____   Signature: _____

                                                        Client name

Date: _____   Signature: _____

                                                        Witness name

APPENDIX 4.2
Non-Engagement Letter
(Conflict of Interest—Client Declines Retainer)

[date]

[file number]

[client name and address]

Dear [client name]:

Re: [File name]

As we discussed during our [telephone conversation/meeting/initial consultation] on [date], a preliminary search revealed that [paralegal firm name] has a conflict of interest in this matter. We provided you with details of the conflict and asked you to decide whether you wished to consent to the retainer based on this disclosure. You have now advised that you do not wish to retain us.

Please be aware that whatever claim you have may be barred by the passage of time. Since time limitations may be critical to your case, we recommend that you immediately contact another paralegal or a lawyer for assistance regarding your matter. If you do not have another paralegal or lawyer in mind to represent you, the Law Society maintains a directory of paralegals and lawyers who may be available to assist you at its website (www.lsuc.on.ca), or you may wish to call the Lawyer Referral Service at 1-900-565-4577. There is a charge for the Lawyer Referral Service.

We confirm that we do not have any documents belonging to you. All documents were returned to you at the end of the initial meeting.

Although we were not able to assist you in this matter, we hope that you will consider [paralegal firm name] in the event that you require legal services in the future.

Thank you again for your interest in this firm.

Yours truly,

[paralegal firm name]

[signature]

[signatory name]

Paralegal

[Adapted from the Law Society of British Columbia website (www.lawsociety.bc.ca) and the Law Society of Upper Canada website (www.lsuc.on.ca).]

APPENDIX 4.3
Non-Engagement Letter (Conflict of Interest—Paralegal Firm Declines Retainer)

[date]

[file number]

[client name and address]

Dear [client name]:

Re: [File name]

As we discussed during our [telephone conversation/meeting/initial consultation] on [date], before [paralegal firm name] could agree to represent you in this matter, we had to investigate whether this representation could adversely affect existing or former clients' interests or whether there might be some other reason that we would be unable to adequately represent your interests.

On [date], we performed a conflict of interest check and found that our firm does indeed have a conflict of interest in this case. Unfortunately, we therefore cannot represent you and we must decline to do so in this matter.

Please be aware that whatever claim you have may be barred by the passage of time. Since time limitations may be critical to your case, we recommend that you immediately contact another paralegal or a lawyer for assistance regarding your matter. If you do not have another paralegal or lawyer in mind to represent you, the Law Society maintains a directory of paralegals and lawyers who may be available to assist you at its website (www.lsuc.on.ca), or you may wish to call the Lawyer Referral Service at 1-900-565-4577. There is a charge for the Lawyer Referral Service.

We confirm that we do not have any documents belonging to you. All documents were returned to you at the end of the initial meeting.

Although we were not able to assist you in this matter, we hope that you will consider [paralegal firm name] in the event that you require legal services in the future.

Thank you again for your interest in this firm.

Yours truly,

[paralegal firm name]

[signature]

[signatory name]

Paralegal

[Adapted from the Law Society of British Columbia website (www.lawsociety.bc.ca) and the Law Society of Upper Canada website (www.lsuc.on.ca).]

KEY TERMS

fiduciary relationship	justified disclosure
fiduciary	permitted disclosure
competent paralegal	dispute
substantive law	informed consent
procedural law	independent legal representation
professional judgment	continuing relationship
candid	continuing client
alternative dispute resolution	multi-discipline practice
compromise and settlement	affiliation
error	affiliated entity
omission	guarantee
duty of confidentiality	client property
express (or explicit) consent	valuable property record
implied consent	serious loss of confidence

REFERENCES

Constitution Act, 1982, being Schedule B to the *Canada Act 1982* (U.K.), 1982, c. 11.

Courts of Justice Act, RSO 1990, c. C.43.

Criminal Code, RSC 1985, c. C-46, as amended.

Curtis, Carole, "Dealing with the Difficult Client" (Toronto: 2003); available online at http://www.practicepro.ca/practice/pdf/DealingDifficultClientCaroleCurtis.pdf.

French Language Services Act, RSO 1990, c. F.32.

Income Tax Act, RSC 1985, c. 1, as amended.

Insurance Act, RSO 1990, c. 1-8.

Law Society Act, RSO 1990, c. L.8, as amended.

Law Society of Upper Canada (LSUC), By-Laws (Toronto: LSUC, 2005); available online at http://www.lsuc.on.ca/regulation/a/by-laws.

Law Society of Upper Canada (LSUC), Knowledge Tree—Difficult Clients (Toronto: LSUC); available online at http://rc.lsuc.on.ca/jsp/kt/loadKnowledgeTreePage.do.

Law Society of Upper Canada (LSUC), *Paralegal Bookkeeping Guide* (Toronto: LSUC, 2008); available online at http://rc.lsuc.on.ca/jsp/bookkeepingGuide/paralegal.jsp.

Law Society of Upper Canada (LSUC), Paralegal Professional Conduct Guidelines (Toronto: LSUC, 2008) ("the Guidelines"); available online at http://www.lsuc.on.ca/paralegals/a/paralegal-professional-conduct-guidelines.

Law Society of Upper Canada (LSUC), Paralegal Rules of Conduct (Toronto: LSUC, 2007, as amended) ("the Rules"); available online at http://www.lsuc .on.ca/paralegals/a/paralegal-rules-of-conduct.

Law Society of Upper Canada (LSUC), Rules of Professional Conduct (Toronto: LSUC, 2008, as amended); available online at http://www.lsuc.on.ca/ regulation/a/profconduct.

Law Society of Upper Canada (LSUC), The Minimum Expectations for Professional Development (Toronto: LSUC); available online at http://rc.lsuc.on.ca/jsp/minExpectationforProfDev/index.jsp.

Office of the Privacy Commissioner of Canada, "Fact Sheet: Complying with the *Personal Information Protection and Electronic Documents Act*"; available online at http://www.priv.gc.ca/fs-fi/02_05_d_16_e.cfm.

Ontario Business Corporations Act, RSO 1990, c. B.16, as amended.

Personal Information Protection and Electronic Documents Act, SC 2000, c. 5.

Provincial Offences Act, RSO 1990, c. P.33, as amended.

Rules of the Small Claims Court, O. Reg. 258/98.

REVIEW QUESTIONS

1. Your practice is restricted to Small Claims Court litigation and *Highway Traffic Act* matters. The property manager for a corporate residential landlord for whom you have done some collections work wants to retain you to defend the landlord in a *Provincial Offences Act* prosecution. The landlord has been charged with several offences contrary to the residential tenancies legislation, including harassment and interference with the tenant's enjoyment of the premises. If the landlord is convicted, the maximum fine is $100,000.00.

    Residential tenancies law is an area into which you are eager to expand. You would also like to accept the retainer because the matter is complex and you look forward to the challenge. Should you accept the retainer?

2. A client consults you about commencing a claim for wrongful dismissal in Small Claims Court. Based on what he is telling you and the documents he has produced to you, you do not think that he has a good case. On the other hand, you could use the money, and he appears to be very eager to sue his former employer. "I don't care if I win. I just want to get these guys," he tells you. "I want to jerk them around the way they jerked me around. I can pay."

    What should you do?

3. A client has several invoices that have been outstanding for 90 days. You wish to put them in collection. What procedures should you follow and what information may you disclose to the collection agency?

4. Joseph Kutar meets with you at your office to discuss a *Highway Traffic Act* matter. While you are reviewing the certificate of offence, Joseph reads the labels on some of the client files stacked on your desk. "I know that landlord," he says, indicating one of the files. "I used to live in one of their buildings. A real slum." You move the files to the floor behind your desk. Then you ask Joseph some questions about the *Highway Traffic Act* matter, taking notes of his answers.

   Based on what he tells you of the matter and your review of the certificate of offence, you advise him to plead down to a lesser offence with fewer demerit points. When he hears this, Joseph's behaviour becomes belligerent and threatening. "I'm a courier," he says. "Any more demerit points and I can't drive. I'll find someone else who knows what they're doing!" He grabs the certificate of offence off your desk and leaves your office.

   A few days later you have some matters in traffic court. Outside the courtroom, you get into a conversation with a couple of other paralegals who do a lot of traffic court work. One of them, Alice Fisher, says jokingly to you, "I'm doing some work for a former client of yours, one J.K. He told me he had to fire you because you kept giving him bad advice. What's the real story?" You change the subject, and start talking about how difficult it is becoming to find parking near the courthouse.

   Several people are sitting or standing close by and can overhear your conversation.

   Discuss some professional and practice management issues that arise based on the above facts.

5. Theresa Santos wishes to meet with you to discuss a residential tenancies matter. She wishes to apply for an abatement of rent and other relief, on grounds of non-repair of the residential premises and harassment by the landlord or the landlord's agent. You are familiar with Theresa's landlord, having acted for the landlord in the past in tenant applications similar to Theresa's, though for a different building. You haven't had any work from that landlord for over a year, but you figure your experience from the previous matters will give you an advantage in this application.

   Should you accept the retainer?

6. Before agreeing to a joint retainer in which you have a continuing relationship with one client, for whom you act regularly, what steps must you take?

7. You are considering accepting a position that has just been offered to you at a new paralegal firm. You have appeared opposite this firm on several matters in the past, and you are very impressed by their advocacy skills and high standards of professionalism. What are some issues that both you and the new firm should consider?

8. Your client is Lars Larssen. On January 3, 20—, you receive a TAG Heuer sports watch valued at $7,500.00 from your client, which is to be held in trust pending a court order determining ownership of the property.

On February 14, 20—, pursuant to a written settlement agreement between the parties and a signed direction from your client, you deliver the watch to your client's former partner, Sigrid Gutman.

Complete the valuable property record for this item.

Schwarz and Berryman PC
Paralegals
Valuable Property Record

Client	Description of property	Date received	Received from	Value	Delivered to	Date of delivery

CHAPTER 5

Advocacy

LEARNING OBJECTIVES

After reading this chapter, you will understand:

- What an advocate is.
- The paralegal advocate's duty to the client and the tribunal.
- The paralegal advocate's obligations in the tribunal process.
- Disclosure of documents.
- Procedure when agreeing to a guilty plea.
- Dealing with witnesses.
- Communicating with witnesses giving testimony.
- The paralegal as witness.
- Dealing with unrepresented persons.
- Disclosure of errors and omissions.

GENERAL (RULE 4; GUIDELINE 12)

An **advocate** is a person who assists, defends, or pleads for others before a tribunal. According to rule 1.02(1), the term **tribunal** includes courts, boards, arbitrators, mediators, administrative agencies, and bodies that resolve disputes, regardless of their function or the informality of their procedures. An **adjudicator** is a person who hears or considers a proceeding before a tribunal and makes a decision with respect to that proceeding (guideline 12).

Rule 4 of the Paralegal Rules, which governs advocacy, applies to all appearances and proceedings before bodies that fall within the definition in rule 1.02 (rule 4.01(2)).

THE PARALEGAL AS ADVOCATE (RULE 4.01)

Duty to Clients, Tribunals, and Others (Rules 4.01(1) to (4), (7))

The paralegal advocate must balance a number of duties.

When acting as an advocate, you shall represent your client honourably and resolutely within the limits of the law. At the same time, you shall treat other licensees and the tribunal before which you are appearing with candour, fairness, courtesy, and respect (rule 4.01(1)), and you shall encourage public respect for, and try to improve, the administration of justice (rule 6.01(1)).

You have a duty to represent your client fearlessly and resolutely. Rule 4 does not require to you assist an opposing party or raise matters that are harmful to your client's case, unless the Rules state otherwise. Rule 4 does place limits on how you may conduct yourself when acting as advocate before a tribunal. Your professional obligations to other parties, other licensees, the tribunal, and the administration of justice are paramount. You must meet these obligations every time you appear before a tribunal as an advocate for a client (guideline 12).

Rule 4.01(4) sets out the following requirements for paralegal advocates:

(a) The paralegal shall raise fearlessly every issue, advance every argument, and ask every question, however distasteful, that the paralegal thinks will help the client's case.

(b) The paralegal shall try to obtain for the client the benefit of every remedy and defence authorized by law. A **remedy** is a method of enforcing a right, or preventing or compensating for a wrong.

(c) A paralegal shall never give up or abandon a client's legal rights without the client's informed consent. This rule applies to the client's legal rights generally, and refers specifically to an available defence under a statute of limitations. A **statutory limitation period** is a period of time established by a statute for commencing a proceeding. When the statutory limitation period has expired, any proceeding against your client is **statute-barred**— that is, it is stopped by the expiry of the statutory limitation period. For example, s. 786 of the *Criminal Code* states that in a summary conviction matter, no proceedings shall be commenced more than six months after the time when the subject matter of the proceedings arose, unless the prosecutor and the defendant agree.

Informed consent is consent based on information that is sufficient to allow the client to assess the situation and make an informed decision.

Special rules apply to agreements on guilty pleas. See rules 4.01(8) and (9), and the discussion on pages 135–136.

(d) A paralegal shall avoid and discourage the client from:

- Resorting to frivolous and vexatious objections. An **objection** is an argument by a party that a particular piece of evidence, line of questioning, or other matter is improper or illegal and should not be allowed by the court. A **frivolous and vexatious objection** is an objection that has no legal merit and is made to annoy, harass, or embarrass the other side.

- Trying to gain advantage from mistakes or oversights by the other side that do not go to the merits of the case. The **merits of the case** are the legal principles upon which a party's assertion of rights is based. A mistake or oversight that does not go to the merits of the case does not affect a party's legal rights.

- Using tactics designed merely to delay or harass the other side.

Regarding rule 4.01(4)(d), guideline 12 recommends that a paralegal should not engage in rude or disruptive conduct before a tribunal, or ill-mannered correspondence, language, or behaviour toward opposing parties or their advocates. See also rule 7.01(3), which states that when providing legal services, a paralegal shall not communicate, in writing or otherwise, with a client, another licensee, or any other person in a manner that is abusive, offensive, or otherwise inconsistent with the proper tone of a professional communication from a paralegal.

The Paralegal and the Tribunal Process (Rule 4.01(5))

ABUSE OF TRIBUNAL PROCESS

Malicious Proceedings (Rule 4.01(5)(a))

A paralegal shall not abuse the process of the tribunal by commencing or continuing to act in proceedings that, although legal, are clearly motivated by malice on the part of the client and are brought solely for the purpose of injuring the other party (rule 4.01(5)(a)). Proceedings that have no merit waste the time of the tribunal and its officers, and do not further the cause of justice (guideline 12).

BOX 5.1

Abuse of Tribunal Process

Scenario

A prospective client wishes to commence an application for termination of a tenancy against a tenant. Based on what she tells you and the documents she produces, you do not think she is entitled to what she says she wants. Throughout the consultation, she speaks of the tenant in disparaging terms, with contempt and anger.

Question: Should you accept the retainer?

Discussion: A paralegal must be honest and candid when advising a client (rule 3.02). You must look at both sides of each issue without bias. You must advise the client honestly and candidly of the applicable law, the client's options, possible outcomes, and possible risks. Your advice should enable the client to make informed decisions and give appropriate instructions in the matter.

You should advise the client that, in your opinion, the proceeding has no legal merit, giving her your reasons. If she disregards your advice and insists on going forward, consider whether she is motivated solely by malice.

If you are satisfied that she is motivated solely by malice, you should decline the retainer. You should send her a non-engagement letter, confirming that you have decided to decline the retainer. You should also confirm that any documents in your possession have been returned to her.

Question: What are the consequences of going forward with the application?

Discussion: You will be in breach of rule 4.01(5)(a), which prohibits paralegals from starting or continuing actions that have no merit and are brought solely to harm the other party. In this case, you have concluded that the proceeding has no merit, and you believe that the client's motives are malicious. Unmeritorious proceedings waste the time of the tribunal and its officers, and do not further the cause of justice. ◇

Complainants (Rule 4.01(5)(l))

A **complainant** is a person who alleges that he or she was the victim of a crime, and who takes part in the prosecution of the person(s) accused of committing the crime.

When representing a complainant or potential complainant, a paralegal shall not try to gain a benefit for the complainant by threatening to lay a criminal charge or by offering to seek or procure the withdrawal of a criminal charge.

MISLEADING THE TRIBUNAL (RULES 4.01(5)(C), (D), (H))

A paralegal must ensure that neither the paralegal nor the client misleads the tribunal. To arrive at an appropriate decision, the tribunal must receive everything that is relevant to the issues to be decided in a matter (guideline 12). If the tribunal is mistaken about or misunderstands some aspect of the facts or the law in a case, the paralegal should do what is necessary to correct the mistake or misunderstanding.

A paralegal shall not knowingly attempt to deceive a tribunal or influence the course of justice by (rule 4.05(5)(c)):

- offering false evidence,

- misstating facts or law,

- presenting or relying upon a false or deceptive affidavit,

- suppressing something that should be disclosed, or

- otherwise assisting in any deception, crime, or illegal conduct.

BOX 5.2

What Is an Affidavit?

An **affidavit** is a written statement of facts that is confirmed under oath or by affirmation by the person making it. The person making the affidavit is called the **deponent**.

The content of an affidavit is evidence. Swearing or affirming a false or deceptive affidavit or assisting another person to do so with intent to mislead is an offence contrary to s. 131 of the *Criminal Code*. ◇

You must represent your client fearlessly and resolutely, but you shall not knowingly engage in dishonest conduct that misleads the tribunal and others in order to protect your client or gain an advantage for your client.

A paralegal shall not deliberately refrain from informing the tribunal of any binding authority that he considers to be directly on point and that has not been mentioned by an opponent (rule 4.01(5)(d)). **Binding authority** (also known as binding precedent) is a judicial decision by a higher court that must be followed by lower courts.

A paralegal shall not knowingly misstate the contents of a document, the testimony of a witness, the substance of an argument, or the provisions of a statute or similar authority (rule 4.01(5)(h)). The tribunal must be able to rely upon correct information when reviewing a case and arriving at a decision.

BOX 5.3

Binding Authority (Rule 4.01(5)(d))

Scenario

You represent the defendant in a Small Claims Court proceeding. During some last-minute online research before the trial, you find a very recent appellate decision that is unfavourable to your client and favourable to the plaintiff. The decision is binding on the Small Claims Court. There are some minor legal and factual differences between the matter dealt with in the appellate decision and the matter before the court.

To your surprise, during submissions, the licensee representing the plaintiff does not refer to the decision.

Are you required to inform the court of a binding precedent that may prejudice your client's case?

Discussion

You are required to represent your client resolutely and honourably within the limits of the law, while treating the tribunal and other licensees with candour, fairness, courtesy, and respect, and upholding the high ethical standards of the paralegal profession (rule 4.01(1)). You are not required to assist an adversary or advance matters that may harm your client's case, unless the Rules provide otherwise (rule 4.01(3)).

You must balance your duty to your client with your duty to treat the tribunal and other licensees with candour and fairness. Your opponent has not mentioned the appellate decision. You may not deliberately refrain from informing the tribunal of the appellate decision if you think the principles stated in the decision are relevant and applicable to this case, regardless of the minor legal and factual differences. You must consider whether the court is likely to arrive at an inappropriate decision if it does not know about the case. ◇

IMPROPERLY INFLUENCING THE TRIBUNAL (RULE 4.01(5)(e), (g))

Adjudicators must be fair, impartial, independent, and neutral. An adjudicator's decision making must not be influenced by private or partisan interests, which may give rise to actual bias or to an appearance of bias in favour of a particular person.

A paralegal shall not appear before an adjudicator if the paralegal, the paralegal's partner, a paralegal employed by the paralegal's firm, or the paralegal's client has a business or personal relationship with the adjudicator that either affects the adjudicator's impartiality or may reasonably appear to affect the adjudicator's impartiality (rule 4.01(5)(e)).

A paralegal shall not attempt or allow anyone else to attempt, directly or indirectly, to influence the decision or action of a tribunal or its officers in any case or matter except by open persuasion as an advocate (rule 4.01(5)(g)).

Guideline 12 states that the only appropriate way to influence a tribunal's decision is by appearing before the tribunal in the presence of, or on notice to, other parties, offering appropriate evidence in support of your client's case, and making persuasive submissions based upon applicable legal principles, unless the tribunal's rules of procedure permit or require otherwise.

You should never communicate directly with the adjudicator in the absence of other parties, unless the tribunal's procedural rules permit you to do so (guideline 12).

DISHONEST CONDUCT (RULES 4.01(5)(b), (c), (f))

A paralegal shall not knowingly assist or permit the client to do anything that the paralegal considers to be dishonest or dishonourable (rule 4.01(5)(b)).

A paralegal shall not knowingly attempt to deceive a tribunal or influence the course of justice by offering false evidence (including false or deceptive affidavits), misstating facts or law, suppressing relevant information, or otherwise assisting in any deception, crime, or illegal conduct (rule 4.01(5)(c)).

BOX 5.4

Offering False Evidence

Scenario

You are acting for the plaintiff in an unliquidated action in Small Claims Court. The defendant failed to file a defence within the prescribed time, and has been noted in default. You have prepared a motion in writing for an assessment of damages, and a supporting affidavit.

When the client reviews the supporting affidavit, she objects to several statements because they are harmful to her case. "If the judge reads this, I'll get less money," she says. "Why should I say anything that's going to take money out of my pocket? I never would have told you that stuff if I'd known you were going to use it against me. I want you to leave it out completely, or change it to say something that will get me what I'm asking for."

The client provided the material to you during a telephone conversation just after the defendant was noted in default. You phoned her because you wanted to clarify some issues before you got started on the supporting affidavit. You took detailed notes of what she said, and went over them with her before ending the call. The statements in the affidavit accurately reflect your notes of the conversation. The statements contain information that is relevant to issues in the matter.

The client is correct that the material is harmful to her case. You did not obtain her consent to disclose the harmful information.

Question: Is the harmful material confidential?

Discussion: You have a duty to hold all client information in strict confidence, unless disclosure is expressly or impliedly authorized by the client or required by law (rule 3.03(1)). You have neither implied nor express consent to disclose this information.

Question: Is disclosure required by law?

Discussion: Unless otherwise provided by the Rules, you are not required to assist an adversary or advance matters that harm your client's case (rule 4.01(3)).

In this case, there is no adversary. The defendant has been noted in default, and is not entitled to notice of the motion for an assessment of damages. However, the court file is public, and its contents—including the affidavit supporting the motion for an assessment of damages—are available to the defendant, should he decide at some point to come forward and dispute the matter. If the harmful material is included in the affidavit, it may come to the attention of the defendant.

In cases where you are dealing with an unrepresented party and the matter is uncontested, you should consider taking particular care to ensure that the tribunal has all the information necessary to come to an appropriate conclusion.

The client is not disputing the truth of the harmful statements, and you have taken careful steps to confirm their accuracy. Her concern is the harmful effect that their disclosure may have on her case.

The only material that the judge will have before her on the motion is the material that you file with the court. The harmful material is accurate, and relevant to issues in the case. If the material is deleted from the affidavit, you may be knowingly attempting to deceive a tribunal and influence the course of justice by relying upon a deceptive affidavit and suppressing information that ought to be disclosed, contrary to rule 4.01(5)(c). You may be knowingly deceiving the tribunal because you are not providing all the information that the judge will need to properly review the matter and arrive at an appropriate decision. You may be knowingly attempting to influence the course of justice because you are suppressing relevant material in order to obtain a more favourable result for your client.

You may be knowingly assisting or permitting the client to do something that is dishonest and dishonourable, contrary to rule 4.01(5)(b).

You must carefully weigh your duties of confidentiality and loyalty to the client against your duty to the tribunal and the administration of justice, keeping in mind your obligations under rules 4.01(4) and (5).

Question: Should you alter the harmful material so that it is favourable to your client's case?

Discussion: If you change the material to make it favourable to your client, the supporting affidavit will contain false statements. If you alter evidence you know to be true in order to gain an advantage for your client, you are knowingly attempting to deceive the tribunal and influence the course of justice by offering false evidence, relying upon a false or deceptive affidavit, and assisting in a crime, contrary to rule 4.01(5)(c). You are knowingly deceiving the tribunal because you are knowingly relying upon false evidence in support of the motion. You are knowingly attempting to influence the course of justice, because you are offering evidence you know to be false in order to obtain a more favourable result for your client.

You are knowingly assisting or permitting the client to do something that is dishonest and dishonourable, contrary to rule 4.01(5)(b).

Giving false evidence (spoken or written) under oath with intent to mislead is an offence contrary to s. 131 of the *Criminal Code*.

Question: What next?

Discussion: You should advise the client that you have a duty to provide the tribunal with everything it needs to arrive at an effective, appropriate decision. You cannot suppress or alter relevant evidence to obtain a more favourable result for her, or assist her in swearing an affidavit you know to be false. You should advise her that swearing a false affidavit with intent to mislead is an offence. If she persists in her instructions, you may be required to withdraw from representation pursuant to rule 3.08. ◇

A paralegal shall not knowingly assert a fact to be true when its truth cannot reasonably be supported by the evidence, or as a matter of which notice may be taken by the tribunal (rule 4.05(5)(f)).

BOX 5.5

Judicial Notice

What is meant by "a matter of which notice may be taken by the tribunal" (rule 4.05(5)(f))? This is known in the courts as **judicial notice**. Adjudicators may notice, or accept as true, certain notorious facts (that is, matters of common knowledge) without hearing evidence and without inquiry. Other lesser-known facts (for example, matters that can be checked in a standard reference work and are not easily disputed) may be judicially noticed after inquiry. ◇

DISCLOSURE OF DOCUMENTS (RULE 4.01(6))

Where the procedural rules of a tribunal require the parties to produce documents, a paralegal advocate:

(a)   shall explain to the client the necessity of making full disclosure of all documents relating to any matter in issue, and the duty to answer any proper question relating to any issue in the action to the best of his knowledge, information, or belief;

(b)   shall assist the client in fulfilling his obligation to make full disclosure; and

(c)   shall not make frivolous requests for production of documents or frivolous demands for information.

The requirements for disclosure may vary from tribunal to tribunal. You should carefully review the procedural rules of the tribunal and other relevant law to determine the extent and timing of required disclosure.

Timely, complete, and accurate disclosure lets the parties know the case they have to meet. It promotes settlement because it allows each party to assess the strengths and weaknesses of her own case and those of opposing parties. It also makes the hearing process more efficient and fair (guideline 12).

ADMISSIONS BY THE CLIENT IN CRIMINAL PROCEEDINGS (RULES 4.01(5)(b), (c), (f))

Guideline 12 states that when defending an accused person, a paralegal's duty is to protect the client from being convicted, except by a tribunal of competent jurisdiction and upon legal evidence sufficient to support a conviction for the offence with which the client is charged. Accordingly, a paralegal may properly rely upon any evidence or defences, including technicalities, as long as they are not known to be false or fraudulent.

The paralegal must advise the client that any admissions made by the client to the paralegal may impose strict limitations on how the paralegal conducts the client's defence (guideline 12). The Rules require that the paralegal shall not:

- knowingly assist or permit the client to do anything that the paralegal considers to be dishonest or dishonourable;

- knowingly attempt to deceive the tribunal; or

- knowingly assert that a fact is true when its truth cannot be supported by the evidence.

Where the client has admitted to the paralegal any or all of the elements of the offence with which the client is charged, the paralegal must not do or say anything before the tribunal—including call any evidence, or make any arguments or submissions—that would contradict the facts admitted to the paralegal by the client (guideline 12). This would be misleading the tribunal.

Where the client admits all of the elements of the offence to the paralegal and the paralegal is convinced that the admissions are true and voluntary, the paralegal is restricted in how he conducts the client's defence. The paralegal may object to the jurisdiction of the tribunal, or to the form or admissibility of the evidence, or may

> ### BOX 5.6
>
> ## Elements of the Offence
>
> The **elements of the offence** are the legal requirements of the offence. They are the components of the offence that must be proven beyond a reasonable doubt by the prosecution in order to obtain a conviction. They are found in the statute that creates the offence, and in the jurisprudence interpreting the statute. The essential components of an offence are:
>
> 1. *Actus reus* (guilty act): the physical components of the offence, including conduct, circumstances, and consequences.
> 2. *Mens rea* (guilty mind): the mental component, including intention or knowledge, blameworthiness, or fault.
>
> To obtain a conviction, the prosecution must call evidence that proves all of the elements of the offence beyond a reasonable doubt. ◇

question whether the evidence is sufficient to prove beyond a reasonable doubt that the accused committed the offence (guideline 12).

Where the client admits all the elements of the offence to the paralegal, the paralegal shall not (guideline 12):

- suggest that someone else committed the offence,

- try to establish a defence of alibi, or

- call any evidence that the paralegal believes is false because of the client's admissions.

Where the client admits all of the elements of the offence to the paralegal, the paralegal is also limited in the extent to which he may attack the evidence for the prosecution. The paralegal may test the evidence given by each witness for the prosecution. The paralegal may argue that the evidence, as a whole, is not sufficient to prove the client guilty beyond a reasonable doubt. The paralegal should go no further than that (guideline 12).

AGREEMENT ON GUILTY PLEAS (RULES 4.01(8), (9))

Unless the client instructs otherwise, a paralegal acting for an accused or a person who is about to be charged in a criminal or quasi-criminal matter may discuss with the prosecutor a possible resolution to the case (rule 4.01(8)).

Before agreeing to a guilty plea on behalf of the client, the paralegal should obtain and review disclosure and complete any investigation that is appropriate in the circumstances. The paralegal may then enter into an agreement with the prosecutor about a guilty plea if the following conditions are met (rule 4.01(9)):

(a) the paralegal advises the client about the prospects for an acquittal or a finding of guilt if the matter goes to a hearing;

(b) the paralegal advises the client of the implications and possible consequences of a guilty plea, including the fact that the court is not bound by any agreement between the prosecutor and the paralegal, that it may refuse to accept the guilty plea, that it may order a trial, and in particular that it may impose a sentence that is harsher than the sentence agreed to by the prosecutor and the paralegal;

(c)   the client is prepared voluntarily to admit the factual and mental elements of the offence charged; and

(d)   the client voluntarily instructs the paralegal to enter into an agreement for a guilty plea.

Guideline 12 recommends that you take any steps that are reasonable in the circumstances to ensure that the client's instructions to enter into the agreement on a guilty plea are informed and voluntary. You should ensure that these instructions are in writing.

INTERVIEWING WITNESSES (RULE 4.02)

General (Rule 4.02(1) and 4.01(5)(i), (j), (k), (m))

Subject to rules 4.02(2) and (3), a paralegal may seek information from any potential witness in a proceeding, including witnesses appearing for opposing parties. The witness need not be under subpoena. You may not contact a witness who is represented, except as provided in rules 4.02(2) and (3).

When contacting witnesses, you should identify yourself to the witness and explain that you are a paralegal. You must give the witness your client's name and status in the proceeding, and ensure that the witness understands that you are acting exclusively in your client's interest. You should make a special effort to be clear on these points when speaking to a witness who does not have legal representation (guideline 12).

A witness has no obligation to talk to you. If a witness tells you he does not want to speak with you, you should leave the witness alone. You are not permitted to harass a witness (rule 4.01(5)(j)).

When interviewing witnesses, you shall take care not to subvert or suppress any evidence. You must not coach a witness to leave out evidence or to say things that are not completely true in order to benefit your client.

When interviewing witnesses, you shall take care not to procure the witness to stay out of the way—in other words, you shall not cause or persuade a witness not to give evidence at trial.

Additional restrictions on a paralegal advocate's conduct when dealing with witnesses are set out at rule 4.01(5). Among other things, this rule requires that, when acting as an advocate, a paralegal shall not:

- knowingly permit a witness or party to be presented in a false or misleading way, or to impersonate another;

- needlessly abuse, hector, harass, or inconvenience a witness; or

- persuade a witness not to give evidence, or encourage a witness not to attend a hearing.

Interviewing Represented Persons (Rules 4.02(2), (3), (6))

You shall not approach or deal with a person who is represented by another licensee, except through or with the consent of the licensee (rule 4.02(2)).

If you are acting for a party in a matter involving a corporation or organization represented by another licensee, you shall not, without the licensee's consent or unless otherwise authorized or required by law (rule 4.02(3)):

(a) approach directors, officers, or persons likely to be involved in the decision-making process for the corporation or organization; or

(b) approach employees and agents of the corporation or organization whose acts or omissions in connection with the matter may expose the corporation or organization to quasi-criminal, criminal, or civil liability.

For purposes of rule 4.02(3), an "organization" includes a partnership, limited partnership, sole proprietorship, association, union, unincorporated group, government department, government agency, tribunal, and regulatory body (rule 4.02(6)).

Rule 4.02 applies to communications with any person, whether or not that person is a party to a formal adjudicative proceeding, contract, or negotiation, who is represented by a licensee in the matter to which the communication relates (rule 4.02(4)).

A paralegal is prohibited from communicating with a represented person if the paralegal has direct knowledge that the person is represented, or where the circumstances are such that the paralegal should be able to determine that the person is represented (rule 4.02(5)). See Figure 5.1.

COMMUNICATION WITH WITNESSES GIVING TESTIMONY (RULE 4.03)

When preparing for a hearing, you may contact any witness, whether the witness is sympathetic to your client's cause or not. Different rules apply during a hearing. Your ability to speak to a witness who is giving testimony is restricted, to ensure that you do not influence what the witness says in the stand.

During a proceeding, whether or not you may speak to a witness depends upon

- whether the witness gives evidence that supports your (and your client's) cause or the cause of an opposing party, and

- what stage the witness is at in giving evidence.

A witness who gives evidence that supports your cause is called a **sympathetic witness**. A witness who gives evidence that supports an opposing party's cause is called an **unsympathetic witness**.

Whether a paralegal is representing a plaintiff, a defendant, a third party, or an accused, there are certain key stages in the process during which the paralegal may have discussions with the witness:

FIGURE 5.1   Represented Parties: Permitted and Prohibited Communication (Rule 4.02)

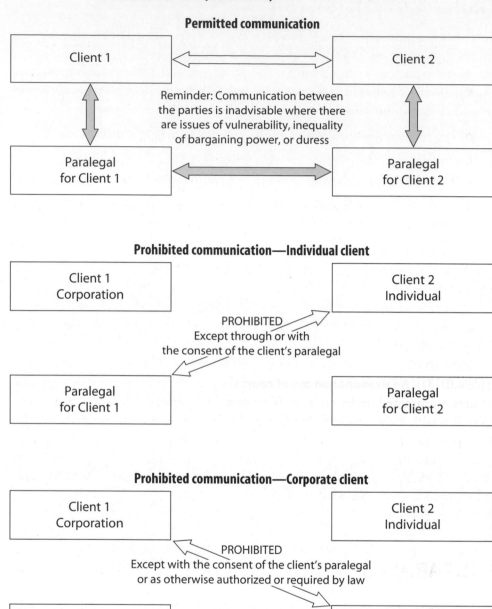

- during examination-in-chief, when a paralegal examines her own witness in support of her client's case;

- any interval between commencement of examination-in-chief and completion of examination-in-chief (for example, if the court takes a recess before examination-in-chief of the witness has been completed);

- after the paralegal has finished examination-in-chief of the witness but before cross-examination of the witness by another licensee;

- during cross-examination of a witness by an opposing licensee;

- after an opposing licensee has finished cross-examination of the witness but before the paralegal begins any re-examination of the witness;

- during re-examination, when the paralegal re-examines her own witness on matters arising out of the cross-examination.

Subject to the direction of the tribunal, you shall observe the rules set out in rule 4.03(1) respecting communication with witnesses giving evidence. For a summary of those rules, see Table 5.1.

If you are uncertain whether entering into discussions with a witness is proper under rule 4.03(1), you should obtain either the consent of the opposing licensee or leave of the tribunal before doing so (rule 4.03(2)).

Rule 4.03(1) applies, with necessary modifications, to examinations out of court (rule 4.03(3)). An **examination out of court** is a procedure during which a party or witness is examined under oath or affirmation by opposing parties or their representatives with a view to obtaining facts and information that will assist the parties to prepare their case. In Superior Court of Justice proceedings, examinations out of court include oral or written examinations for discovery (Rules of Civil Procedure, rule 31), taking of evidence before trial (Rules of Civil Procedure, rule 36.01), and cross-examination on an affidavit for use on a motion or application (Rules of Civil Procedure, rule 39.02). See rule 34.01 of the Rules of Civil Procedure.

THE PARALEGAL AS WITNESS (RULE 4.04)

As an advocate, the paralegal's role is to advance the client's case within the limits of the law. The role of a witness is to give evidence that may or may not assist in advancing the case of any of the parties to a proceeding. Because these roles are different, you may not be able to carry out the functions of both advocate and witness at the same time.

Subject to any contrary provisions of the law or the discretion of the tribunal before which you are appearing, when acting as an advocate for a client before a tribunal you shall not submit your own affidavit to the tribunal (rule 4.04(1)). An affidavit is sworn, written evidence. If you submit an affidavit in a proceeding, you are acting as a witness.

When acting as an advocate for a client before a tribunal, you shall not testify before the tribunal unless permitted to do so by the rules of the court or the rules of procedure of the tribunal, or unless the matter is purely formal and not subject to dispute (rule 4.04(2)).

Table 5.1 Communication with Witnesses Giving Testimony (Rule 4.03(1))

Rule 4.03(1)	Stage of proceeding	Witness in stand	Witness called by	Permitted communication
1.	Examination-in-chief conducted by you	Your witness	You	During a recess, you may only discuss with the witness any matter not covered in the examination to that point
3.	Interval between completion of examination-in-chief and commencement of cross-examination	Your witness	You	You shall not discuss with the witness the evidence given in chief or relating to any matter touched on during examination-in-chief
4.	Cross-examination by opposing licensee	Your witness	You	You shall have no conversation with the witness about the witness's evidence or any issue in the proceeding
5.	Interval between completion of cross-examination and commencement of re-examination	Your witness	You	You shall have no conversation with the witness about evidence to be dealt with on re-examination
2.	Examination-in-chief conducted by another licensee	Witness unsympathetic to your cause	Another licensee	You may discuss the witness's evidence with the witness*
6.	Cross-examination conducted by you	Witness unsympathetic to your cause	Another licensee or another party	You may discuss the witness's evidence with the witness*
8.	Re-examination by opposing licensee	Witness unsympathetic to your cause	Opposing licensee	You may discuss the witness's evidence with the witness*
7.	Cross-examination conducted by you	Witness sympathetic to your cause	Another licensee or another party	You may only discuss with the witness any matter not covered in the cross-examination to that point*
8.	Re-examination by opposing licensee	Witness sympathetic to your cause	Opposing licensee	You shall not discuss with the witness the evidence to be given during re-examination

* Reminder: A witness has no obligation to speak to you. If a witness tells you she does not want to speak with you, you should leave the witness alone. You are not permitted to harass a witness (rule 4.01(5)). You should not attempt to approach or deal with a person who is represented by another licensee, except as set out in rules 4.02(2) and (3).

You shall not express personal opinions or beliefs, or assert as a fact anything that is not properly subject to legal proof, cross-examination, and challenge (rule 4.04(4)). This is improper and may put your credibility in issue.

A paralegal who is required to testify before a tribunal shall entrust the conduct of the client's case to another licensee (rule 4.04(3)).

DEALING WITH UNREPRESENTED PERSONS (RULE 4.05)

When providing legal services, you may find yourself dealing with opposing parties or other individuals with an interest in the matter who are not represented by a paralegal or a lawyer. A conflict of interest may arise if the unrepresented person comes to believe that you are protecting his or her interests.

Rule 4.05 states that, when dealing on a client's behalf with an unrepresented person, you shall:

(a) urge the unrepresented person to obtain independent legal representation from a competent paralegal or lawyer with no personal interest in the matter;

(b) take care to see that the unrepresented person is not proceeding under the impression that you will protect his interests; and

(c) make it clear to the unrepresented person that you are acting exclusively in the interests of the client, and that your comments may be partisan.

Making it clear to the unrepresented person that you are acting exclusively in the interests of your own client may require more than simply telling the unrepresented person this. Guideline 12 recommends that, to avoid misunderstandings, you should confirm in writing to the unrepresented person the steps you have taken to fulfill the requirements of rule 4.05.

You may be able to act for unrepresented persons who have an interest in the matter, such as a co-accused, but you must consider rules 3.04(8) to (14) governing joint retainers.

ERRORS AND OMISSIONS (RULE 4.01(7))

If a paralegal does, or fails to do, something which may involve a breach of rule 4, the paralegal shall:

- disclose the error or omission to the client and, if necessary, the tribunal; and

- do all that can reasonably be done to correct it.

Any disclosure by the paralegal when making reasonable attempts to correct the error or omission is subject to rule 3.03 relating to confidentiality. Confidential information can only be disclosed with the client's authorization, as required by law, or if the disclosure is justified under the Rules.

If the client instructs you to engage in or continue a course of conduct prohibited by rule 4, you must advise the client that the conduct is prohibited and explain that you cannot accept the instructions. If the client persists in instructing you to engage in or continue the prohibited conduct, you must withdraw from representing the client. See rule 3.08 relating to withdrawal from representation, and the discussion at pages 111 to 116.

CHAPTER SUMMARY

The paralegal advocate must balance a number of duties, as explained in rule 4 and guideline 12. You must represent your client honourably and resolutely within the limits of the law; treat other licensees and the tribunal before which you are appearing with candour, fairness, courtesy, and respect; and encourage public respect for, and try to improve, the administration of justice.

You have a duty to represent your client fearlessly and resolutely. You must balance that duty against the limits set by rule 4 on how you may conduct yourself when acting as advocate for a client. Your professional obligations to other parties, other licensees, the tribunal, and the administration of justice are paramount.

You shall avoid and discourage the client from resorting to frivolous and vexatious objections, trying to gain advantage from mistakes or oversights by the other side that do not go to the merits of the case, and using tactics designed merely to delay or harass the other side. You shall not knowingly assist or permit the client to do anything that you consider to be dishonest or dishonourable.

You shall not abuse the process of the tribunal by commencing or continuing to act in proceedings that, although legal, are clearly motivated by malice on the part of the client and are brought solely for the purpose of injuring the other party.

You shall not appear before an adjudicator if you, your partner, a paralegal employed by your firm, or your client has a business or personal relationship with the adjudicator that either affects the adjudicator's impartiality or may reasonably appear to affect the adjudicator's impartiality.

You must ensure that neither you nor your client misleads the tribunal. You shall not attempt, directly or indirectly, to influence the decision or action of a tribunal or its officers in any case or matter except by open persuasion as an advocate. You shall not knowingly attempt to deceive a tribunal or influence the course of justice by offering false evidence, misstating facts or law, suppressing relevant information, or otherwise assisting in any deception, crime, or illegal conduct.

Where the procedural rules of a tribunal require the parties to produce documents, you shall explain the disclosure obligation to the client and assist him to fulfill his obligation to make full and fair disclosure.

In criminal and quasi-criminal matters, you must advise the client that any admissions he makes to you may impose strict limitations on how you conduct his defence.

Before agreeing to a guilty plea on behalf of the client, you must obtain and review disclosure and complete any investigation that is appropriate in the circumstances. When entering into an agreement with the prosecutor about a guilty plea, you must take any reasonable steps to ensure that the client's consent to the plea is informed and voluntary.

You may seek information from any potential witness in a proceeding, including witnesses appearing for opposing parties. However, a witness has no obligation to speak to you, and you are not permitted to harass a witness.

You shall not approach or deal with a person who is represented by another licensee, except through or with the consent of the licensee.

If you are acting for a party in a matter involving a corporation or organization represented by another licensee, you shall not, without the licensee's consent or unless otherwise authorized or required by law, approach directors, officers, and other decision-makers, or employees and agents whose conduct may expose the organization to liability.

Your ability to speak to a witness who is giving testimony is restricted by the provisions in rule 4.03(1).

When acting as an advocate for a client before a tribunal, you shall not act as a witness before the tribunal unless permitted to do so by the rules of the court or the rules of procedure of the tribunal, or unless the matter is purely formal and not subject to dispute. You shall not express personal opinions or beliefs or appear to give unsworn testimony.

When dealing on a client's behalf with an unrepresented person, you shall urge the unrepresented person to obtain independent legal representation, do nothing to make the unrepresented person think that you will protect his interests, and make it clear that you are acting exclusively in the interests of your own client, in writing if necessary.

KEY TERMS

advocate

tribunal

adjudicator

remedy

statutory limitation period

statute-barred

objection

frivolous and vexatious objection

merits of the case

complainant

affidavit

deponent

binding authority

judicial notice

elements of the offence

sympathetic witness

unsympathetic witness

examination out of court

REFERENCES

Criminal Code, RSC 1985, c. C-46, as amended.

Law Society of Upper Canada (LSUC), Paralegal Professional Conduct Guidelines (Toronto: LSUC, 2008) ("the Guidelines"); available online at http://www.lsuc.on.ca/paralegals/a/paralegal-professional-conduct-guidelines.

Law Society of Upper Canada (LSUC), Paralegal Rules of Conduct (Toronto: LSUC, 2007, as amended) ("the Rules"); available online at http://www.lsuc.on.ca/paralegals/a/paralegal-rules-of-conduct.

Rules of Civil Procedure, RRO 1990, Reg. 194.

REVIEW QUESTIONS

1. Your client is the plaintiff in a Small Claims Court proceeding. The defendant is self-represented. You have spoken to the defendant about seeking independent legal representation. You also told him several times that you were acting solely in the interests of the plaintiff.

   A date has been set for a settlement conference. Recently, the defendant called you. He wanted information about what a settlement conference was, and what he had to do to prepare for it. "I thought you might be able to help me out here," he tells you. "You've had a lot of experience with this stuff."

   You tell him that you cannot assist him. Is there anything more that you need to do?

2. You represent a defendant in a *Highway Traffic Act* matter. Your client has indicated that she would like to plead down to reduce the fine and demerit points. What steps must you take?

3. You represent the accused on a charge of assault, where the Crown has elected to proceed by way of summary conviction. The accused has admitted to you that she committed the offence.

   What effect does this have upon your conduct of her defence?

4. You are preparing for a trial in a Small Claims Court proceeding in which you represent the defendant.

   a. May you contact a witness for the plaintiff?

   b. When contacting witnesses, what information should you provide?

   c. What if a witness tells you she does not want to talk to you?

5. You are representing the plaintiff in a Small Claims Court action. The defendant, who is represented by another paralegal, is anxious to settle the matter. He has been contacting your client directly to discuss terms of settlement. Your client has indicated that she does not wish to discuss the matter except through you.

   One morning, the defendant calls you to discuss the case and propose terms of settlement.

   What should you do?

6. You are representing the defendant in a Small Claims Court proceeding. The plaintiff is represented by another paralegal. At the trial of the matter, the plaintiff's evidence is given by the plaintiff himself, and two other witnesses (Witness 2 and Witness 3), neither of whom is represented. Your client is the only witness for the defence.

   When answering the following questions, assume that both parties are individuals. Refer to any relevant rules and give reasons for your answer.

a. During examination-in-chief of the plaintiff by the plaintiff's paralegal, may you discuss the plaintiff's evidence with the plaintiff?

b. During your cross-examination of the plaintiff, may you discuss the plaintiff's evidence with the plaintiff?

c. During re-examination of the plaintiff by the plaintiff's paralegal, may you discuss the plaintiff's evidence with the plaintiff?

d. Witness 2 for the plaintiff is unsympathetic to your cause. During examination-in-chief of Witness 2 by the plaintiff's paralegal, may you discuss Witness 2's evidence with her?

e. During your cross-examination of Witness 2, may you discuss Witness 2's evidence with Witness 2?

f. During re-examination of Witness 2 by the plaintiff's paralegal, may you discuss Witness 2's evidence with Witness 2?

g. Witness 3 for the plaintiff is sympathetic to your cause. During your cross-examination of Witness 3, may you discuss Witness 3's evidence with Witness 3?

h. During re-examination of Witness 3 by the plaintiff's paralegal, may you discuss Witness 3's evidence with Witness 3?

i. During your examination-in-chief of the defendant, may you discuss your client's evidence with your client?

j. During the interval between the conclusion of your examination-in-chief of the defendant and the commencement of cross-examination by the opposing licensee, may you discuss your client's evidence with your client?

k. During cross-examination of the defendant by the plaintiff's paralegal, may you discuss your client's evidence with your client?

l. During the interval between the conclusion of cross-examination by the opposing licensee and your re-examination of the defendant, may you discuss your client's evidence with your client?

CHAPTER 6

Duty to Others

LEARNING OBJECTIVES

After reading this chapter, you will understand:

- The general duty to encourage respect for the administration of justice.
- Maintaining security of court facilities.
- Inappropriate public statements.
- Prevention of unauthorized provision of legal services.
- Obligations of suspended paralegals.
- Obligations of paralegals who have undertaken not to provide legal services.
- The duty of courtesy and good faith to licensees and others.
- Communication with the Law Society.
- The duty to report misconduct by yourself or others.
- The duty to report criminal charges and convictions.
- The disciplinary authority of the Law Society.

ENCOURAGING RESPECT FOR THE ADMINISTRATION OF JUSTICE (RULE 6; GUIDELINE 16)

General (Rules 6.01(1), (2))

A paralegal has a duty to conduct himself in a way that maintains the integrity of the paralegal profession (rule 2.01(1)). As part of the duty of integrity, a paralegal shall encourage public respect for the administration of justice, and try to improve it (rule 6.01(1)). A paralegal must take care not to undermine or destroy public confidence in legal institutions or authorities by making irresponsible allegations or comments, particularly when commenting on judges or members of a tribunal (rule 6.01(2)).

BOX 6.1

Irresponsible Allegations

Scenario

You are acting for a tenant/respondent in a landlord application for termination of the tenancy. On the hearing date, you get to the tribunal early. While you are waiting for your client outside the hearing room, you begin chatting with a paralegal colleague. Your colleague starts talking to you about the Landlord and Tenant Board member who is presiding that day. "Every time I appear before her, I get a bad result," your colleague says. "That woman loves landlords. She'll go to any lengths to kick a tenant out in the street." Several people who are standing nearby overhear your colleague's remarks.

Is your paralegal colleague's comment appropriate?

Discussion

Paralegals have a duty to do nothing that could weaken or destroy public confidence in legal institutions and the administration of justice. Your colleague's public complaint about the Board member is inappropriate and unprofessional. His professional knowledge may lend extra weight to his comments in the minds of those who overhear them. You should not permit the conversation to continue along these lines. You may consider pointing out that Board members are required to be impartial and unbiased in their decision-making, and must comply with the *Residential Tenancies Act* and its regulations, the *Statutory Powers Procedure Act*, the Principles of Member Conduct, the Board's Rules of Practice, and the interpretation guidelines. ◇

Security of Court Facilities (Rules 6.01(3) and 3.03)

As part of a paralegal's duty to the justice system, the paralegal must help ensure that its facilities remain safe. A paralegal who has reasonable grounds to believe that a dangerous situation is likely to develop at a court facility shall inform the local police force and give particulars.

Guideline 16 recommends that, in a situation to which rule 6.01(3) applies, you should suggest solutions to the situation, such as additional security. You should also consider notifying other licensees who may be affected by the dangerous situation.

If your reasonable belief is based on information from or about a client, you must carefully consider your obligations under rule 3.03 regarding confidentiality when deciding what action to take.

If your reasonable belief is based on information from or about someone who is not your client, you may disclose whatever information you think is appropriate when advising the police or court security staff about the dangerous situation.

Public Appearances and Statements (Rules 6.01(4), (4.1))

A paralegal may communicate information to the media and may make public appearances and statements, so long as there is no violation of the paralegal's duty to (rule 6.01(4)):

- maintain client confidentiality;
- uphold the integrity of the paralegal profession;
- encourage public respect for courts and tribunals; and
- encourage public respect for and improvement of the administration of justice.

A paralegal shall not communicate information to the media or make public statements about a matter before a tribunal if she knows or ought to know that there is a substantial likelihood that the information or statement will cause material prejudice to a party's right to a fair trial or hearing (rule 6.01(4.1)).

Working with or Employing Unauthorized Persons (Rules 6.01(5), (6))

The *Law Society Act* requires that anyone who provides legal services or practises law in Ontario must be licensed by the Law Society, unless they are exempt from licensing or are deemed not to be providing legal services or practising law. When carrying out its regulatory functions under the Act, one of the principles that the Law Society shall have regard to is its duty to protect the public interest (s. 4.2).

A person who provides legal services or practises law without a licence may cause harm to the public. For the protection of the public, licensees are required to meet standards of learning, professional competence, and professional conduct that are appropriate for the legal services they provide. Although they may have ability and skill, unlicensed individuals are not required to meet appropriate standards of learning, professional competence, and professional conduct. A client who hires an unlicensed individual does not benefit from the protections enjoyed by clients of regulated legal service providers. These include (guideline 16):

- adherence to a mandatory code of conduct;
- maintenance and operation of a trust account;
- mandatory professional liability insurance coverage; and
- access to a compensation fund for clients who have been victimized by dishonest licensees.

As a member of the Law Society, a paralegal shall assist in preventing the unauthorized practice of law and the unauthorized provision of legal services (rule 6.01(5)).

BOX 6.2

Speaking to the Media

The following material has been adapted for paralegals from "Speaking to the Media," an online publication available at the Lawyers' Professional Indemnity Company website (www.practicepro.ca).

Before you agree to speak to the media or make any public communication, you should carefully consider all aspects of the matter, including the following:

- What are your motives? You may speak to the media if you are satisfied that it is in the client's best interests that you do so. If you are motivated by self-interest, you should decline to speak. A paralegal should not use public communications about a client matter as an opportunity for self-promotion.

- What is the scope of the retainer? If the retainer agreement contains terms about public communications and statements to the media, you must review them carefully. If the retainer agreement is silent about public communications and statements to the media, then you must obtain your client's voluntary, informed consent in writing before you make a public statement.

- Keep in mind that an insurer may not be bound by any agreement between you and the client. If your comments result in a claim by a dissatisfied client, insurance coverage for such a claim may be denied on grounds that the claim does not fall within the definition of "professional services."

- Whether or not you speak to the media is your decision. Even with a client's enthusiastic consent, you should decline to make a public communication if you are not satisfied that it is in accordance with your professional obligations to the client, the profession, the courts, or the administration of justice.

- If the client matter is ongoing, do not discuss any confidential information or information about the strategy of your client's case or position. Do not discuss any confidential information at any time, except with the client's informed, voluntary consent in writing.

- If the matter is ongoing, you shall not communicate information to the media or make public statements if you know or ought to know that there is a substantial likelihood that the information or statement will cause material prejudice to a party's right to a fair trial or hearing.

- Identify your key messages ahead of time and rehearse different ways to communicate them. Work your key messages into every answer that you provide.

- Avoid answering questions in the heat of the moment, before you have had a chance to think.

- If it is practicable, discuss the reporter's objectives for the interview ahead of time, and request a copy of the questions in advance.

- Ensure that you understand the question or point. If you do not, ask for clarification before responding. If the question is too broad, ask for clarification before responding.

- If you do not know the answer to a question, say so. Do not guess or speculate.

- Keep your remarks brief. Resist the temptation to expand your answer to fill dead air time.

- Be aware that you will have no control over the editing of your statements or the context in which they will be presented when published.

- Recognize that the duties you owe to your client, the paralegal profession, the court or tribunal, and the administration of justice are paramount. ◈

Except with the express approval of a committee of Convocation appointed for the purpose, a paralegal shall not (rule 6.01(6)):

- retain,

- share office space with,

- use the services of,

- partner or associate with, or

- employ in any capacity having to do with the provision of legal services any person who, in Ontario or elsewhere,

  (a) is disbarred and struck off the Rolls,

  (b) is a person whose license to practise law or to provide legal services is revoked,

  (c) as a result of disciplinary action, has been permitted to resign his or her membership in the Law Society or to surrender his or her licence to practise law or to provide legal services, and has not had his or her license restored,

  (d) is suspended,

  (e) is a person whose license to practise law or to provide legal services is suspended, or

  (f) is subject to an undertaking not to practise law or to provide legal services.

Suspended Paralegals (Rule 6.01(7))

A paralegal whose license to provide legal services is suspended shall comply with the requirements of the By-laws and shall not (rule 6.01(7))

  (a) provide legal services, or

  (b) represent or hold herself out as a person entitled to provide legal services.

A suspended paralegal shall comply with By-law 7.1 (Part II) and By-law 9 (Part II.1).

By-law 7.1 (Part II)

The following definitions apply for purposes of By-law 7.1, Part II.

An existing client means (1) a client who is a client of a suspended paralegal when a suspension order is made against the paralegal, or (2) a person who becomes a client of the suspended paralegal after the suspension order is made but before the suspension begins.

A former client is a person who was a client of a suspended paralegal before a suspension order was made against the paralegal but was not a client when the order was made.

A prospective client is a person who seeks to retain a suspended paralegal after the suspension order is made against the paralegal but before the suspension begins.

BOX 6.3

Unauthorized Persons

Scenario

You are a licensed paralegal with a large office space. To reduce your business expenses, you decide to enter into a space-sharing arrangement with a possibility of referrals. One of the people who responds to your advertisement tells you that she is a lawyer who has been running a consulting service for small business start-ups for several years. She seems like a very nice person who would be perfect for your space-sharing arrangement. After she leaves, you search her name at the Law Society website. To your surprise, her name does not appear. When you call to check her status, you are informed that she was disbarred.

May you enter into a space-sharing arrangement with this person?

Discussion

Except with the express approval of a committee of Convocation appointed for the purpose, you shall not occupy office space with any person who, in Ontario or elsewhere, is disbarred and struck off the Rolls or falls within any of the other categories set out in rule 6.01(6). You must decline to share office space with her.

Further Comments

The procedure to follow when applying for permission to work with or employ an unauthorized person is available in the "Lawyer Regulation" section of the Law Society website, in a document entitled "Working With a Suspended Lawyer." An applicant must satisfy the Law Society that he can effectively supervise a disbarred or suspended person.

Disbarment or disciplinary suspension results from serious professional misconduct. The Law Society will consider the character, attitudes, and abilities of the disbarred or suspended person with whom the applicant proposes to work, including the following:

- pre-discipline character, standing, and professional reputation;

- ethical standards while in practice;

- the type of misconduct that led to discipline/suspension;

- post-discipline attitude, conduct, and reformation;

- the elapsed time since the discipline;

- ability and capacity to perform tasks as proposed by the applicant;

- sincerity and frankness in discussing issues relating to his or her circumstances, including any discipline;

- pre- and post-discipline cooperation with the Society; and

- outstanding obligations to the Society, LawPRO, clients, and other investigatory and regulatory bodies and agencies. ◈

NOTICE REQUIREMENTS AND OTHER OBLIGATIONS BEFORE SUSPENSION BEGINS

On or before the date the suspension begins, a suspended paralegal shall (s. 9(1)):

(a) notify every existing client, on whose matters the work will not be completed by the suspended paralegal before the suspension begins, of the suspension order, and that

    (i) the suspended paralegal will be unable to complete the work,

    (ii) the client will need to retain another licensee to complete the work, and

    (iii) the suspended paralegal will transfer the file to a licensee retained by the client to complete the work, or return the file to the client.

The above notice requirements do not apply if the only remaining work on the client's matter is a final report to the client, or the fulfillment of one more undertakings given by the suspended paralegal (s. 9(2)). See the discussion of ss. 12 and 13 below.

If the only work to be completed by the suspended paralegal on the client matter is a final report to the client, the suspended paralegal shall, before the suspension begins, retain another licensee who is authorized to do so to review the client's file and to complete and send the final report to the client (s. 12).

At the time a prospective client seeks to retain a suspended paralegal, the suspended paralegal shall notify the prospective client of the suspension order (s. 11).

On or before the date the suspension begins, a suspended paralegal shall return to the Law Society any photo identification card issued to her by the Society (s. 16).

NOTICE REQUIREMENTS AND OTHER OBLIGATIONS DURING SUSPENSION

During the suspension, a suspended paralegal shall (s. 10):

(a) notify all persons who contact the suspended paralegal's place of business of the suspension order; and

(b) notify any existing or former client who contacts the suspended paralegal's place of business of the name and contact information of another licensee who has been given possession of the clients' documents and files.

If, on the date the suspension begins, the only work to be completed by the suspended paralegal on the client's matter is fulfillment of one or more undertakings given by the suspended paralegal, the suspended paralegal shall retain another licensee or person who is authorized to do so to take all steps necessary to fulfill the undertakings (s. 13).

A suspended paralegal shall, not later than 30 days after the suspension begins, complete and file with the Society a report confirming and providing details of the suspended paralegal's compliance with By-law 7.1, Part II (s. 18).

A suspended paralegal may apply in writing to the Society for an exemption from or a modification of a requirement mentioned in Part II, and the Society may exempt the suspended paralegal from the requirement, or modify the requirement, subject to such terms and conditions as the Society may impose (s. 19).

BOX 6.4

Transfer of Client Files by Suspended Paralegal

A suspended paralegal may, with the client's authorization, transfer the client's file to another paralegal in good standing in the firm where the suspended paralegal is a partner or an employee. A **paralegal in good standing** is a paralegal licensee who has fulfilled all membership requirements and who is not suspended or disbarred. ◇

By-law 9 (Part II.1)

By-law 9 sets out special requirements for record-keeping and handling of client money and other client property by licensees.

At a minimum, a paralegal firm should maintain two bank accounts: a general account and a mixed trust account.

The general account is the firm's operating account. This is the account you use to:

- deposit payments from clients you have billed for completed legal services;

- pay your office expenses, such as rent, office supplies, staff salaries, bank charges, and so on;

- pay disbursements on behalf of your clients; and

- pay yourself.

No money belonging to clients should be in the general account.

Client money, such as a money retainer, remains the property of the client and must be held for the benefit of the client. A money retainer is paid to you for future legal services. You must hold the money retainer for the benefit of the client until the legal services contracted for have been provided and the client has been properly invoiced for them.

Whenever you receive a money retainer, settlement funds payable by the client to another party, or settlement funds payable to the client by another party, you must deposit them to your trust account. Trust accounts are the accounts you use to:

- deposit money you receive from your clients to be paid to another party;

- deposit money you receive from other parties on behalf of your clients;

- deposit money you receive from clients for future legal services and disbursements;

- disburse money as directed by your clients;

- reimburse your practice for proper expenses you have made on behalf of your clients; and

- transfer money to your general account for fees *after* you have sent a bill to your client for completed legal services.

By-law 9, Part II.1 sets out restrictions on handling of client money or other client property by a suspended paralegal.

HANDLING OF CLIENT MONEY OR OTHER PROPERTY (S. 2.2(1))

During the suspension, a suspended paralegal shall not:

- receive from or on behalf of a person or group of persons any money or other property, or

- otherwise handle money or property that is held in trust for a person or group of persons.

Exceptions (s. 2.2(2))

During the suspension, a suspended paralegal may receive money from or on behalf of a person or group of persons:

- in payment of fees for services performed by the suspended paralegal for the person or group; or

- in reimbursement for money properly spent, or for expenses properly incurred, on behalf of the person or group.

TRUST ACCOUNT (S. 2.3(1))

Within 30 days of the beginning of the suspension, a suspended paralegal shall withdraw from trust and pay to the appropriate person (s. 2.3(1)(a)):

(i)   money properly required to pay a person on behalf of a client;

(ii)   money required to reimburse the suspended licensee for money properly spent or expenses properly incurred on behalf of a client;

(iii)   money required for payment of fees for services performed by the suspended licensee; and

(iv)   all other money that belongs to the suspended licensee or to a person other than the client.

After all payments have been made pursuant to s. 2.3(1)(a), the suspended paralegal shall withdraw from trust all money belonging to the client and pay the money to (s. 2.3(1)(b)):

(i)   the client,

(ii)   another licensee as directed by the client, or

(iii)   another licensee who has agreed with the suspended licensee to accept payment in the event that the suspended licensee is unable to pay the money to the client or as directed by the client.

The suspended paralegal shall then close every trust account kept in his name, and cancel or cause to be cancelled his signing authority on every trust account kept in the name of the firm of licensees where he is a partner or an employee (s. 2.3(1)(c)).

REPORT TO LAW SOCIETY ON COMPLIANCE WITH PART II.1 (S. 2.3(4))

Not later than 30 days from the beginning of the suspension, the suspended paralegal shall complete and file with the Law Society a report confirming and providing details of his compliance.

PERMISSION TO BE EXEMPT FROM REQUIREMENT (S. 2.4)

A suspended paralegal may apply in writing to the Society for an exemption from or a modification of a requirement mentioned in Part II, and the Society may exempt the suspended paralegal from the requirement, or modify the requirement, subject to such terms and conditions as the Society may impose.

BOX 6.5

How Does By-law 9, Part II.1 Work?

Elizabeth May is a paralegal sole practitioner. She uses two bank accounts in her firm: a general account and a mixed trust account.

Elizabeth is suspended effective April 1. As of April 1, Elizabeth is holding $8,000.00 in trust on account of settlement funds paid by another party for the benefit of Client A. In the period from her last interim invoice to Client A until April 1, Elizabeth has provided unpaid legal services worth $600.00 in Client A's matter.

Question: Is Elizabeth permitted to invoice Client A and pay the invoice from the funds held in trust for Client A?

Discussion: Yes, if there is a term in her retainer agreement with the client that she may pay her fees from settlement funds, and if she does so on or before April 30. Section 2.3(1)(a)(iii) permits a suspended paralegal to withdraw money from trust for payment of proper fees and disbursements within 30 days of the beginning of the suspension.

After she has billed Client A, Elizabeth may properly withdraw funds from the trust account and transfer them to her general (operating) account. The invoice received by the client will show a balance owing of zero, because it has been paid in full out of trust.

Question: What about the balance of the settlement funds that Elizabeth is holding in her trust account for the benefit of Client A?

Discussion: Having paid herself, Elizabeth must now pay the balance of the money in trust to the client or to another licensee as directed by the client (s. 2.3(1)(b)). Any direction by the client with respect to payment of the funds should be in writing.

On or before the end of the 30-day period, all funds held in Elizabeth's trust account must be properly disbursed in accordance with Part II.1. The mixed trust account must be closed. Elizabeth must provide to the Law Society an accounting of all transactions carried out during the 30-day period (s. 2.3(4)). ◇

Undertakings Not to Provide Legal Services (Rules 6.01(8), (9))

A paralegal who gives an undertaking to the Law Society not to provide legal services shall not (rule 6.01(8)):

(a) provide legal services, or

(b) represent or hold herself out as a person entitled to provide legal services.

A paralegal who gives an undertaking to the Law Society to restrict her provision of legal services shall comply with the undertaking (rule 6.01(9)).

Guidelines for Paralegals Who Are Suspended or Who Have Undertaken Not to Provide Legal Services

The Law Society has published a document outlining general guidelines for paralegals who are suspended or who have given an undertaking not to provide legal services. The following is adapted from those guidelines, which are available in the "Paralegals" section of the Law Society website (www.lsuc.on.ca).

MANDATORY ACTIVITIES

Before the effective date of the suspension or undertaking not to provide legal services, the paralegal who is suspended or who has given an undertaking not to provide legal services shall do the following:

(a) The paralegal shall remove from the business premises or any other location any sign or representation, in English or any other language, giving the impression that the premises are a legal services firm or that the former paralegal is able to provide legal services. Unacceptable language includes "paralegal office," "law office," "legal office," "paralegal," "law clerk," "court agent," "Licensee of the Law Society of Upper Canada," "Licensed by the Law Society of Upper Canada," "notary public," or similar words.

(b) The paralegal shall remove or cross out the words or terms set out above from stationery, letterhead, business cards, forms, stamps, accounts, electronic mail forms, Internet sites, and any other advertisements or publications bearing her name.

(c) The paralegal shall disconnect her telephone and facsimile lines, or arrange for a voice message advising callers that her professional business is closed until further notice and providing clients with the name and number of another licensee to call for information regarding their files.

(d) Suspended paralegals under definite suspension (that is, suspension for a fixed term) may leave a message advising when the office will reopen.

PROHIBITED ACTIVITIES

Effective from the date of suspension or undertaking not to provide legal services, a suspended paralegal shall not:

(a) accept legal work for new clients;

(b) accept new legal work for existing clients;

(c) notarize documents pursuant to the *Notaries Act*, or commission affidavits or statutory declarations pursuant to the *Commissioners for taking Affidavits Act*;

(d) report to clients, other than to

(i) advise of the suspension or the undertaking not to provide legal services, and

(ii) deliver an account for services rendered in the period before the suspension or undertaking not to provide legal services began;

(e) give to another licensee or receive on behalf of a client, other individual, corporation, or other entity, any undertaking with respect to any legal matter;

(f) occupy or share office space with a licensee contrary to rule 6.01(6) of the Rules; or

(g) provide services to a licensee in relation to that licensee's professional business contrary to rule 6.01(6) of the Rules.

PERMITTED ACTIVITIES

During the term of the suspension or undertaking not to provide legal services, the suspended paralegal may:

(a) see clients for the sole purpose of assisting them in transferring their past or present legal work to another licensee;

(b) if requested by the client, suggest a referral to a particular licensee to continue work on the client's file (the client must decide whether to accept the suggested referral, or seek the legal services of another licensee);

(c) collect accounts receivable;

(d) bill clients for work completed before the effective date of the suspended paralegal's suspension or undertaking not to provide legal services; and

(e) arrange for payment of the licensee whom the suspended paralegal has retained to complete outstanding reporting letters and undertakings.

RESUMPTION OF LEGAL SERVICES

Upon termination of a suspension or undertaking not to provide legal services, a suspended paralegal shall not resume the provision of legal services until she receives written confirmation of the termination of the suspension or undertaking not to provide legal services from the Law Society. This confirmation will be promptly given.

DUTY OF COURTESY AND GOOD FAITH TO LICENSEES AND OTHERS (RULE 7; GUIDELINE 17)

A paralegal's general duty of courtesy and good faith is set out at rule 2.01(2). A paralegal shall be courteous and civil, and shall act in good faith with all persons with whom she has dealings in the course of her practice.

You should guard against letting your personal dislike of another licensee cloud your judgment in a matter. You should not allow a client's animosity toward other parties in an adversarial proceeding to influence your conduct and demeanour toward those parties or their licensees. Ill-mannered or hostile behaviour between paralegals brings the administration of justice into disrepute, and may harm their clients' interests. Personal animosity between paralegals may impair their ability to focus on their clients' interests and to advance the matter without unnecessary delay or cost (guideline 17).

Rule 7.01 sets out various types of conduct that are prohibited. If a complaint is made about a paralegal whose conduct does not comply with rule 7.01, the Law Society will review that conduct.

Sharp Practice (Rule 7.01(1))

A paralegal shall avoid sharp practice and shall not take advantage of or act without fair warning on slips, irregularities, or mistakes on the part of other licensees if these do not go to the merits and do not involve any diminution of the client's rights. See also rule 4.01(4)(d).

Sharp practice is the dishonourable taking of advantage. A paralegal engages in sharp practice when she obtains, or tries to obtain, an advantage for herself or her client through dishonourable means (guideline 17). Examples of sharp practice include:

- lying to another licensee,

- trying to trick another licensee,

- making an oral promise to another licensee with the intention of reneging on the promise later, and

- taking advantage, without fair warning, of another licensee's innocent mistake or error.

BOX 6.6

Sharp Practice

Scenario

Your client is the plaintiff in a Small Claims Court action for $9,000.00 based on damage to property. The defendant is represented. Your client has told you that, to avoid the expense of a trial, she is prepared to settle for less than the full amount claimed.

The defendant's paralegal phones you one day and says, "Why don't we settle on terms that my guy will pay your client $7,000.00?"

Should you accept the offer?

Discussion

Be wary. The defendant's paralegal is making what should be a formal offer in a very informal fashion. He may be using the negotiating process in bad faith, to fish for information about the kinds of concessions he can push for. You should tell him to get instructions from his client and send you the offer in writing. You can then take it up with your client. ◇

BOX 6.7

Taking Advantage Without Fair Warning

Scenario

Your client is the defendant in a Small Claims Court action. There is a lot of animosity between your client and the plaintiff. The plaintiff is represented by a paralegal whom you dislike and distrust.

A date has been scheduled for a settlement conference for October 15. The plaintiff's paralegal sends you what is, in your opinion, a completely unnecessary and mildly insulting letter reminding you of your disclosure obligations under Small Claims Court Rule 13.03. You note that, according to the letter, she thinks the settlement conference is scheduled for November 15.

When you advise your client of the error, he is delighted. "If they don't show up, they'll look like clowns," he comments. He tells you to act as though you did not notice the incorrect date.

Should you follow your client's instructions?

Discussion

This is an innocent mistake that does not go to the merits. Whatever your personal opinion of the plaintiff's paralegal, you are obliged to contact her and correct the error.

As far as your client's instructions go, you must advise him that the Paralegal Rules prohibit you from taking advantage of this kind of error, and that his rights are not diminished by having the settlement conference go forward on the scheduled date. If he persists in his instructions, you may have to withdraw from representation. See rules 3.08 and 4.01(1), (4)(d), and (5)(b). ◇

Reasonable Requests (Rule 7.01(2))

A paralegal shall agree to reasonable requests by other licensees concerning trial dates, adjournments, waiver of procedural formalities, and similar matters that do not prejudice the rights of the client.

Abusive Communication (Rule 7.01(3))

When providing legal services, a paralegal shall not communicate with a client, another licensee, or any other person in a manner that is abusive, offensive, or otherwise inconsistent with the proper tone of a professional communication from a paralegal. This rule applies to written and spoken communications.

Unfounded Criticism of Other Licensees (Rule 7.01(4))

A paralegal shall not engage in ill-considered or uninformed criticism of the competence, conduct, advice, or charges of other licensees. However, a paralegal should be prepared to represent a client in a complaint involving another licensee when requested to do so.

Prompt Communication (Rule 7.01(5))

A paralegal shall answer with reasonable promptness all professional letters and communications from other licensees that require an answer. A paralegal shall be punctual in fulfilling all commitments.

Communication with Represented Persons (Rule 7.01(6))

A paralegal shall not communicate with or attempt to negotiate settlement of a matter directly with any person who is represented by another licensee, except with the consent of that licensee. See also rule 4.02(2), discussed in Chapter 5 (pages 137–138).

Recording Conversations (Rule 7.01(7))

A paralegal shall not use a tape recorder or other device to record a conversation between the paralegal and a client or another licensee, even if lawful, without first informing the other person of his intention to do so.

BOX 6.8

Courtesy and Good Faith

Scenario

Your client is the plaintiff in a Small Claims Court matter. There is a lot of animosity between your client and the defendant. The defendant is represented by another paralegal.

A date has been set for trial. One week before the trial date, the defendant's paralegal phones you in a panic. He has just discovered that he has an out-of-town hearing in another court on the date set for the Small Claims trial. It will be impossible for him to appear on both matters.

You have provided full disclosure, reviewed the file, and interviewed and summoned all your witnesses. "I can't believe that anyone—even you—can just forget a trial until one week before it's supposed to happen," you tell him. "I have to wonder how you manage to get dressed in the morning. Or does your wife have to dress you?" You say this in a pleasant, even tone of voice. The other paralegal cuts off the call.

You telephone your client to discuss the situation with her. "The man's a cretin," you tell her in the course of the conversation. "They're handing out licences like popcorn these days."

Question: Should you agree to the adjournment?

Discussion: Rule 7.01(2) requires that you agree to reasonable requests concerning trial dates and other procedural matters. This request is being made on very short notice. You are ready to go forward with the trial. An adjournment will result in further delay for your client, and may result in additional expense. The defendant's paralegal does not have a good reason for requesting the adjournment. Arguably, you are not obliged to agree to an adjournment in these circumstances.

Instead of seeking your consent, the defendant's paralegal should notify the court clerk that he requires an adjournment, and seek direction from a judge. If the trial date is not adjourned, he should make arrangements for another licensee to appear on one of his scheduled matters.

Question: Were you justified in your response to the other paralegal's request?

Discussion: No, you were not. Rule 7.01(3) states that, when providing legal services, you shall not communicate with another licensee in a manner that is abusive, offensive, or otherwise inconsistent with the proper tone of professional communication from a paralegal. Your response was made in a polite tone of voice, but its content was extremely offensive. You are going to have to continue to deal with the paralegal on this matter until its conclusion, and you have just done something that was unprofessional, and that may make that task a lot more difficult and consequently may harm your client's interests.

Question: Should you have made the comments about the other paralegal to your client?

Discussion: No. Rule 7.01(4) states that you shall not engage in ill-considered or uninformed criticism of the competence, conduct, or advice of other licensees. Your comments criticize the paralegal's competence and conduct, and go beyond that to suggest that a paralegal licence is a worthless accreditation. Such remarks bring the paralegal profession and the administration of justice into disrepute. ◇

RESPONSIBILITY TO THE LAW SOCIETY (RULE 9; GUIDELINE 21)

The Law Society is the governing body for all persons licensed to practise law or provide legal services in Ontario. Licensees owe a number of duties to the Law Society, to enable it to carry out its regulatory mandate efficiently and effectively, and ensure that the public is protected from inappropriate conduct by lawyers and paralegals. These include:

- the duty to respond promptly and completely to a Law Society communication;

- the duty to report misconduct;

- the duty to report criminal charges and convictions; and

- the duty to submit to the disciplinary authority of the Law Society.

Communications from the Law Society (Rule 9.01(1))

A paralegal shall reply promptly to any communication from the Law Society, and shall provide a complete response to any request from the Law Society. In addition to the duty to respond promptly and completely to a request for information, a paralegal has a duty to cooperate with a person conducting an investigation of a complaint under the *Law Society Act* (guideline 21).

The Law Society is mandated to protect the public interest. The Law Society will investigate a complaint against you if the complaint raises any genuine regulatory issues—in the case of a complaint by a client, any issues of whether your conduct may harm the public. Even if you consider a complaint trivial and without merit, it is your duty to respond promptly and completely, and to cooperate in the investigation of the complaint. If you fail to observe these duties, you may be disciplined on grounds of failure to respond, whatever the outcome of the complaint that triggered the investigation.

For more information, see the article by Dan Abrahams entitled "*Mostly Common Sense*: Staying Out of Trouble with the Law Society."

Duty to Report Misconduct (Rules 9.01(2) to (8))

A paralegal must assist the Law Society in upholding the integrity of the paralegal profession by reporting professional misconduct in accordance with rule 9.01(2). A paralegal shall report to the Law Society:

(a) the misappropriation or misapplication of trust monies by a licensee;

(b) the abandonment of a law practice by a lawyer or a legal services practice by a client;

(c) participation in serious criminal activity related to a licensee's practice;

(d) the mental instability of a licensee if it is of such a serious nature that the licensee's clients are likely to be seriously prejudiced; and

(e) any other situation where a licensee's clients are likely to be severely prejudiced.

Rule 9.01(2) does not require a paralegal to report any of the above if to do so would involve a breach of client confidentiality. Nothing in rule 9.01(2) is intended to interfere with the paralegal's duty to the client (rule 9.01(3)).

Guideline 21 comments that evidence of what may seem like isolated incidents or "minor" transgressions of the Rules may, when investigated, disclose more serious misconduct, or may indicate the commencement of a course of conduct that may lead to serious breaches in the future.

A report of misconduct under rule 9.02(2) must be made in good faith, with a view to protecting the public. It must not be motivated by malice, a desire to cause harm to another licensee, or other ulterior motive.

The rule 9.01(2) obligation to report requires a paralegal to report her own misconduct as well as that of other licensees. A paralegal who knows of misconduct and does not report it contravenes rule 9 and may be subject to discipline by the Law Society. If you are uncertain of whether or not to report another licensee's conduct, you should consider seeking assistance from the Law Society directly, through the Practice Management Helpline (416-947-3315 or 1-800-668-7380 ext. 3315), or indirectly, through another licensee (guideline 21).

ENCOURAGING A CLIENT TO REPORT DISHONEST CONDUCT (RULES 9.01(5) TO (8))

If your client has a claim against an apparently dishonest licensee, you must try to persuade the client to report the facts to the Law Society before seeking private remedies against that licensee (rule 9.01(5)).

If the client refuses to report a claim against an apparently dishonest licensee to the Law Society, you shall obtain instructions in writing from the client to proceed with the client's private remedies without notice to the Law Society (rule 9.01(6)).

You shall inform the client of the provision of the *Criminal Code* (currently s. 141) stating that everyone who asks for, obtains, or agrees to receive or obtain any valuable consideration for himself or any other person by agreeing to conceal an indictable offence is guilty of an indictable offence and is liable to imprisonment for a term not exceeding two years (rule 9.01(7)).

If the client wishes to pursue a private agreement with the apparently dishonest licensee, you must withdraw from representation if the agreement constitutes a breach of s. 141 of the *Criminal Code*.

Duty to Self-Report Criminal Charges and Convictions (Rule 9.01(9))

If a paralegal is charged with an offence described in By-law 8, he shall inform the Law Society of the charge and of its disposition in accordance with the By-law.

By-law 8, s. 2(1)(a) requires licensees to report to the Law Society in writing that they have been charged with any of the following:

(i) an indictable offence under the *Criminal Code* (defined in By-law 8 as (1) an offence for which an offender may be prosecuted only by indictment, and (2) a hybrid offence—that is, an offence for which an offender may be prosecuted by indictment or that is punishable by summary conviction, at the instance of the prosecution);

(ii) an offence under the *Controlled Drugs and Substances Act* (Canada);

(iii) an offence under the *Income Tax Act* (Canada) or under an Act of the legislature of a province or territory of Canada in respect of the income tax law of the province or territory, where the charge alleges, explicitly or implicitly, dishonesty on the part of the licensee or relates in any way to the professional business of the licensee;

(iv) an offence under an Act of the legislature of a province or territory of Canada in respect of the securities law of the province or territory, where the charge alleges, explicitly or implicitly, dishonesty on the part of the licensee or relates in any way to the professional business of the licensee; or

(v) an offence under another Act of Parliament, or under another Act of the legislature of a province or territory of Canada, where the charge alleges, explicitly or implicitly, dishonesty on the part of the licensee or relates in any way to the professional business of the licensee.

By-law 8, s. 2(1)(b) requires licensees to report to the Law Society in writing of the disposition of a charge mentioned in s. 2(1)(a).

A licensee shall report a charge to the Law Society as soon as reasonably practicable after she receives notice of the charge, and shall report the disposition of the charge as soon as reasonably practicable after she receives notice of the disposition (s. 2(3)).

REQUIREMENT TO REPORT—PRIVATE PROSECUTION

Section 504 of the *Criminal Code* permits anyone (other than a peace officer, a public officer, the attorney general, or the attorney general's agent) who, on reasonable grounds, believes that a person has committed an indictable offence, to appear before a justice and lay an information in writing and under oath. A licensee who has been charged under s. 504 is only required to inform the Society of the charge and of its outcome if there is a finding of guilt or a conviction (By-law 8, s. 2(2)). If the licensee is acquitted, there is no obligation to report the private prosecution to the Law Society.

In a private prosecution, a licensee shall report a charge and its outcome as soon as reasonably practicable after she receives notice of the disposition (By-law 8, s. 2(4)).

> **BOX 6.9**
>
> ## Reminder: The By-law 8 Obligation to Report Criminal Charges
>
> By-law 8, s. 2(1) requires you to self-report to the Law Society any criminal charge, whether it is related to your practice or not. By-law 8, s. 2(2) requires you to self-report to the Law Society any criminal charge in a private prosecution if and when you are convicted.
>
> Rule 9.01(2) imposes the following obligations on a paralegal:
>
> - to self-report misconduct, including criminal activity, to the Law Society, unless to do so would be unlawful or would involve a breach of client confidentiality; and
>
> - to report misconduct by other licensees, including criminal activity, to the Law Society, unless to do so would be unlawful or would involve a breach of client confidentiality.
>
> The rule 9.01(2)(c) obligation to report criminal activity is restricted to serious criminal activity related to a licensee's practice. ◈

DISCIPLINARY AUTHORITY OF THE LAW SOCIETY (RULES 9.01(10) TO (13); GUIDELINE 22)

The *Law Society Act* prohibits a paralegal from engaging in professional misconduct or conduct unbecoming a licensee (s. 33).

The Law Society may discipline a paralegal for professional misconduct (rule 9.01(11)) or for conduct unbecoming a paralegal (rule 9.01(12)).

Rule 9.01(13) provides definitions of professional misconduct and conduct unbecoming a paralegal.

Professional misconduct refers to conduct by a paralegal that tends to bring discredit upon the paralegal profession. This may include:

- violating or attempting to violate the Rules, or a requirement of the *Law Society Act* or the regulations and by-laws under the Act;

- knowingly assisting or inducing another licensee to violate or attempt to violate the Rules, or a requirement of the *Law Society Act* or the regulations and by-laws under the Act;

- knowingly assisting or inducing a non-licensee partner or associate of a multi-discipline practice to violate or attempt to violate the Rules, or a requirement of the *Law Society Act* or the regulations and by-laws under the Act;

- misappropriating or otherwise dealing dishonestly with a client's or a third party's money or property;

- engaging in conduct that is prejudicial to the administration of justice;

- stating or implying an ability to influence improperly a government agency or official; or

- knowingly assisting a judge or judicial officer in conduct that is a violation of applicable rules of judicial conduct or other law.

Conduct unbecoming a paralegal refers to conduct in a paralegal's personal or private capacity that tends to bring discredit upon the paralegal profession. This may include:

- committing a criminal act that reflects adversely on the paralegal's honesty, trustworthiness, or fitness as a paralegal;

- taking improper advantage of the youth, inexperience, lack of education, unsophistication, ill health, vulnerability, or unbusinesslike habits of another; or

- engaging in conduct involving dishonesty.

The Law Society may discipline a paralegal regardless of whether the paralegal is acting in a professional capacity as a paralegal or in a personal capacity, if the paralegal's conduct tends to bring discredit upon the paralegal profession and raise issues of the paralegal's professional integrity (rules 9.01(11) and (12)).

A paralegal is subject to the disciplinary authority of the Law Society regardless of where the paralegal's conduct occurs (rule 9.01(10)). If you engage in conduct unbecoming while on vacation in British Columbia, and it comes to the Law Society's attention, you may be disciplined.

The Rules cannot address every situation. Paralegals are required to comply with both the letter and the spirit of the Rules. Complying with the letter of a rule means complying with its literal meaning—the words on the page—but not necessarily with the intent or principle behind it. Complying with the spirit of a rule means that you conduct yourself in accordance with the intent or principle behind the rule, even though that intent or principle may not be expressly stated in the rule (guideline 22).

CHAPTER SUMMARY

As a paralegal, you have a duty to conduct yourself in a way that maintains the integrity of the paralegal profession. As part of this duty, you shall encourage public respect for the administration of justice, and try to improve it. You must take care not to undermine or destroy public confidence in legal institutions or authorities by making irresponsible allegations or comments, particularly when commenting on judges or members of a tribunal.

As part of your duty to the justice system, you must help to ensure that its facilities remain safe. If you have reasonable grounds to believe that a dangerous situation is likely to develop at a court facility, you shall inform the local police force and give particulars. If your belief is based on information from or about a client, you must consider your obligations to the client under rule 3.03 regarding confidentiality when deciding what action to take.

You may communicate information to the media and make public appearances and statements as long as you do not violate your duty to maintain client confidentiality, to uphold the integrity of the paralegal profession, to encourage public respect for courts and tribunals, and to encourage public respect for and improvement of the administration of justice.

You shall not communicate information to the media or make public statements about a matter before a tribunal if you know or ought to know that there is a substantial likelihood that the information or statement will cause material prejudice to a party's right to a fair trial or hearing.

As a member of the Law Society, you shall assist in preventing the unauthorized practice of law and the unauthorized provision of legal services. You shall not retain, share office space with, use the services of, partner or associate with, or employ in any capacity having to do with the provision of legal services any person who, in Ontario or elsewhere, is not a member in good standing of the Law Society.

A paralegal whose licence to provide legal services is suspended shall not provide legal services or represent or hold himself out as a person entitled to provide legal services. He shall also comply with the By-law 7.1 (Part II) and By-law 9 (Part II.1) requirements regarding notice requirements and other obligations during suspension, and restrictions on handling of client money or other property by a suspended paralegal.

A paralegal who gives an undertaking to the Law Society not to provide legal services shall not provide legal services or represent or hold himself out as a person entitled to provide legal services. A paralegal who gives an undertaking to the Law Society to restrict his provision of legal services shall comply with the undertaking.

As a paralegal, you have a general duty of courtesy and good faith. You shall be courteous and civil, and shall act in good faith with all persons with whom you have dealings in the course of your practice.

You should guard against letting your personal dislike of another licensee cloud your judgment in a matter, or allowing a client's animosity toward other parties in an adversarial proceeding to influence your conduct and demeanour toward those parties or their licensees.

Rule 7.01 sets out various types of prohibited conduct. If a complaint is made about a paralegal whose conduct does not comply with rule 7.01, the Law Society will review that conduct.

Licensees owe various duties to the Law Society, including the duty to respond promptly and completely to a Law Society communication; to report misconduct, criminal charges, and convictions; and to submit to the disciplinary authority of the Law Society.

The *Law Society Act* prohibits a paralegal from engaging in professional misconduct or conduct unbecoming a licensee. The Law Society may discipline a paralegal for such conduct if it tends to bring discredit upon the paralegal profession and to raise issues of the paralegal's professional integrity, regardless of whether the paralegal is acting as a paralegal or in a personal capacity and regardless of where the conduct occurs.

KEY TERMS

paralegal in good standing

sharp practice

professional misconduct

conduct unbecoming a paralegal

REFERENCES

Abrahams, Dan, "*Mostly Common Sense*: Staying Out of Trouble with the Law Society" (LSUC: May 2008); available online at http://rc.lsuc.on.ca/pdf/kt/ mostlyCommonSense.pdf.

Commissioners for taking Affidavits Act, RSO 1990, c. C.17.

Law Society Act, RSO 1990, c. L.8, as amended.

Law Society of Upper Canada (LSUC), By-Laws (Toronto: LSUC, 2005); available online at http://www.lsuc.on.ca/regulation/a/by-laws.

Law Society of Upper Canada (LSUC), Guidelines for Paralegals Who Are Suspended or Who Have Given an Undertaking Not to Provide Legal Services; available online at http://www.lsuc.on.ca/paralegals/a/guidelines-for-suspended-paralegals.

Law Society of Upper Canada (LSUC), Paralegal Professional Conduct Guidelines (Toronto: LSUC, 2008) ("the Guidelines"); available online at http://www .lsuc.on.ca/paralegals/a/paralegal-professional-conduct-guidelines.

Law Society of Upper Canada (LSUC), Paralegal Rules of Conduct (Toronto: LSUC, 2007, as amended) ("the Rules"); available online at http://www.lsuc .on.ca/paralegals/a/paralegal-rules-of-conduct.

Law Society of Upper Canada (LSUC), "Working With a Suspended Lawyer"; available online at http://www.lsuc.on.ca/regulation/a/working-with-a-suspended-lawyer.

Lawyers' Professional Indemnity Company, "Speaking to the Media"; available online at http://www.practicepro.ca/information/speakingtomedia.asp.

Notaries Act, RSO 1990, c. N.6.

REVIEW QUESTIONS

1. You are attending at court on a summary conviction matter. While waiting outside the courtroom for your matter to be called, your client starts talking with some other people. "These judges," he says. "As far as I can see, they're all in the prosecutor's pocket." The others grin and nod. "You've got that right," one of them comments.

   You are not a part of this conversation. What, if anything, should you do?

2. In the course of a court proceeding, your client's conduct, both in and out of the courtroom, has become increasingly erratic and hostile to the judge. She has made several comments in your presence about how she

would like to "kill that judge." You are getting very concerned, because she has a history of violence.

What should you do?

3. You have been approached by the local media to participate in a press conference about a client matter that is ongoing. Your client is enthusiastic. She wants to get her message out to the press. You are flattered, because you believe that the publicity will be good for you and your firm, and may bring in a lot of new business.

What are some issues you need to consider?

4. "A suspended paralegal may continue to advertise her legal services during the period of the suspension." True or false? Give reasons for your answer.

5. "A suspended paralegal may continue to receive money in payment of outstanding invoices after commencement of the suspension." Please comment.

6. You are attempting to negotiate settlement in a client matter. The opposing paralegal has called you several times to discuss settlement. During the course of several telephone conversations, she has made statements and later denied them. Sometimes she claims that she said something else, or that you misunderstood what she said. You find this very annoying and a waste of time. To pin her down once and for all, you would like to start taping your conversations with her. May you do so?

7. You have just received a request for information from the Law Society concerning a client complaint. In your opinion, the complaint is trivial, silly, and a complete waste of your time. You are very busy in your practice at the moment, and would rather use your time and energy to provide good service to your clients. You figure you will get back to the Law Society when your workload lightens up a bit.

Discuss.

CHAPTER 7

Practice Management

LEARNING OBJECTIVES

After reading this chapter, you will understand:

- Reasonable fees and disbursements.
- Contingency fees.
- Fee splitting.
- Referral fees.
- Professional responsibility.
- Financial responsibility.
- Supervisory responsibility.
- Delegation.
- Making legal services available.
- Marketing.
- Advertising of fees.
- Compulsory errors and omissions insurance.
- File management.
- Time management.
- Technology management.

FEES AND RETAINERS

General

WHAT ARE FEES?

Fees are what a client pays to a paralegal for legal services provided by the paralegal to the client, including advice, correspondence, drafting pleadings and other documents, and time spent in court.

There are four methods of determining the amount of the fee:

- fees based on an hourly rate,

- fixed or flat fees,

- fees by stages, and

- contingency fees.

When determining what type of fee to charge a client, you should consider which method best suits the matter and the client (guideline 13).

Fees Based on an Hourly Rate

When you charge **fees based on an hourly rate**, you are paid for actual time spent on the client matter. In order to calculate this kind of fee, you must establish an hourly rate that is reasonable in the circumstances, and you must keep track of time spent on the client matter by you and anyone to whom you delegate work. When you bill the client, you determine the fee owing to the date of the invoice by multiplying your hourly rate (or that of others who have completed work on the file) by the amount of time spent on the client matter to the date of the invoice.

You may wish to consider establishing different hourly rates for yourself for different types of matters, depending on their complexity, the time and effort required, and so on.

For a client matter where you are charging an hourly rate, you should **docket**, or record, your time for all tasks completed on the file. Time records may be maintained manually or electronically. The time record should state the client name, the matter number or code, the person performing the task, details of the task, and the amount of time spent on the task.

Your **docketed time**—the total time you record to a client matter—may not necessarily turn into **billable time**, or the time that you actually charge to the client on an invoice. In certain situations, you may determine that it is reasonable to **write off time**—that is, not to include some time when calculating your fee. Or you may designate certain tasks on the file as **non-billable time**. You should consider keeping complete time records of all time spent on a client matter, whether the time is billed to the client or not. These records provide a useful tool for determining what activities are unproductive or inefficient.

Fixed, Flat, or Block Fees

A **fixed, flat, or block fee** is a fixed amount charged for a particular task or client matter. Regardless of how much time is spent on the matter, the fee charged to the client does not change.

Fixed fees are often used in high-volume practice areas with routine procedures, such as *Highway Traffic Act* matters and civil collections.

You should consider docketing your time on fixed fee matters, as a tool for determining whether the fixed fee you are charging is appropriate in all of the circumstances.

Fees by Stages

With **fees by stages**, you break the matter down into stages and charge the client based on a reasonable estimate of the fee for each stage or step in the matter. When estimating fees, you should consider advising the client of any facts or circumstances that form the basis of the estimate, and any facts or circumstances that may result in an increase or decrease in the estimate.

Contingency Fees

In a **contingency fee** arrangement, payment of part or all of your fee is contingent on the successful disposition or completion of the matter in respect of which services are provided. The amount of your fee may be calculated as a percentage of any amount recovered by the client.

Contingency fees are discussed in more detail below.

WHAT ARE DISBURSEMENTS?

Disbursements are expenses related to the client matter that are paid by the paralegal on behalf of the client and for which the paralegal is entitled to be reimbursed. Guideline 13 gives the following examples of disbursements:

- court and tribunal filing fees,

- photocopying expenses,

- postage and courier fees,

- long distance phone calls,

- mileage,

- expert reports,

- transcripts or certified documents, and

- research (such as Quicklaw or Westlaw charges) or research conducted by third-party professionals related to the client matter.

You cannot charge a client more than the actual cost of the disbursement to you. You cannot profit from disbursements at the client's expense.

Where a disbursement or expense is substantial, you should explain to the client why it is necessary, and obtain the client's approval in writing before paying the disbursement or incurring the expense. This may help prevent a later dispute with the client about whether or not it was a proper disbursement or expense (guideline 13).

Reasonable Fees and Disbursements

A paralegal shall not charge or accept any amount for a fee or disbursement unless it is fair and reasonable and has been disclosed in a timely fashion (rule 5.01(1)).

FAIR AND REASONABLE FEE

Factors to be considered when deciding what is a fair and reasonable fee are set out at rule 5.01(2). They include:

- the time and effort required in the matter;

- the time and effort actually spent on the matter;

- the difficulty and importance of the matter;

- whether special skill or service was required and provided;

- the amount involved or the value of the subject matter;

- the results obtained;

- fees authorized by statute or regulation; and

- special circumstances, such as the loss of other retainers, postponement of payment, uncertainty of reward, or urgency.

Pro Bono Legal Services

Rule 5.01(2) requires a paralegal to determine what is a fair and reasonable fee based on a range of factors. In some situations, the only fair and reasonable fee is a reduced fee, or no fee at all.

Guideline 13 encourages a paralegal to consider, in appropriate cases, providing **pro bono legal services**—that is, legal services at no charge or for a reduced fee, for the good of the public. When a prospective client or a client has limited means to pay, you should consider reducing or waiving the fees you would normally charge.

In a pro bono arrangement, you should also consider, and discuss with the client, how payment of disbursements will be handled. The terms of the pro bono arrangement should be confirmed in writing to the client.

TIMELY DISCLOSURE

Guideline 13 recommends that you discuss charges for fees and disbursements at the outset of the retainer. You should follow the steps below to meet your obligations under rule 5.01:

- Whenever possible, you should provide the client with an estimate of the amount of fees you expect to charge to complete the matter, or to bring the matter to a certain stage.

- You should disclose and discuss with the client all items that will be charged as disbursements, and how those amounts will be calculated.

- If an administrative charge forms part of the amount charged as a disbursement, disclosure of any such charge should be made to the client in advance.

To avoid misunderstandings, you should provide the above information to the client in writing. The client may then make an informed decision about whether to accept or refuse the arrangement.

When estimating fees, you should consider advising the client of any facts or circumstances that form the basis of the estimate, and any facts or circumstances that may result in an increase or decrease in the estimate.

When discussing fees and disbursements with the client, you should provide a reasonable estimate of the total cost. It is inappropriate to provide an unreasonable estimate (for example, quoting a fee that you know is unrealistically low) in order to obtain the client's business. It is also inappropriate to manipulate fees and disbursements in order to provide a lower fee estimate (guideline 13).

Sometimes something happens in a client matter that you did not foresee at the outset. If the result is higher costs than you originally estimated, you must advise the client, explain why the cost of the matter has changed, provide a revised estimate, and obtain the client's instructions based on the new information. The new information, including the revised estimate, should be in writing. Any new client instructions based on the new information should be confirmed in writing.

STATEMENT OF ACCOUNT (RULE 5.01(4))

A **statement of account** tells the client how much she owes the paralegal on account of fees and disbursements as of the date of the account. It is the same thing as an invoice or bill.

In a statement of account to a client, you shall clearly and separately detail amounts charged as fees and amounts charged as disbursements (rule 5.01(4)). The account must also show how much the client must pay on account of the Goods and Services Tax (GST). The GST applies to fees and some disbursements, and should be in a separate line on the account. You must review the account and sign it before it is sent to the client (guideline 13).

Lawyers are permitted to charge interest on outstanding accounts in accordance with s. 33 of the *Solicitors Act*. Interest on unpaid fees, charges, and disbursements is calculated from a date that is one month after the bill is delivered (s. 33(1)). The rate of interest chargeable shall not exceed the rate that is established by s. 128 of the *Courts of Justice Act* (prejudgment interest) in respect of an action that is commenced on the day the bill is delivered.

Paralegals are not prohibited from charging interest on outstanding accounts. Paralegals may wish to consider s. 33 of the *Solicitors Act* and any other applicable law when doing so.

The interest rate chargeable on overdue accounts and the date from which interest is chargeable should be stated in a separate line on the invoice.

Clients in a joint retainer should receive separate statements of account.

If the client disputes the account, you should discuss the matter calmly and respectfully with the client to try to resolve the dispute. Civility and professionalism must govern all discussions, including discussions relating to fee disputes with clients (guideline 13).

You will find sample invoices in Appendixes 7.1 and 7.2.

Hidden Fees (Rule 5.01(3))

The client should be the only person who pays you for services provided in the client matter. If you accept a payment or other reward or benefit in connection with the client matter from anyone except the client, it may undermine the relationship of trust that must exist between the paralegal and the client. It also leaves your honesty and ability to act in the client's best interests open to question.

You are not permitted to accept a fee, reward, costs, commission, interest, rebate, agency or forwarding allowance, or any other compensation related to your employment by the client from anyone other than the client, unless you provide full disclosure to the client and the client gives his or her informed consent.

Contingency Fees (Rules 5.01(6) to (8))

Except in quasi-criminal or criminal matters, a paralegal may enter into a written agreement that provides that the paralegal's fee is contingent, in whole or in part, on the successful disposition or completion of the matter for which the paralegal's services are to be provided (rule 5.01(6)).

A contingency fee is often, but not always, stated as a percentage of any amount recovered by the client. In determining the appropriate percentage or other basis of a contingency fee, the paralegal shall advise the client on the factors that are being used to determine the percentage or other basis for the fee, including (rule 5.01(7)):

- the likelihood of success,

- the nature and complexity of the claim,

- the expense and risk of pursuing the claim,

- the amount of the expected recovery,

- who is to receive an award of costs, and

- the amount of costs awarded.

Regardless of how the contingency fee is determined, it shall be fair and reasonable, taking into consideration the above factors (rule 5.01(8)).

The contingency fee agreement must be clear about how the fee will be calculated. Guideline 13 suggests that you refer to Regulation 195/04 to the *Solicitors Act*, which applies to contingency fees for lawyers, for guidance regarding the terms to be included in a paralegal contingency fee agreement.

Joint Retainers (Rule 5.01(9))

If you are acting for two or more clients in a joint retainer arrangement, you shall divide the fees and disbursements equitably between them, unless the clients have agreed to another arrangement.

Clients in a joint retainer should receive separate statements of account.

Fee Splitting and Referrals (Rules 5.01(11), (12), (13))

Fee splitting occurs when a paralegal shares or splits her fee with another person.

Fees for a matter may be divided between licensees who are not in the same firm if the client consents and the fees are divided in proportion to the work done and the responsibilities assumed by each of the licensees (rule 5.01(10)).

A paralegal shall not share, split, or divide his or her fees with any person who is not a licensee, including an affiliated entity (rule 5.01(11)(a)).

A paralegal shall not give any financial or other reward to any person who is not a licensee, including an affiliated entity for the referral of clients or client matters (rule 5.01(11)(b)).

Rule 5.01(11) does not apply to multi-discipline practices of paralegal and non-licensee partners where the partnership agreement provides for the sharing of fees, cash flows, or profits among members of the firm.

Guideline 13 defines a **referral fee** as:

- a fee paid by a paralegal to another licensee for referring a client to the paralegal, or

- a fee paid to a paralegal by another licensee for the paralegal's referral of a person to the other licensee.

> ### BOX 7.1
>
> ## Reminder: Affiliations and Multi-discipline Practices (MDP)
>
> An affiliated entity is any person or group of persons other than a person or group authorized to provide legal services in Ontario. An affiliation is an arrangement where a paralegal services firm provides legal services to the public jointly with a non-legal entity whose members practise a profession, trade, or occupation that supports or supplements the paralegal's provision of legal services.
>
> A multi-discipline practice (MDP) is a business arrangement that permits paralegal licensees to provide clients the services of a non-licensee who practises a profession, trade, or occupation that supports or supplements the provision of legal services.
>
> Affiliations and multi-discipline practices are discussed in Chapter 4 (pages 100 to 102). ◇

A paralegal who refers a matter to another licensee because of the expertise and ability of that licensee to handle the matter may accept, and the other licensee may pay, a referral fee if the following conditions apply (rule 5.01(13)):

(a) the referral was not made because of a conflict of interest;

(b) the referral fee is reasonable and does not increase the total amount of the fee charged to the client; and

(c) the client is informed and consents.

> ### BOX 7.2
>
> ## Referrals
>
> ### Scenario
>
> You have been approached by one Sandra Hobbins. Sandra is a non-licensee who wishes to refer a client to you. In return for the referral, she proposes that you pay her 15 percent of your fee when the client matter is concluded. She also tells you that she will act as "liaison" between the client and you. "It's a good deal for you," she says. "This guy can pay. And if you do a good job, there will be lots of repeat business."
>
> May you enter into this arrangement?
>
> ### Discussion
>
> Sandra is a non-licensee. You must inform her that you cannot enter into a fee split-ting arrangement with, or give any financial or other award to, a non-licensee (rule 5.01(11)).
>
> As far as her proposal to act as "liaison" goes, you should explain to her that she is not the client, and may not continue to be involved in the client matter. Unless the client provides you with informed, written instructions to the contrary, you can-not discuss the client's matter with Sandra or accept instructions from her regarding the client matter. ◇

Retainers (Rule 5.01; Guideline 14; By-law 9)

BOX 7.3

Reminder: What Is a Retainer?

In a legal services context, the word "retainer" has several meanings.

- A paralegal–client retainer (referred to in guideline 14 as a retainer) is the contractual relationship between the client and the paralegal whereby the client agrees to hire the paralegal and the paralegal agrees to provide legal services to the client in a particular matter.

- A retainer agreement is a written contract between the paralegal and the client that sets out the scope of the legal services to be provided in the client matter and the likely cost of those services to the client, as well as the other terms of the paralegal–client retainer.

- A money retainer is money paid by the client to the paralegal for future legal services in a particular client matter. ◈

THE RETAINER AGREEMENT (RULE 5.01(1))

Guideline 14 recommends that, as soon as possible after you have been hired by a client in a particular matter, you should discuss with the client two essential terms of the paralegal–client retainer:

- the scope of the legal services to be provided, and

- the likely cost of those services.

Every client matter is unique. When estimating fees, you should consider advising the client of any facts or circumstances that form the basis of the estimate, and any facts or circumstances that may result in an increase or decrease in the estimate.

Other terms that you may wish to consider discussing with the client are:

- your billing practices—that is, how frequently the client will be billed for fees and disbursements;

- whether and how often a money retainer may be required from the client; and

- how client settlement funds are to be handled.

You must ensure that the client understands the scope of the legal services to be provided; how fees, disbursements, and GST will be charged; and any other terms of the paralegal–client retainer.

It is advisable to confirm the terms of the retainer in writing. Depending on the nature of the client matter, confirmation in writing may be done by:

- a retainer agreement signed by the client;

- an engagement letter delivered by the paralegal to the client; or

- a confirming memo delivered to the client by mail, email, or fax.

If the client has agreed that any outstanding fees or disbursements may be paid from client settlement funds received in trust, that arrangement should be confirmed in writing. In this context, **client settlement funds** are money paid by another person to your client in settlement of a client matter. Your written confirmation of the retainer should contain a term that any settlement funds payable to your client are to be paid to you in trust, and that you may withhold any amounts owing for invoiced fees and disbursements before paying the balance out of trust to the client.

BOX 7.4

Reminder: Retainer Agreements

The retainer agreement is a valuable tool for managing client expectations about all aspects of the paralegal–client retainer. See the discussion of retainer agreements in Chapter 3 (pages 39 to 40) and in Chapter 4 (pages 72 and 111). You will find a sample retainer agreement, adapted for a paralegal firm, in Appendix 3.1. Sample retainer agreements are also available at the Lawyers Professional Indemnity Company website (www.practicepro.ca).

A retainer agreement should be adapted to reflect the terms of the agreement between the paralegal and the client in a particular client matter. ◇

MONEY RETAINERS (RULE 5.01; BY-LAW 9, PART IV)

A money retainer is a payment made by the client to the paralegal for future legal services and disbursements in the client matter. A money retainer must be deposited to your trust account and held for the benefit of the client until part or all of those services have been provided and invoiced to the client. Proper disbursements and proper expenses in the client matter may be paid directly from client funds held in trust (By-law 9, s. 9(1)).

It is appropriate to request a money retainer at the outset of the paralegal–client retainer. Guideline 14 recommends that, when determining the amount of the money retainer, you should consider the circumstances of the particular client matter; the client's circumstances; and the estimated fees, disbursements, and GST. Many of the factors to consider are the same as those set out in rule 5.01(2) for determining if a fee is fair and reasonable, including urgency, the time and effort required in the matter, its difficulty and importance, and the amount involved in the matter, or its value.

You should consider requesting additional money retainers from time to time as the client matter goes forward, interim accounts are delivered, and the funds held in trust to the credit of the client matter are depleted. Any arrangement with respect to money retainers should be discussed with the client at the outset of the retainer, and confirmed in the retainer agreement or otherwise in writing.

Money retainers may be inappropriate in some client matters—for example, where the paralegal and the client have entered into a contingency fee agreement.

The Trust Account (Rule 5.01(5); Guideline 15; By-law 9, Part IV)

Client money, such as a money retainer or settlement funds, remains the property of the client. It must be deposited to your trust account and held for the benefit of the client.

A paralegal shall not appropriate any funds of the client held in trust or otherwise under the paralegal's control, for or on account of fees, except as permitted by By-law 9 (rule 5.01(5)).

Generally, a paralegal practice will have one general (operating) account and one mixed trust account. A **mixed trust account** is a trust account that holds money for more than one client. By-law 9 requires you to keep special trust records for the mixed trust account so that you can keep track of what money belongs to which client. Where you are retained on more than one matter for a client, you must also keep track of the trust funds to be credited to each active matter for that client.

You may not remove money from trust in a client matter to pay your fees unless (By-law 9, s. 9):

■ you have provided the legal services for which you are charging the client,

■ you have delivered a bill or invoice to the client, and

■ there is money in trust with which to pay all or part of the amount billed to the client matter.

You must never disburse from trust an amount in excess of the amount actually held in trust in a particular client matter. You are personally responsible for reimbursing the trust account for any amount paid out in error.

When you invoice a client, you may transfer funds held in trust to the credit of that client matter out of the trust account into your general (operating) account, in payment of the invoice. The payment from trust must be stated in a separate line on the invoice. Any amount still owing after payment has been made from trust must also be stated in a separate line on the invoice. If the amount invoiced was paid in full out of trust, the amount owing on the invoice will be stated in a separate line as zero.

If the funds held in trust to the credit of the client matter are not adequate to pay the total amount of the invoice, you may deduct only the amount actually held in trust from the invoice, and transfer only the amount actually held in trust to the general account. The client is responsible for paying any balance still owing after the funds held in trust to the credit of the client matter are deducted from the client's bill and transferred to your general account. Where the client pays an outstanding balance on an invoice, any payment may be deposited directly to your general (operating) account, because it is for legal services that have been performed and billed to the client.

You do not have to wait until a client matter is concluded to bill the file. An **interim invoice** is an invoice that is delivered to the client before the client matter is completed, for fees and disbursements to the date of the interim invoice. You should consider interim billing in any client matter that is ongoing over a period of time. Interim billing should take place at reasonable intervals. If interim billing depletes the funds held in trust to the credit of the client matter, you may require additional money retainers at reasonable intervals as well.

When determining the frequency and amount of the money retainers required of clients, you should consider your obligation to continue to represent clients in certain circumstances, despite non-payment of fees. You may not withdraw from representing a non-paying client if serious prejudice to the client would result.

The client should be advised of your billing practices and of the circumstances in which additional money retainers will be required at the outset of the retainer. Any arrangement with respect to billing practices and money retainers should be confirmed in the retainer agreement or otherwise in writing.

Presenting interim accounts at reasonable intervals in a lengthy client matter is an effective way of managing client expectations about the cost of a matter.

BOX 7.5

Billing the Client

You are holding money in your mixed trust account as follows:

Client	Matter number	Amount
A	001	$500.00
B	002	$1,000.00
C	003	$400.00
D	004	$600.00

Total monies held in trust: $2,500.00

Assume that all matters are being billed at an hourly rate.

Scenario 1

You have completed legal services in Matter 001 for Client A. The total of fees, disbursements, and GST is $650.00. You have $2,500.00 in your mixed trust account.

Can you pay the total amount owing from trust?

Discussion

No, you cannot. Money in the mixed trust account is held to the credit of particular client matters. You cannot take trust money from other client matters to pay the invoice in Matter 001. The trust money held to the credit of the other client matters belongs to those clients, not to Client A and not to you.

You are holding $500.00 in trust to the credit of Matter 001. The invoice will show payment from trust of $500.00. The amount still owing after the payment from trust is $150.00.

An amount owing on an invoice is a **receivable**—that is, money owed to you by the client. Payment of receivables may be deposited directly to your general account.

Remember that on the invoice, fees and disbursements must be clearly and separately detailed. GST owing, the payment of $500.00 from trust, and the final amount owing should appear on separate lines. You must review the invoice and sign it before it is sent to the client. If you are charging interest on outstanding accounts, the interest rate and when it becomes chargeable should be stated in a separate line on the invoice.

Depending on what stage Matter 001 is at, you may wish to consider requesting a further money retainer from Client A.

Scenario 2

You have completed legal services in Matter 004. The amount of the final invoice is $400.00.

Can you pay the total amount owing from trust?

Discussion

You are holding $600.00 in trust to the credit of Matter 004. The invoice will show payment from trust of $400.00. The final amount owing on the invoice will be zero. You must review the invoice and sign it before it is sent to the client.

When the $400.00 payment is transferred from trust to your general account, there will be $200.00 left in trust. That is the client's money. Matter 004 is now concluded, and the money left in trust should be returned promptly to the client, unless you have written instructions from the client to transfer that money to the credit of another ongoing matter.

Scenario 3

Matter 002 is ongoing. You have completed several steps in the proceeding, including the settlement conference. To date, your legal services total $850.00 including GST. A trial date has been set for three months' time. For the trial, you will need to interview and summon at least three witnesses in addition to your client. You will also require an expert's report, which will cost $500.00.

What are your next steps?

Discussion

You are holding $1,000.00 in trust to the credit of Matter 002. You should consider sending the client an interim invoice for your legal services to date, which may be paid in full from trust. You should also consider requesting a further money retainer from the client.

You should advise the client about the expert's report, why it is needed, and its cost before incurring that expense. You should obtain her approval in writing, in order to avoid a possible dispute with her about whether it was a proper disbursement or expense.

Before retaining the expert, you should also consider your obligations under rule 8.01(2) regarding financial responsibility. You should clarify the terms of the third-party retainer in writing. The third-party retainer should specify the fees, the nature of the services to be provided, and the person responsible for payment. If you do not assume responsibility for payment of the expert's fees, you should, if practicable, help make satisfactory arrangements for payment.

Remember that at the outset of the retainer, the client should be advised of your billing practices. The client should also be advised if and when further money retainers will be required. You should confirm this in writing to the client, in the retainer agreement or otherwise. ◇

PRACTICE MANAGEMENT (RULE 8)

Running an effective paralegal practice involves a range of responsibilities. You must make decisions about what procedures and systems you need to have in place to make the business successful, while ensuring compliance with and being responsible for your professional obligations under the Rules and the by-laws.

Supervision and Delegation (Rules 8.01(1), (3), (4), (5); By-law 7.1, Part I; Guideline 18)

DELEGATION

A paralegal shall, in accordance with the by-laws, assume complete professional responsibility for all business entrusted to her (rule 8.01(1)). A paralegal must take any action necessary to ensure compliance with the *Law Society Act*, the by-laws, Rules, and the Law Society's policies and guidelines.

In appropriate circumstances, a paralegal should consider providing legal services with the assistance of competent non-licensee employees. A competent support person may take on a range of tasks on client matters as set out in rule 8.01 and By-law 7.1 (Part I), permitting the paralegal to spend more time providing legal services to clients. This may result in more efficient service and lower costs to clients.

By-law 7.1, s. 3(1) permits a paralegal to assign tasks and functions to an employee in connection with a paralegal's provision of legal services to the paralegal's clients, in accordance with Part I.

A paralegal shall not assign to an affiliated entity or its staff tasks or functions in connection with the paralegal's provision of legal services to clients, unless the client consents (s. 3(2)).

Assignment of Tasks or Functions—Direct Supervision (By-law 7.1, s. 4)

When assigning tasks and functions to an employee, you shall comply with the following (the list is not exhaustive):

(a) You shall not permit an employee to accept a client on your behalf.

(b) You shall maintain a direct relationship with the client throughout the paralegal–client retainer.

(c) You shall assign to employees only tasks and functions that the employee is competent to perform.

(d) You shall ensure that the employee does not act except with your instructions.

(e) You shall review at frequent intervals the employee's performance of the tasks and functions assigned to him.

(f) You shall ensure that the tasks and functions assigned to the employee are performed properly and promptly.

(g) You shall assume responsibility for all tasks and functions performed by the employee, including all documents prepared by the employee. You must review all correspondence and other documents prepared by the employee.

(h) You shall ensure that the employee does not, at any time, act finally in a client's affairs.

Guideline 18 states that the extent of your supervision of an employee will depend on a number of factors, including the nature of the task and the experience of the employee. Tasks or functions that are routine—that is, standardized and repetitive—may require less direction and supervision, if the employee is familiar with them. Tasks or functions that are more complex or unusual may require extra direction and supervision. A task or function with which the employee is unfamiliar may also require extra direction and supervision.

It is your responsibility to ensure that the employee is properly trained to perform assigned tasks and functions, and to supervise the manner in which employees complete the work assigned to them (guideline 18).

Assignment of Tasks or Functions—Express Instruction and Authorization (By-law 7.1, s. 5(1))

You shall give an employee express instruction and authorization prior to permitting the employee to:

(a) give or accept an undertaking on your behalf;

(b) appear on your behalf before an adjudicative body with respect to a scheduling matter or other related routine administrative matter; or

(c) take instructions from your client.

Assignment of Tasks or Functions—Prior Consent and Approval (By-law 7.1, s. 5(2))

Before you permit an employee to conduct routine negotiations with third parties with respect to the client's matter, you shall obtain the client's consent. You shall approve the results of the negotiation before any action is taken based on the outcome of the negotiations.

Tasks and Functions That May Not Be Assigned (Rule 8.01(4); By-law 7.1, s. 6)

You shall not permit an employee to (rule 8.01(4)):

(a) provide legal services;

(b) be held out as a licensee; or

(c) perform any duty that only paralegals may perform or do anything that paralegals may not do.

Employees must clearly identify themselves as non-licensees when communicating with clients, prospective clients, courts or tribunals, or the public. This applies to both spoken and written communications.

In your supervisory role, as the person responsible for all business entrusted to you, you cannot permit an employee to do anything that paralegals may not do, including engaging in unauthorized practice. If a paralegal employs a lawyer, the lawyer employee cannot practise law, because the paralegal employer does not have the education, training, and knowledge to supervise someone engaged in the practice of law. A paralegal employer may supervise a lawyer employee if the lawyer employee practises within the permitted scope of practice for paralegals.

You shall not permit an employee to (By-law 7.1, s. 6):

(a)   give a client legal advice;

(b)   appear in a proceeding before an adjudicative body on behalf of a person, except as set out in s. 5(1), unless the non-licensee is authorized by the *Law Society Act* to do so (that is, falls within one of the By-law 4 exemptions);

(c)   conduct negotiations with third parties, except as set out in s. 5(2);

(d)   sign correspondence, other than correspondence of a routine administrative nature; or

(e)   forward to your client any document, other than a routine document, that has not been reviewed by you.

Collection Letters (By-law 7.1, s. 7)

Special restrictions apply to collection letters. You shall not permit a collection letter to be sent to any person unless:

(a)   the letter is sent in connection with a client matter;

(b)   the letter is prepared by you or by an employee under your direct supervision;

(c)   where the letter is prepared by an employee under your direct supervision, it is reviewed and approved by you before being sent;

(d)   the letter is on your firm letterhead; and

(e)   the letter is signed by you.

Multi-discipline Practice (Rules 3.04(15) and 8.01(1), (5))

A multi-discipline practice is a business arrangement that permits paralegal licensees to provide to clients the services of a non-licensee who practises a profession, trade, or occupation that supports or supplements the provision of legal services (By-law 7, s. 18(1)). The paralegal licensee must have effective control over the non-legal professional's provision of services to clients of the multi-discipline practice (By-law 7, s. 18(2)2).

A paralegal in a multi-discipline practice is required to assume complete professional responsibility for all business entrusted to him or her (rule 8.01(1)). In accordance with By-Law 7.1 and rule 8.01(5), a paralegal in a multi-discipline practice shall ensure that non-licensee partners and associates comply with By-law 7 (Part III), the Rules, and all ethical principles that govern paralegals in the discharge of their professional obligations, including the duty to hold all client information in strict confidence and the duty to avoid conflicts of interest, when providing non-legal professional services within the paralegal practice and when carrying on business or fulfilling professional undertakings outside of the paralegal practice.

A paralegal in a multi-discipline practice must ensure that the client understands legal services are provided by the paralegal, and supplemented by the non-legal professional services of non-licensee partners and associates.

Table 7.1 Delegation to Non-Licensee Employees (Rule 8.01; By-law 7.1)

Task, function, or conduct	Is an employee permitted to perform the task or function?	Authority
Accept a client on the paralegal's behalf	No	By-law 7.1, s. 4
Act without the paralegal's instruction	No	By-law 7.1, s. 4
Act finally in a client's affairs	No	By-law 7.1, s. 4
Give or accept an undertaking on behalf of the paralegal	Yes, with the paralegal's express instruction and authorization permitting the employee to do so	By-law 7.1, s. 5(1)
	No, in any other circumstances	
Appear before an adjudicative body	Yes, on scheduling or other routine administrative matters and with the paralegal's express instruction and authorization permitting the employee to do so	By-law 7.1, s. 5(1)
	Yes, if non-licensee falls within the exemptions	*Law Society Act*, s. 1(8) By-law 4
	No, in any other circumstances	By-law 7.1, s. 6
Give a client legal advice	No	By-law 7.1, s. 6
Take instructions from a client	Yes, with the paralegal's express instruction and authorization permitting the employee to do so	By-law 7.1, s. 5(1)
	No, in any other circumstances	
Conduct negotiations with third parties	Yes, in routine negotiations, with the client's prior consent and with the paralegal's approval of the results of the negotiations before any further action following from the negotiations	By-law 7.1, s. 5(2)
	No, if it is not a routine negotiation	By-law 7.1, s. 6
Sign correspondence	Yes, if correspondence is of a routine administrative nature	By-law 7.1, s. 6
	No, in any other circumstances	
Forward a document to the client without review by the paralegal	Yes, if it is a routine document	By-law 7.1, s. 6
	No, in any other circumstances	
Provide legal services	No	Rule 8.01(4)
Hold himself out as a licensee	No	Rule 8.01(4)
Perform any duty that only a paralegal may perform	No	Rule 8.01(4)
Do anything that a paralegal may not do	No	Rule 8.01(4)

HIRING AND TRAINING OF STAFF (GUIDELINE 18)

Hiring Staff

In order to run your practice efficiently and comply with your obligations to clients under the Rules and the by-laws, you must take steps to hire trustworthy, competent staff and train them properly. Proper hiring and training of staff will assist you to manage your practice effectively, as required by rule 3.01(4)(h).

During the hiring process, you should obtain information about a potential employee to assess her competence and trustworthiness, keeping in mind your obligation to comply with privacy legislation. If the position involves handling money, you should obtain the applicant's consent to a criminal record check and a credit report.

When designing your interview questions, review rule 2.03 regarding harassment and discrimination and the *Human Rights Code* to ensure that your questions are appropriate and do not contravene the Code.

When considering whether to offer employment to a candidate, you should confirm the information in the candidate's resumé. You should verify education and previous employment experiences, and consult references before you offer the position to a candidate.

Training Staff

You are responsible for all business entrusted to you. You must take any action necessary to ensure compliance with the *Law Society Act*, the by-laws, the Rules, and the Law Society's policies and guidelines. As part of this professional obligation, you should ensure that staff receive appropriate training before delegating tasks or functions to them. Training ensures that staff have the knowledge, skill, and ability to perform their employment duties effectively. It also ensures that they are aware of their professional obligations in a legal services practice.

You should educate staff with respect to the following (guideline 18):

- the tasks and functions they can perform;

- the tasks and functions they cannot perform;

- their obligation to conduct themselves with courtesy and professionalism;

- the definitions of harassment and discrimination, and the prohibition against conduct that constitutes harassment or discrimination;

- the duty to maintain client confidentiality and procedures to protect client confidentiality (for example, appropriate file management procedures);

- the duty to avoid conflicts of interest, and how to use the conflict-checking system;

- proper handling of client property, including money; and

- proper record-keeping.

An office procedures manual is a valuable tool for assisting staff to perform their duties effectively and professionally.

Financial Obligations (Rule 8.01(2); Guideline 23)

A paralegal shall promptly meet financial obligations incurred in the course of the paralegal practice on behalf of clients unless, before incurring the obligation, the paralegal clearly indicates in writing to the person to whom the obligation is owed that it is not to be a personal obligation of the paralegal.

In the course of providing legal services, a paralegal often incurs financial obligations to others on behalf of clients. These obligations include:

- charges for medical reports;

- disbursements payable to tribunal offices;

- fees charged by expert witnesses, sheriffs, and court reporters; and

- the accounts of paralegal agents retained in other jurisdictions.

To help avoid disputes about payment of accounts, where a paralegal retains a person on behalf of a client the paralegal should clarify the terms of the third-party retainer in writing. The third-party retainer should specify the fees, the nature of the services to be provided, and the person responsible for payment. If the paralegal does not assume responsibility for payment of the fees, the paralegal should, if practicable, help make satisfactory arrangements for payment.

If there is a change of representation, the paralegal who retained the third party should advise that person of the change, and provide contact information for the new paralegal or lawyer, if any.

Marketing Legal Services (Rules 8.02, 8.03; Guideline 19)

A paralegal shall make legal services available to the public in an efficient and convenient way (rule 8.02(1)).

BOX 7.6

Making Legal Services Available

Rule 8.02(1) imposes an obligation on paralegals to make legal services available to the public. This does not mean that you must accept every retainer that is offered. You have a general right to decline representation (except when assigned as representative by a tribunal). That right should be exercised prudently, especially if your refusal would make it difficult for a person to obtain legal advice or representation. Guideline 19 recommends that you should not refuse a retainer for the following reasons:

- because a person seeking legal services or that person's cause is unpopular or notorious;

- because powerful interests or allegations of malfeasance or misconduct are involved; or

- because of your personal opinion of the guilt of an accused.

If you decline representation, you shall assist in obtaining the services of another licensee qualified in the particular field who is able to act. ◇

A person requiring legal services should be able to find a qualified paralegal with a minimum of delay and inconvenience. A paralegal assists in this process by promoting his or her legal services to the public. A paralegal's promotional strategies must comply with the Rules. They must be in the best interests of the public, and consistent with a high standard of professionalism.

Rule 8.02(2) places restrictions on the manner in which a paralegal promotes his or her practice. A paralegal shall not use methods that:

(a) are false or misleading;

(b) amount to coercion, duress, or harassment;

(c) take advantage of a person who is vulnerable or who has suffered a traumatic experience and has not yet recovered;

(d) are intended to influence a person who has retained another licensee to change the person's representation for the matter, unless the change is initiated by the person or by the other representative; or

(e) otherwise bring the paralegal profession or the administration of justice into disrepute.

A paralegal shall not advertise services that are beyond the permissible scope of paralegal practice (rule 8.02(3)).

Marketing includes advertisements and similar communications in various media, as well as firm names (including trade names), letterhead, business cards, and logos (rule 8.03(1)).

A paralegal may market legal services if the marketing (rule 8.03(2)):

(a) is demonstrably true, accurate and verifiable,

(b) is neither misleading, confusing, or deceptive, nor likely to mislead, confuse or deceive, and

(c) is in the best interests of the public and is consistent with a high standard of professionalism.

A paralegal may advertise fees charged for legal services by the paralegal if (rule 8.03(3)):

(a) the advertising is reasonably precise as to the services offered for each fee quoted,

(b) the advertising states whether other amounts, such as disbursements and taxes, will be charged in addition to the fee, and

(c) the paralegal adheres to the advertised fee.

A paralegal must be able to market his services to the public in a way that differentiates those services from services provided by other licensees, including lawyers. A paralegal must ensure that his marketing does not suggest that he is a lawyer, and should take steps to correct any misunderstanding in that respect on the part of a client or prospective client.

Guideline 19 provides the following examples of marketing practices that may contravene rule 8.03:

- stating an amount of money that the paralegal has recovered for a client, unless there is a further statement that the amount recovered and other litigation outcomes will vary according to the facts in individual cases;

- referring to the paralegal's degree of success in past cases, unless there is a further statement that past results are not necessarily indicative of future results and that litigation outcomes will vary according to the facts in individual cases;

BOX 7.7

Marketing a Paralegal Firm

Scenario

Your paralegal firm does a lot of work for multi-unit residential landlords. Most of the matters involve terminating tenancies and evicting tenants for non-payment of rent. You are designing a brochure to advertise your firm to potential landlord clients. You want to use this logo on your brochure:

Is the logo an acceptable marketing strategy?

Discussion

In its list of marketing practices that may contravene rule 8.03(2), guideline 19 includes marketing that

- raises unjustifiable expectations,

- suggests or implies that the paralegal is aggressive, or

- disparages or demeans other persons or groups.

The logo of a fist clutching dollar bills suggests that you will obtain good results for a client by using aggressive conduct. Suggesting or implying that aggressive behaviour achieves good results may be misleading or deceptive, and is inconsistent with the best interests of the public and a high standard of professionalism. The logo may also be misleading or deceptive in that the fistful of dollars raises unjustifiable expectations about the results you will achieve. Finally, in the context of your target market, the logo suggests that force is needed when dealing with tenants. That is disparaging and demeaning to tenants.

You should carefully reconsider your artwork. ◈

- suggesting that the quality of the paralegal's services is superior to the quality of service provided by other licensees;

- creating unjustifiable expectations;

- suggesting or implying that the paralegal is aggressive;

- disparaging or demeaning other persons, groups, organizations, or institutions;

- taking advantage of a vulnerable person or group; and

- using testimonials or endorsements that contain emotional appeals.

INTERNET MARKETING

Advertising by paralegals using electronic media, such as websites, network bulletin boards, and email, is governed by the Rules.

In addition to the Rules, paralegals who are contemplating marketing their services using electronic media should review and consider the Law Society's Ethical Considerations and Technology publication regarding the use of technology by law firms, as well as the "Technology in Your Practice" document in the Knowledge Tree in the "Practice Resources" section at the Law Society website.

Internet advertising is not limited to a particular geographic area, and access is not confined to a particular group of users. Anyone anywhere in the world who has Internet access can view your website.

To prevent confusion in the minds of users as to your identity, location, and qualifications, you should provide the following information:

- your name,

- your status as a licensed paralegal,

- the name of your paralegal firm,

- your mailing address,

- your licensed jurisdiction of practice, and

- the email address of at least one paralegal responsible for communication.

You should consider stating the areas of law in which paralegals are authorized to provide legal services in Ontario, in accordance with rule 8.02(3).

There are restrictions on indiscriminate distribution of marketing material using electronic media on grounds that it produces widespread and unwanted communication, and is incompatible with the public interest, the best interests of the profession, and the administration of justice.

The "Technology" section of the Law Society's Practice Management Guidelines (available in the "Practice Resources" section of the Law Society website) provides the following examples of unacceptable marketing strategies using electronic media:

- advertising legal services, where the advertisement is directly and indiscriminately distributed to a large number of newsgroups or electronic mail addresses (spamming); and

- posting advertisements to newsgroups, listservers, or bulletin boards whose posting topic does not match what is being advertised in the posting (misleading or deceptive advertising).

Compulsory Errors and Omissions Insurance (Rule 8.04; By-law 6, Part II)

Errors and omissions insurance is professional liability insurance that is intended to reimburse clients for any damage or loss suffered as a result of a paralegal's negligence or wrongdoing when working on a client matter.

All paralegals practising in Ontario shall obtain and maintain adequate errors and omissions insurance as required by the Law Society (rule 8.04(1)).

When a claim of professional negligence is made against a paralegal, he shall assist and cooperate with the insurer to the extent necessary to enable the claim to be dealt with promptly (rule 8.04(2)). In cases where liability is clear and the insurer is prepared to pay its portion of the claim, the paralegal shall pay the balance (rule 8.04(3))—that is, pay the deductible.

MANAGEMENT SYSTEMS IN A LEGAL SERVICES PRACTICE

In addition to the practice management responsibilities covered by rule 8, a paralegal should consider putting systems in place to manage a client's documents and information, and to manage time spent in the practice. A paralegal should also consider the ways in which technology may benefit the practice. Effective practice management helps ensure that clients receive timely, effective service.

An office policies and procedures manual is a useful management tool for improving staff efficiency and ensuring that staff, including field placement students, follow appropriate systems and procedures in a paralegal practice. You will find a sample excerpt from an office procedures manual in Appendix 7.3.

You should consider reviewing and updating, as required:

- all practice management systems;
- firm checklists, procedural and substantive; and
- precedents.

File Management

Much of the following material has been adapted from the "File Management" section of the Law Society's Practice Management Guidelines.

Appropriate file management systems enable you to manage the client's information and documents while complying with professional obligations such as the duty of confidentiality and avoidance of conflicts.

You should implement systems to:

- store and easily retrieve key information regarding all firm clients, as well as related persons and opposing parties;

- open and maintain active client files;

- check for conflicts;

- check for limitation periods and procedural deadlines;

- close client files; and

- retain and dispose of closed client files.

You should also review your management systems at reasonable intervals and, if necessary, adapt them to meet changing standards, techniques, and practices.

OPENING AND MANAGING ACTIVE CLIENT FILES

When Should a New Client File Be Opened?

A new client file should be opened for any new matter for:

- a new client,

- a current client, and

- a former client.

For current or continuing clients, a new file should be opened for each client matter as you are retained.

It may not always be practicable or necessary to open a new file for a prospective client whose contact with your firm is brief and informal. However, you should consider opening a new file for any prospective client with whom you have an initial consultation, even if the client does not retain you or you decline the retainer. The prospective client's information should be entered into your conflict-checking system. The conflict search results, your notes of the consultation, and the non-engagement letter, if any, should be filed in the client file. If you decline the retainer, you should recommend that the prospective client seek other legal representation and suggest resources that will assist the client in that search, such as the Paralegal Directory or the Lawyer Referral Service at the Law Society website.

Naming and Coding Active Client Files

You should consider using a standard file information checklist to obtain information about a client or prospective client, related persons, and opposing parties, for use at the initial consultation or when the retainer is established.

You should consider setting up a standard file opening protocol or checklist for staff to follow when opening new files. The file opening checklist should include a requirement that a conflict check be performed as soon as possible after the initial contact with a potential client, and the results given to the paralegal for review.

Each new file should have a unique file name and reference or matter number assigned to it. The file name should include the name of the client, and the reference or matter number. Electronic files should be cross-referenced to paper files, and vice versa.

Organization of File Contents

File contents and information should be organized in subfiles according to the class or type of document or information, for efficient storage and retrieval.

In a paralegal practice, depending on the type of client matter, you should consider setting up subfiles for the following:

- communications, including correspondence, file memoranda, notes of telephone conversations and meetings with the client, and so on, arranged chronologically;

- pleadings and other tribunal documents;

- the retainer agreement, engagement letter, or billing memorandum;

- original documents and disclosure;

- legal research; and

- other subfiles, if appropriate.

Handling and Storage of Active Client Files

You should keep active client files out of sight of the public. They should be worked on in a private area, where others cannot see them.

Electronic files should be worked on in a location where the computer monitor is not visible to the public. If that is not practicable, the monitor should be turned so that it is not visible to the public. You should consider installing a filter on the monitor.

All documentation relating to the client file should be stored in an appropriate subfile in the client file.

You should store active client files separately from closed client files. Active client files should be filed in an orderly fashion for easy retrieval. When not in use, active client files should be stored in a cabinet that can be locked. If practicable, the cabinet should be in a secure location away from public areas. File cabinets containing active client files should be locked when no one is in the office.

If practicable, you should consider limiting staff access to particular client files to only those staff who are working on the files.

You should train staff in the importance of client confidentiality and the risks of improper handling of client information.

An office procedures and policies manual is a valuable tool for training staff. It also provides a reference guide for day-to-day operations. It should be reviewed and updated at reasonable intervals.

CONFLICT-CHECKING SYSTEM

General

A conflict of interest is any circumstance that may negatively affect a paralegal's ability to fulfill her ethical and professional obligations to the client. Rule 3.04(1) defines a conflict or conflicting interest as an interest, financial or otherwise,

(a) that would be likely to have an adverse effect on a paralegal's judgment on behalf of, or loyalty to, a client or prospective client; or

(b) that a paralegal might be prompted to give preference to over the interests of a client or a prospective client.

Examples of a potential conflict might include a personal financial interest in a business, and serving as a director on a corporate board.

The Rules require paralegals to manage potential and real conflicts of interest. Paralegals should consider implementing and maintaining a conflicts database, including, where practicable, the following information about former, current, and prospective clients:

- the client's name, and aliases and former names, if applicable;

- the names and contact information of related persons, and of conflicting or adverse parties (if available), cross-referenced to the client matter by active file name or, where applicable, the closed file code;

- the date when a client file was opened and closed; and

- the subject matter of the file.

If appropriate, you should consider preparing a list of potential conflicts, which should be considered before accepting the retainer.

When to Check for Conflicts

Conflicts of interest may arise at any time in a client matter, as the matter evolves, new parties are added, and new circumstances or information come to light. You should check for conflicts when a potential client first contacts your firm. If office staff are the first contact the prospective client has with your firm, they should be trained to ask for certain information at the initial contact, and to enter any information they obtain into the conflicts database. They should perform a conflicts check at that point in the matter. The results of the search should be delivered to you for your review and consideration.

The conflicts database should be checked thereafter at critical points in the client matter, including when you have more information about the client and about related or adverse parties. If a retainer is entered into, you should conduct a conflict search any time a new party is added in a proceeding. If a conflict arises after you are retained, you may be required to withdraw from representing the client.

CLOSING, RETAINING, AND DISPOSING OF CLIENT FILES

Your file storage procedure should:

- provide for proper distribution or disposal of the contents of files in client matters that have been concluded,

- assign a closed file code to the file,

- provide for secure storage of closed files separate and apart from active client files, and

- provide for destruction of closed client files when appropriate.

You should not close a client file until after all matters related to the file have been completed and any appeal period has expired.

Distribution and Disposal of File Contents

Prior to closing the file, you should remove any unnecessary documents from the file. The following documents should be delivered to the client:

- the client's original documents;

- documents and disclosure from opposing parties;

- reports and other documents related to issues in the matter; and

- any tribunal or legal documents not already provided to the client, such as pleadings, affidavits, or similar documents.

You should consider having the client sign an acknowledgment of receipt of the documents provided to her.

You should consider destroying or disposing of any documents that may be obtained in the future from a tribunal or government registry, if you are satisfied that you will not require the information for purposes of your own defence. Confidential information should be shredded before it is disposed of.

You should consider keeping photocopies of documents returned to the client, for use in your defence in the event that the client sues you for negligence, makes a complaint of misconduct to the Law Society, or disputes your invoice. Photocopies of client documents must be made at your own expense. You may wish to keep copies of the following:

- correspondence and communications, including email, file memoranda, and notes of telephone conversations or meetings;

- the retainer agreement;

- client authorizations and directions;

- documents containing client instructions and changes to instructions;

- documents confirming the client's refusal to follow your advice; and

- drafts and the final version of any agreements as evidence of client instructions.

You should consider removing the following from the file and retaining for later use:

- legal research;

- case law, or a list of case law; and

- documents to be used as precedents.

You are entitled to keep any documents that were not prepared for the client's benefit and that the client did not have to pay for. These include:

- copies of original documents photocopied at your own expense;

- your working notes, including summaries of evidence and trial submissions;

- time entries or dockets;

- accounting records, client invoices, trust statements, and other financial information relating to the client matter; and

- other documents prepared for your own benefit and protection at your expense.

You should assign to the file a closed client file code that is different from the active client file code.

Storage of Closed Client Files

You should arrange for storage of closed paper files in a secure storage location that is separate and apart from active client file storage. Closed electronic files should be stored in a secure location that is separate and apart from active electronic files.

The storage facility or location should protect files from destruction or damage, and should maintain client confidentiality.

Closed client files should be stored in a manner that allows for easy retrieval.

Closed electronic files should be stored or saved in a format that will be retrievable in the future. You should review your storage procedures for closed electronic files from time to time, as technology evolves.

Retention and Destruction of Closed Client Files

You should consider whether a client file will be retained indefinitely, or eventually be destroyed. How long you retain a closed client file will depend on the circumstances, including the following:

- whether information contained in the file is available from other sources, such as tribunal records or government registries;

- a paralegal's potential liability for errors and omissions; and

- any applicable limitation periods.

If you decide that a file should be destroyed, you should determine the date the file should be destroyed, taking into consideration:

- any legal or regulatory requirements to maintain certain file contents, and

- any limitation periods relating to your potential liability for errors and omissions.

Files should be destroyed in a manner that preserves client confidentiality. For example, you should consider shredding paper files.

Time Management

Much of the following material has been adapted from the "Time Management" section of the Law Society's Practice Management Guidelines.

Time management systems help you organize and make more effective use of your time. They increase your productivity and improve client service.

You should consider implementing and maintaining the following systems in your paralegal practice:

- a time planning system,

- a reminder system, and

- a time docketing or recording system.

TIME PLANNING

Planning your time in an advocacy practice presents challenges, due to frequent absences from the office on tribunal appearances, hearings, and so on. If practicable, you should consider maintaining regular office hours. You should schedule time each day to

- address urgent or pending matters,

- return phone calls and emails from clients and opposing parties,

- deal with correspondence, and

- ensure docket entries are recorded and assigned to client files.

On a weekly or monthly basis, you should plan for the following:

- meetings with clients;

- completing work on client files, including drafting, research, and reviewing documents;

- out-of-office attendances, including client meetings and tribunal appearances;

- meetings with firm staff and colleagues;

- attending to administrative or business aspects of the practice;

- completing the trust bank reconciliation by the 25th day of each month;

- attending to other accounting, bookkeeping, or filing requirements; and

- conducting periodic reviews of all active client files.

You should also set aside time monthly or yearly to attend continuing education relating to professional development (refer to rule 3.01(4)(h)).

TICKLER OR REMINDER SYSTEMS

On a daily or weekly basis, you should consider using a to-do list setting out tasks to be accomplished in order of importance.

You may use a manual or electronic diary or calendar to plan your time on a daily, weekly, and yearly basis. Your calendar should contain particulars of the following:

- appointments;

- steps to be taken in particular client matters;

- court, tribunal, or other attendances on client matters; and

- crucial dates, including limitation periods and deadlines for Law Society filings and other requirements.

Your calendar should also contain reminders that an appointment, tribunal attendance, or other task or deadline is approaching. The frequency and timing of the reminders will depend on the importance of the approaching deadline or task, the amount of preparation required, its complexity, and so on.

You may consider delegating, to your office assistant or other staff, responsibility for diarizing key dates in time management systems and following up to ensure compliance with deadlines. Before doing so, you should satisfy yourself that the staff member to whom the task is delegated is competent to perform it. Keep in mind that you are ultimately responsible for meeting deadlines and limitation periods.

You should conduct monthly reviews of all active client files to ensure that work on all files is being completed in a timely and cost-effective manner.

TIME DOCKETING OR RECORDING SYSTEMS

Every time you complete a task on a file, you should docket, or record, that time to the file. Time dockets may be maintained manually or electronically. Whatever its form, the docket entry should state the client name, the matter number or code, the date and time, the name or initials of the person doing the work, details of the task, and the amount of time spent on the task.

When using daily time sheets to record time spent on different client matters, you should

- docket your time for each task immediately after completing the activity or task, and

- ensure that docket entries are recorded to client files on a daily basis.

You should consider keeping complete time records of all time spent on client matters, regardless of whether the time is billable or non-billable and regardless of the fee structure. Your time records are a useful tool for determining which activities are unproductive or inefficient. For example, you can use your dockets of time spent on fixed fee matters to determine whether the fixed fee is appropriate, given the average amount of time you spend on those types of matters.

Time records are also useful for determining whether, and how frequently, you should deliver interim invoices on a file. Your billing practices on a client file will also depend on your firm billing policy, if any, and on any agreement you have entered into with the client regarding billing practices, as set out in writing in the retainer agreement or otherwise.

When implementing a time docketing system, you should select one that will permit you to do all of the following:

- explain services to be performed;

- accumulate total time spent on the file by each paralegal;

- record billable and non-billable time;

- produce interim and final invoices; and

- produce time data for monthly, quarterly, and annual reports to assist in management of the paralegal firm.

Technology

The following material is adapted from the Law Society's Practice Management Guidelines regarding technology, available in the "Practice Resources" section at the Law Society website, and from the Law Society's Ethical Considerations and Technology article.

A paralegal may use technology to assist with marketing, client service, and practice management.

OFFERING AND ADVERTISING LEGAL SERVICES

When offering and advertising legal services, you must comply with rules 8.02 and 8.03, discussed above at pages 188 to 192.

PRACTICE MANAGEMENT

General

To assist you in providing legal services conscientiously, diligently, and in a timely and cost-effective manner, you should consider using the following technology tools:

- legal research tools such as CanLII or Quicklaw, Internet-based legal research, or CD-ROM databases;

- document management systems such as case management or litigation support software, and document assembly software to create legal forms and documents;

- analysis support software such as spreadsheets or calculators;

- word-processing software to reduce time spent on dictation, writing, or drafting;

- communication tools such as voicemail, email, facsimile transmission, and video or telephone conferencing;

- database management systems for maintaining client information and checking for conflicts of interest;

- calendaring and scheduling systems for managing deadlines and other crucial dates, including limitation periods and deadlines for Law Society filings; and

- time docketing and accounting systems to meet record-keeping requirements and to allow you to accurately invoice clients.

Managing Technology

You should develop a reasonable understanding of the technology tools used in your practice, or should have access to someone who possesses such an understanding. If you use outside service providers to set up, maintain, or repair technology tools that store or use client information, you must ensure that the client information remains confidential.

You should consider implementing and enforcing firm policies for the acceptable use of electronic communications to ensure that discriminatory material is not distributed. Your policy may include:

- restrictions against downloading, viewing, or circulating electronic material of a discriminatory nature; and

- mandatory deletion of unsolicited material of a discriminatory nature received from a third party.

When using electronic means of communication, you shall take steps to secure confidential information transmitted in an electronic form. You should:

- develop and maintain an awareness of how to minimize the risk of disclosure, discovery, or interception of such communications;

- use appropriate technical means to minimize such risks;

- with extremely sensitive information, use and advise clients to use encryption software; and

- develop and maintain office procedures that offer reasonable protection against inadvertent discovery or disclosure of confidential information transmitted electronically.

You should implement security measures to manage the risks of using technology tools, such as:

- unauthorized copying of electronic data,

- accessing of electronic files by hackers,

- destruction of electronic information and hardware by viruses,

- damage to electronic information and hardware by power failures and electrical storms, and

- theft of electronic information stored in stolen hardware.

To manage the risks of using technology tools, you should consider using security measures such as:

- installation of firewalls and anti-virus software,

- use of passwords to limit access to electronic data,

- installation of surge protection hardware, and

- installation of encryption software.

When using technology, you must exercise appropriate judgment to avoid an error or omission. Anyone using the Internet to communicate has a reasonable and justified expectation of privacy. Communicating on the Internet without encryption does not violate the principle of confidentiality. Encryption makes theft or interception more difficult, but even strong encryption can be defeated. In ordinary circumstances, you are not expected to anticipate the theft of confidential communications on the Internet.

One of the risks of using email is inadvertent disclosure of sensitive or confidential information to persons who are not entitled to see it. You must take care that you do not inadvertently send sensitive information or a confidential communication to the wrong person.

You should consider advising the client of the risks of electronic communication, and encrypting all electronic communications to preserve client confidentiality. You should also consider using encryption on electronic devices that you carry with you, such as laptops and cell phones, if they have confidential client information stored on them. That way, if your laptop is stolen or you lose your cell phone, the confidential information is protected.

You should have backup and disaster recovery plans to deal with the loss or destruction of electronic information. You should consider implementing some or all of the following procedures:

- performing regular backup of data,

- storing backup disks in a secure off-site location,

- performing routine checks to ensure data can be restored, and

- having insurance in place to cover the cost of recovering lost hardware or electronic information.

You should ensure that information stored in electronic form will be accessible in the future. You should review your storage procedures for electronic information from time to time, as technology evolves, to ensure that you can retrieve the information.

CHAPTER SUMMARY

A paralegal shall not charge or accept any amount for a fee or disbursement unless it is fair and reasonable and has been disclosed in a timely fashion. At the outset of the paralegal–client retainer, you should discuss with the client the scope of the legal services to be provided and the likely cost of those services. You should also consider discussing particulars of your billing practices.

You must ensure that the client understands the scope of the legal services to be provided; how fees, disbursements, and GST will be charged; and any other terms of the retainer. It is advisable to confirm the terms of the retainer in writing.

In a statement of account to a client, you shall clearly and separately detail amounts charged as fees and amounts charged as disbursements, and show how much the client must pay on account of the GST. The client should be the only person who pays you for legal services provided in the client matter.

Except in quasi-criminal or criminal matters, you may enter into a written agreement that provides that your fee is contingent, in whole or in part, on the successful disposition or completion of the matter for which your services are to be provided.

If you are acting for two or more clients in a joint retainer arrangement, you shall divide the fees and disbursements equitably between or among them, unless the clients have agreed to another arrangement. Each joint client shall receive a separate invoice.

You shall not share, split, or divide your fees with any person who is not a licensee, including an affiliated entity.

You shall not give any financial or other reward to any person who is not a licensee, including an affiliated entity, for the referral of clients or client matters. If you refer a matter to another licensee because of his expertise and ability to handle the matter, you may accept, and the other licensee may pay, a referral fee if certain conditions are met.

You shall assume complete professional responsibility for all business entrusted to you. You are permitted to assign tasks and functions to an employee in connection with your provision of legal services in accordance with By-law 7.1 (Part I). You shall carefully review rule 8.01(4) and By-law 7.1 (Part I) to determine tasks that may and may not be delegated to employees. Employees shall perform their tasks under your direct supervision.

In order to run your practice efficiently and effectively, you must take steps to hire trustworthy, competent staff, and ensure that they receive appropriate training before you delegate tasks or functions to them.

You shall promptly meet financial obligations incurred in the course of your practice on behalf of clients unless, before incurring the obligation, you clearly indicate in writing to the person to whom the money is owed that it is not to be a personal obligation.

A paralegal shall make legal services available to the public in an efficient and convenient way. A paralegal must be able to market his services to the public in a way that differentiates those services from services provided by other licensees, including lawyers. A paralegal shall not use marketing strategies that are false or misleading, not in the best interests of the public, or inconsistent with high standards of professionalism.

Advertising by paralegals using electronic media is governed by the Rules. There are restrictions on indiscriminate distribution of marketing material using electronic media.

All paralegals practising in Ontario shall obtain and maintain adequate errors and omissions insurance as required by the Law Society.

Effective practice management helps ensure that clients receive timely, effective service. In addition to the practice management responsibilities covered by rule 8, you should consider putting systems in place to manage a client's documents and information, and time spent in the practice. You should also consider the benefits of technology, and, when using technology tools, implement appropriate measures to manage risks and avoid errors and omissions.

An office policies and procedures manual can improve staff efficiency and ensure that all staff follow appropriate systems and procedures. You should consider reviewing and updating, as required, all practice management systems, procedural and substantive firm checklists, and precedent documents.

APPENDIX 7.1
Sample Invoice—No Money Retainer

Judith N. Black, Paralegal
123 Radiant Way, Suite 200
Brampton, Ontario X1X 2Y3

tel: 905 122 3333   fax: 905 123 4444   email: jblack@paralegal.com

GST Registration No.:	12568 8666 RT
File No.:	JB00328
Invoice No.:	859
Date:	June 30, 20—

Sylvia Cisco
1234 Pleasant Valley Crescent
Mississauga, Ontario X1X 3Y4

Re: Cisco v. Jones

For Professional Services Rendered:

To all services rendered on your behalf in connection with the above-noted matter for the period ending June 30, 20—

MY FEE:	$ 700.00
TOTAL FEE:	$ 700.00

DISBURSEMENTS	Disbursements	
Photocopies	36.25	
Court work*	35.00	
Issue claim*	75.00	
Service*	35.00	
Default judgment*	35.00	
Total		$ 206.25
TOTAL FEES AND DISBURSEMENTS		$ 906.25
5% GST on account		36.81
		$ 943.06
Transferred from Trust to General		0.00
Previous balance		0.00
Previous payments		0.00
BALANCE DUE AND OWING		$ 943.06

* Tax-exempt

THIS IS MY ACCOUNT HEREIN

Judith N. Black
Paralegal

APPENDIX 7.2
Sample Invoice—Money Retainer

Judith N. Black, Paralegal
123 Radiant Way, Suite 200
Brampton, Ontario X1X 2Y3

tel: 905 122 3333   fax: 905 123 4444   email: jblack@paralegal.com

GST Registration No.: 12568 8666 RT

File No.:	JB00329
Invoice No.:	860
Date:	June 30, 20—

Francesca Ciccone
87 Harwood Boulevard
Georgetown, Ontario X1X 4Z5

Re: Ciccone—Careless driving charge

For Professional Services Rendered:

To all services rendered on your behalf in connection with the above-noted matter for the period ending June 30, 20—

	MY FEE:	$ 1,000.00
	TOTAL FEE:	$ 1,000.00

DISBURSEMENTS	Disbursements	
Photocopies	36.45	
Total		$ 1,036.45
TOTAL FEES AND DISBURSEMENTS		$ 1,036.45
5% GST on account		$ 51.82
		$ 1,088.27
Transferred from Trust to General		1,000.00
Previous balance		0.00
Previous payments		0.00
BALANCE DUE AND OWING		$ 88.27

THIS IS MY ACCOUNT HEREIN

Judith N. Black
Paralegal

APPENDIX 7.3
Office Procedures Manual—File Management

1.00   OFFICE PROCEDURES MANUAL

Definitions

1.01   In this manual:

ACL2 refers to the Automated Civil Litigation 2 software package that is used by [paralegal firm name] to create Small Claims Court forms.

By-laws refers to the by-laws of the Law Society.

ESI Law refers to the ESI Law practice management software that is used by [paralegal firm name] to manage this practice, including conflicts, client accounts, trust accounts, disbursements, calendaring, and time management.

Law Society refers to the Law Society of Upper Canada.

Paralegal refers to a paralegal licensed by the Law Society.

Rules refers to the Paralegal Rules of Conduct published by the Law Society and contained in Appendix [number].

Staff refers to all persons employed by [paralegal firm name] in any capacity, including paralegal licensees employed by [paralegal firm name].

Standard Form refers to a form developed by [paralegal firm name]. The current (read-only) versions of all standard forms are located in the S:/[paralegal firm name] Common/Forms directory.

Purpose

1.02   This Office Procedures Manual is intended to provide all [paralegal firm name] staff and placement students with a step-by-step guide to all aspects of [paralegal firm name]'s legal services.

Any questions regarding office procedures and policies should be directed to [name of paralegal].

Correction and Improvement

1.03   The current (read-only) version of this manual is located at S:/[paralegal firm name] Common/Procedures/Procedure_Manual.doc. A manual is identified by its version number and issue date, which are printed on each page of the manual.

1.04   Whenever a situation is encountered that is not covered by this manual or where this manual is not clear on what procedure is to be followed, staff and placement students should bring the matter to the attention of [name of paralegal] by email so that the procedure can be clarified or the oversight corrected as quickly as possible.

1.05   Updated versions of this manual will be issued by email to all staff every three months. Where a significant change is required, an interim version will be issued immediately. Where there are no changes, a new version will not be issued and staff will be notified by email that the current version stands unchanged.

2.00   CONFIDENTIALITY

General

2.01   Staff shall review the firm confidentiality policy, rule 3.03 of the Rules, and any applicable guidelines, and comply with their contents.

2.02   Upon commencement of employment with the firm, non-paralegal staff shall take an oath of confidentiality. The oath shall be placed in the staff member's employment file.

2.03   Upon commencement of their placement with the firm, field placement students shall review the firm confidentiality policy, rule 3.03 of the Rules, and any applicable guidelines, and comply with their contents.

2.04   Upon commencement of their placement with the firm, field placement students shall take an oath of confidentiality. The oath shall be placed in the field placement student's file. Any breach shall result in immediate termination of the field placement.

2.05   No information about firm clients may be disclosed without express instructions from the client, or otherwise in accordance with the Rules.

In-Office Confidentiality

2.06   All client meetings shall be conducted in the conference room. The room may be booked by using the "CONF" calendar in ESI Law. Please show the appropriate consideration for anyone who has booked the room after you.

2.07   Client meetings may be held in a staff office only if there is no alternative. All client files other than the file of the client with whom you are meeting must be secured. Computer applications not related to the client matter shall be closed down before the client enters the office.

2.08   The workstation in the reception area is fitted with a filter to prevent clients from observing confidential information. Only the file currently being worked on should be open. Its contents should be concealed if an unauthorized person approaches the desk.

2.09   When the reception area is left unattended, all files must be secured and the workstation shut down or placed in lock mode by the person leaving the area unattended.

General Inquiries

2.10   Appendix [number], Telephone Response, contains scripts for handling inquiries, taking client calls, and taking calls from opposing parties or their representatives. Follow the instructions in the appropriate script. If necessary, refer the matter to a paralegal. Note: When speaking to clients, you must follow the portion of the script that identifies you as a non-licensee to the caller.

2.11   When a potential client or a continuing client with a new matter contacts [paralegal firm name], reception shall complete the general inquiry form, and the information shall be entered into the conflicts database.

2.12   Every inquiry shall be referred to a paralegal, along with a preliminary conflict check. This applies even where the person making the inquiry indicates that they are not interested in retaining our services at this time.

3.00   ACTIVE FILES

Client Identification/Verification

3.01   By-law 7.1 Part III requires [paralegal firm name] to identify and verify clients. "Identification" refers to information about who the client is provided by the client to the firm. "Verification" refers to information the firm must obtain to confirm the identification provided by the client.

3.02   Client identification must be confirmed by the paralegal opening a file for a new client, or an existing client whose identification has not been confirmed and/or verified in accordance with the by-law. The paralegal is also responsible for verification of client identification where the matter requires verification. If there is any doubt as to whether verification is required, it must be obtained. Client identification and verification shall be documented on the appropriate forms.

3.03   New client identification and verification documents shall be filed in the client file.

3.04   A database shall be maintained of all clients whose identification has been confirmed and verified where verification is required.

Opening a New File

3.05   Each new matter shall be assigned a unique file code when the file is entered.

3.06   The new matter checklist for opening a file shall be completed (see Appendix [number]). The checklist shall be filed in the client file. This will ensure that all firm policies on naming files, retainer agreements, money retainers, non-engagement letters, and conflict-checking have been followed.

3.07   Each new matter checklist shall be reviewed and signed by the supervising paralegal.

Conflicts Database

3.08   At the initial contact, before the initial consultation, or immediately after new parties are added or additional information is obtained in a client matter, a conflict report must be run.

3.09   The search shall be noted on the file information sheet and the results shall be referred to the supervising paralegal. The paralegal shall review, date, and sign the search, noting any further action to be taken on the file.

Ticklers

3.10   When a file is added to the system, any limitation period or procedural deadline must be calculated, and the date and particulars entered into the calendaring system with a tickler time that will allow sufficient time for the completion of the task prior to the deadline.

3.11   As each task in the calendaring system is completed, it must be entered as completed, noting the time and person completing the task. If necessary, subsequent tasks shall be calendarized as preceding tasks are completed.

Organization of File Contents

3.12   The contents of client files should be organized into colour-coded subfiles. In electronic format, subfiles will be subfolders. The main paper file (Tan) and all subfiles must be clearly labelled using the template in S:/[paralegal firm name] Common/ file_labels.doc on the main file and each subfile. All file contents are to be arranged in reverse chronological order, and dated and initialled by the person filing the document where the document is not signed and dated.

3.13   Client files must contain the following colour-coded subfiles where applicable:

Correspondence (Red): All correspondence related to the matter should be filed in this subfile, including notes of telephone conversations as well as hard copies of any emails.

Pleadings (Blue): All court documents are kept in this subfile.

Documents (Green): The originals of all documentary evidence should be kept in this subfile, with an inventory form stapled to the front cover of the file. Any documents moved from this file must be inventoried out and in (if returned).

Account (Yellow): Identification, verification(s), retainer agreement, instruction authorizations, and billing information.

Research (Purple): Relevant case law and legal research.

3.14   The status of the file is designated by a coloured "dot" sticker to the right of the label on the main client file. The codes are green for active, yellow for unpaid (matter complete but amount outstanding), orange for undistributed (account paid but contents not distributed), and red for closed. The active file dot (green) shall only be placed on a file by the responsible paralegal when the file-opening checklist has been completed. The current status dot is pasted over the existing dot.

3.15   Where a client makes a request by email, a copy of the response, including the initial message, shall be printed and placed in the file. If the email contains instructions, the source must be verified by emailing a reply to the email address provided by the client for instructions in the matter file. Copies of all emails will automatically be stored in the ESI Law folder for the client. Printed copies of all emails shall be placed in the correspondence subfile.

3.16   When a client call comes to reception, a message shall be taken and recorded in the telephone log and the message (pink) sent to the paralegal responsible for the file. The paralegal responding to the message must note the date and time of the return call on the pink copy and file it in the communications folder of the file, along with any other notes of the conversation.

3.17   When a client call is taken by voice mail, the paralegal must log the call in her telephone log, noting the time the message was left and the time it was received. When responding to the message, the paralegal shall note the date, time, and particulars of the return call and file it in the correspondence subfile of the client file.

3.18   Where a return call is taken by voice mail, the pink copy should remain with the paralegal until the client has been contacted. Paralegals should review all unanswered return calls on a regular basis, and leave an additional message where the client has not responded.

Filing Cabinets

3.19   All filing cabinets are in the storage room. All filing cabinets are fire-retardant and waterproof. They are to be locked at all times when an authorized person is not in the room. There are separate cabinets for active and closed files. Files older than five years old are stored in off-site facilities.

3.20   In case of emergency, any staff working in the storage room shall place all client files in the most accessible space in any secured filing cabinet, lock all cabinets, and depart the room. Do not attempt to carry files with you.

Storage of Active Files

3.21   When in use, active client files shall not be left in any area to which the public has access. Files that are being worked on must be secured in a locked drawer or cabinet when left unattended.

3.22   Computer screens shall be filtered, and all electronic data of a confidential nature will be password protected and encrypted.

3.23   When not in use, all documentation connected with an active client file shall be properly stored within its file and filed with the active files by matter number.

4.00   CLOSING, RETAINING, AND DISPOSING OF CLIENT FILES

File-Closing System

4.01   When all work has been completed and after the supervising paralegal has sent out a final reporting letter along with a final account, the paralegal shall review all file contents and reconfirm that the appropriate information has been entered into the conflict-checking database. A sample closing checklist is contained in Appendix [number]. A tickler must be entered into ESI Law as a reminder for the expiry of any appeal period.

4.02   If the account has been settled in full, the file may be designated as undistributed. Otherwise the account is designated as unpaid. Generally, file contents are not to be distributed until the account is paid, unless the client has retained [paralegal firm name] or another licensee to appeal the matter. If another licensee has been retained for the appeal, file contents belonging to the client shall be returned to the client or delivered to the licensee on the client's written direction.

4.03   Undistributed files and files with unpaid accounts are kept with active files. The person taking the final payment on an unpaid account should mark the file as undistributed.

4.04   By the 10th day of each month, the receptionist shall examine all files in the active filing cabinet and confirm that the status marked on the file is correct or bring any inconsistencies to the attention of the responsible paralegal.

Distributing File Contents

4.05   If the account has been paid or the file has been transferred to another licensee on the client's direction, the supervising paralegal shall return any documents that are the client's property to the client, unless directed in writing by the client to deliver the documents to another person.

Closing and Storing Closed Files

4.06   Files are to be closed within 30 days of the final distribution of file contents to the client or as directed by the client. The matter is to be designated as "closed" in ESI Law. Closed files shall be assigned a closed file code, and stored separately from active files. Closed files shall be stored by closed file code in the limited-access secured filing cabinet that is labelled "Closed Files." ESI Law can be searched on a variety of parameters and will provide the closure date for a file when the matter is called up.

4.07   The supervising paralegal shall ensure that the closed file contains copies of any documents that might serve as evidence in defence of any possible future claims of malpractice or misconduct, or assessment of accounts.

Closed File Retention

4.08   By-law 9 requires paralegals to maintain trust accounting records for at least ten years. All other documents shall be maintained for at least six years. This shall be considered a minimum standard at [paralegal firm name].

4.09   In March of each year, closed files older than five years shall be reviewed by a paralegal partner, packaged in secure containers, and moved to secure, off-site storage facilities. Depending on the circumstances, some client files may be retained indefinitely. When we have files older than 15 years, the retention policy will be reviewed.

4.10   Contact a partner if you require access to a file that is stored off site. All files, on or off site, can be accessed through ESI Law.

KEY TERMS

fees based on an hourly rate	pro bono legal services
docket	statement of account
docketed time	fee splitting
billable time	referral fee
write off time	client settlement funds
non-billable time	mixed trust account
fixed, flat, or block fee	interim invoice
fees by stages	receivable
contingency fee	marketing

REFERENCES

Contingency Fee Agreements, O. Reg. 195/04.

Law Society of Upper Canada (LSUC), By-Laws (Toronto: LSUC, 2005); available online at http://www.lsuc.on.ca/regulation/a/by-laws.

Law Society of Upper Canada (LSUC), Ethical Considerations and Technology (Toronto: LSUC); available online at http://rc.lsuc.on.ca/pdf/pmg/tech_guidelines.pdf.

Law Society of Upper Canada (LSUC), Knowledge Tree—Technology in Your Practice (Toronto: LSUC); available online at http://rc.lsuc.on.ca/jsp/kt/loadKnowledgeTreePage.do.

Law Society of Upper Canada (LSUC), Paralegal Professional Conduct Guidelines (Toronto: LSUC, 2008) ("the Guidelines"); available online at http://www.lsuc.on.ca/paralegals/a/paralegal-professional-conduct-guidelines.

Law Society of Upper Canada (LSUC), Paralegal Rules of Conduct (Toronto: LSUC, 2007, as amended) ("the Rules"); available online at http://www.lsuc.on.ca/paralegals/a/paralegal-rules-of-conduct.

Law Society of Upper Canada (LSUC), Practice Management Guidelines (Toronto: LSUC, 2008); available online at http://rc.lsuc.on.ca/pdf/pmg/pmg.pdf.

Solicitors Act, RSO 1990, c. S-15.

REVIEW QUESTIONS

1. You are going through a slow period in your paralegal practice. A client approaches you about an assault charge, where the Crown has elected to proceed by way of summary conviction. Ordinarily, you would charge an hourly rate of $100.00 for your fees in such a matter, but you need the business, so you give the client an estimate of the total cost based on an hourly rate of $70.00. You figure you can always adjust your fee later, pleading unforeseen circumstances. You also plan to make a little extra by padding the disbursements.

   Discuss, referring to the applicable rule(s) and other authorities, if any.

2. You have a trial date coming up in a Small Claims Court matter. At trial, you intend to rely upon an expert report. The fee for the expert report is $800.00. The deadline for service of the expert report on other parties is fast approaching. What should you do?

3. a. What are five issues that you should discuss with the client at the outset of the retainer?

   b. How should these discussions be confirmed?

   c. What if something happens that you could not reasonably have foreseen at the outset of the retainer?

4. You have just received a money retainer from a new client. You have some bills you need to pay, and you are running short of cash in the general account. You would like to deposit the new client's money retainer directly to the general account and use it to pay the bills. You plan to replace it later.

   Discuss.

5. A client sends you a cheque for payment of an outstanding invoice. What do you do with the money?

6. You are holding $800.00 in trust in a client matter. You completed the preliminary steps in the matter, and have delivered an interim invoice for $600.00 to the client. May you use the money held in trust to pay the invoice?

7. What is a contingency fee, and when may it be used?

8. You specialize in residential tenancies matters. A landlord whom you have never represented telephones you seeking legal services. When you perform a conflict check, you discover a conflicting interest. You refer the landlord to another paralegal, who is also a residential tenancies specialist. The other paralegal wishes to pay you a referral fee. She has her client's consent. May she pay, and may you accept, the referral fee?

9. Indicate which of the following are permitted for a non-licensee staff in a paralegal firm, and which are prohibited. State the rule or other authority upon which you are relying.

- accepting a client on a paralegal's behalf

- giving legal advice

- taking instructions from a client

- holding himself out as a licensee

- giving or accepting an undertaking on behalf of the paralegal

- appearing before an adjudicative body

- negotiating with third parties

- signing correspondence

- forwarding a document to the client without review by the paralegal

- doing anything that a paralegal may not do

10. To market your firm, you are planning to send out an email containing your firm name and contact information, and the slogan "We are quite simply THE BEST!! We are AWESOME!!" For maximum impact, you plan to distribute the email to a large number of newsgroups and email addresses.

   Discuss, referring to any rules or other authorities upon which you are relying.

11. What are some strategies for maintaining client confidentiality when handling active client files?

12. What is a tickler or reminder system, and what is it used for?

13. What is a time docketing system and what is it used for?

CHAPTER 8

Accounting, Bank Accounts, and Bookkeeping

LEARNING OBJECTIVES

After reading this chapter, you will understand:

- The purpose and importance of keeping proper books and records.
- The general (operating) account.
- The trust account.
- Financial institutions for trust accounts.
- Trust receipts.
- Trust disbursements.
- Special procedures for cash.
- Financial records in a paralegal practice.

WHY KEEP BOOKS AND RECORDS?

A paralegal practice is a regulated business. You cannot run your business effectively without complete, accurate, and up-to-date books and records. They provide the information you need to make financial decisions in your practice.

Accurate books and records also help you to fulfill reporting and filing obligations, including:

- Canada Revenue Agency filing requirements for income tax and GST/HST;

- your Annual Report to the Law Society, which includes information on your trust books and records, and your general books and records; and

- reports to the Law Foundation of Ontario regarding interest accrued on your mixed trust account.

By-law 9 sets out minimum requirements for books and records in a legal services practice. These requirements are intended to protect the public, and therefore focus on trust records.

Accounting Systems

The *Paralegal Bookkeeping Guide* points out that there are several different kinds of accounting systems available, including

- manual double entry,

- one write,

- spreadsheet programs,

- general accounting software (not designed for trust accounting), and

- legal accounting software (designed for trust accounting).

When selecting an accounting system, you should consider the number of transactions you have, whether you plan to do your own bookkeeping or hire someone to do it for you, how well you understand bookkeeping, your comfort level with computers and software, and what you can afford.

The financial records By-law 9 requires you to maintain permanent records. If you choose a manual accounting system, where transactions are entered and posted by hand, the entries must be entered and posted in ink, or drafted in pencil and then photocopied.

If you use spreadsheet programs, accounting software, or other computerized systems for bookkeeping and accounting, you must ensure that you can produce hard copies of all documents for your own records and for production to the Law Society upon request. You must implement appropriate security measures, including installation of firewalls and antivirus software, and use passwords to limit access. You should put backup and disaster recovery plans in place to ensure that your books and records can be replaced or recovered if they become damaged or lost.

Regardless of the type of accounting system you choose, you may wish to consider delegating the bookkeeping and accounting functions in your firm to others who have experience with legal bookkeeping and trust accounting, if it is practicable to do so. However, you must understand the basic principles of legal bookkeeping and trust accounting, because you are the person who is ultimately responsible for ensuring that client money is properly handled and accounted for, as required by By-law 9. It is your responsibility to monitor your books and records for:

- overdrawn or inactive client trust ledger accounts,

- items on the trust bank reconciliation that have not been corrected or explained, and

- failure to deposit trust receipts by the close of the following banking day.

It is also your responsibility to act promptly to correct any errors.

BANK ACCOUNTS IN A PARALEGAL PRACTICE

There are no restrictions on how many accounts you may open in your practice. However, additional bank accounts mean additional bank charges and record-keeping obligations. Generally, one general account and one trust account will be sufficient. You may wish to consider opening a separate interest-bearing bank account to hold any goods and services tax (GST) or harmonized sales tax (HST) to be remitted to the Canada Revenue Agency.

General Account

The **general account** is your operating account. It is a business account, and should be separate and apart from any personal accounts you may hold. The general account is used to pay for business expenses, such as staff salaries, rent, telephone, bank fees, and office supplies. You pay your Law Society membership fees and liability insurance premiums from the general account. If you are holding no client money in trust, or insufficient money in trust, you pay proper disbursements and expenses in the client matter from the general account. You draw money from the general account to pay yourself.

The money in the general account comes from the following sources:

- payment for completed legal services for which the client has received an invoice;

- payment you have received from the client for proper disbursements and expenses incurred in the client matter; and

- you, if you have made a contribution to the firm's liquidity.

Liquidity refers to the amount of cash, or assets that can be easily converted to cash, that the firm has available to meet its short-term (one year or less) financial commitments.

There should be no client money in the general account. Client money is any money that is held for or on behalf of the client, and includes money that a client has paid to you as a money retainer for future legal services. Client money continues to belong to the client until you have performed the legal services contracted for and delivered an invoice to the client.

When opening your general account, you should ensure that the financial institution will provide you with bank statements and passbooks, along with cashed cheques, including cashed certified cheques, for your general account, as required by By-law 9.

BOX 8.1

The General Account

Scenario

All work in Matter 101 has been completed. You are not holding a money retainer in trust. You deliver a final invoice to the client. The client sends you a cheque in payment of the invoice.

How should you handle the money?

Discussion

Matter 101 is completed, and the client has received a final invoice for completed legal services. The money belongs to your firm, and may be deposited directly to the general account. ◇

GENERAL RETAINERS

As a rule, client money must never be deposited directly to your general account. By-law 9, s. 8 sets out a limited number of exceptions. You may deposit a general money retainer directly to your general account (s. 8(2)1). A **general retainer** is money paid by a client to a legal services firm to secure its services. It is payment for the service of agreeing to be the client's legal representative. There is no obligation to account for a general retainer.

General retainers are extremely rare. In most cases, a client will give you a money retainer that is specific—that is, intended to be used for future legal services and disbursements in a specific client matter.

If you deposit client money directly to your general account on grounds that it is a general retainer, the Law Society will scrutinize the transaction very carefully. The onus is on you to establish that the retainer is a true general retainer.

Calling the money a general retainer in a written agreement between you and your client will not be considered conclusive. The Law Society will conclude that the retainer is in fact a specific retainer that should be deposited to your trust account if (*Paralegal Bookkeeping Guide*, at 5):

- your client does not understand the general retainer agreement;

- your client intended the payment to be applied to future legal services in a particular client matter; and

- the total amount paid by the client, including the general retainer, is comparable to your usual fee for the services provided.

GENERAL SALES TAX/HARMONIZED SALES TAX

The following is a brief discussion of how the GST works in a legal services practice, adapted from the Law Society's *Guide to Opening Your Practice* and the Goods and Services Tax/Harmonized Sales Tax page at the Canada Revenue Agency website (www.cra-arc.gc.ca). For information about how certain disbursements are characterized for GST/HST purposes, see the Canada Revenue Agency's GST/HST Policy Statement P-209R regarding lawyers' disbursements.

Effective July 1, 2010, provincial sales tax in Ontario will be harmonized with the federal GST, resulting in a federally administered 13 percent tax, of which the Ontario portion will be 8 percent. It is anticipated that procedures for collecting and remitting HST will resemble those for GST.

If the annual revenues from your legal services practice exceed the amount prescribed by the Canada Revenue Agency, you must collect and remit GST on your billings and on some disbursements. For fiscal years beginning after 2007, you have the option of filing GST returns monthly, quarterly, or annually if your annual revenue falls below the threshold prescribed by the Canada Revenue Agency. Your **fiscal year** is an accounting period of 12 months, used for producing annual financial statements in your paralegal practice. The fiscal year does not necessarily coincide with the calendar year. You should consider and compare the cost of annual, quarterly, or monthly filing.

You should also consider opening a separate interest-bearing bank account to hold the GST to be remitted, so that the funds are available for remittance in accordance with the schedule set up by the Canada Revenue Agency. Keep in mind that, when you have billed a client for services to which the GST applies, you are responsible for remitting the GST to the Canada Revenue Agency by the applicable deadline, regardless of whether or not the client has paid for those services.

There are penalties for failure to file a return or make any payment on time.

Trust Account (Rule 5.01(5); Guideline 15; By-law 9)

The trust account is used for client money. If you do not ask for money retainers or otherwise deal with client money in your paralegal practice, you are not required to have a trust account. If you require clients to pay you money in advance for future legal services, expenses, or disbursements, or if you act in client matters that may involve handling settlement funds (for example, residential tenancies matters or Small Claims Court proceedings), then you should have a trust account.

The trust account should be used for client money only. Paralegal funds must never be deposited to the trust account. See By-law 9, ss. 7(1) and 8(2).

A paralegal has special obligations when handling client funds. When you receive money that belongs to a client or is to be held on behalf of a client, you must deposit those funds to your trust account. Client funds held in trust are also known as **trust funds** (guideline 15).

In any business, you must maintain an audit trail of transactions that take place in the business. An **audit trail** is a set of original documents and other records that provide information about a transaction. When handling trust funds, it is very important to maintain an audit trail, not just for business purposes, but to demonstrate compliance with the Law Society's record-keeping requirements for trust accounts.

MONEY TO BE PAID INTO TRUST

You receive money in trust for a client if you receive any of the following from a person (By-law 9, s. 7(2)):

- money that belongs in whole or in part to the client;

- money that is to be held on behalf of a client;

- money that is to be held on a client's direction or order;

- money that is advanced to you on account of fees for future or unbilled legal services; or

- money that is advanced to you on account of future disbursements.

You are not required to deposit money received in trust from or for a client to your trust account if (By-law 9, s. 8(1)):

(a) the client requests in writing that the money shall not be deposited to trust;

(b) you deposit the money into an account in the client's name, or in the name of a person designated by the client, or in the name of an agent of the client other than you; or

(c) you pay the money immediately upon receiving it to the client or to a person on behalf of the client, following normal business practices.

When dealing with client money that is not paid into trust, you must maintain an audit trail of how it was handled. Where the client requests in writing that the money be deposited to a separate interest-bearing trust account, you must maintain proper trust records in accordance with By-law 9.

When you receive money in trust for a client, you shall pay the money into your trust account immediately, and by no later than the end of the next banking day (By-law 9, s. 1(3)).

You shall not appropriate any trust funds except as permitted by By-law 9 (rule 5.01(5)). If you inadvertently withdraw from your trust account money that is not permitted to be withdrawn from the trust account, you shall pay the money back into the trust account immediately using your general account.

If you bill a client and receive an overpayment for your billed services, you must immediately deposit the amount received to your trust account, to the credit of the particular client matter. As soon as is practical, you must then transfer the actual amount owed to you to your general account. You may either return the overpayment to the client or hold it in trust for future fees and disbursements, depending on the client's instructions.

BOX 8.2

Overpayment

Scenario

In Matter 102, you are not holding a money retainer in trust. You deliver an interim invoice for $853.00 to the client. The client sends you a cheque for $1,000.00 in payment of the invoice.

How should you handle the money?

Discussion

The client has paid you more than you are owed. You must deposit the cheque to your trust account, to the credit of Matter 102. As soon as is practicable, you should transfer $853.00 in payment of the interim invoice to your general account. You should then seek the client's instructions about whether he would prefer to have the overpayment returned or held in trust for future fees and disbursements in Matter 102, which is ongoing. The client's instructions should be confirmed in writing. ◈

Financial Institutions for Trust Accounts (By-law 9, s. 7)

You may open trust accounts at the following financial institutions:

- a chartered bank,

- a provincial savings office,

- a credit union or caisse populaire, or

- a registered trust corporation.

There is no requirement that you have your general account at the same institution as your mixed trust account. However, it will probably be more convenient and efficient for you to have both accounts at the same institution.

Types of Trust Accounts

MIXED TRUST ACCOUNT

The mixed trust account is an account into which money belonging to many different clients is deposited and held. This is the type of trust account that most paralegal firms are likely to use.

Interest on Money Held in the Mixed Trust Account

The interest that accrues on client money held in your mixed trust account is deemed to be held in trust for the Law Foundation of Ontario (*Law Society Act*, s. 57). The mixed trust account must bear interest at a rate approved by the trustees of the Law Foundation.

When selecting a financial institution for your mixed trust account, you must obtain its agreement to this arrangement. You must provide the institution with a letter directing it to forward interest on the mixed trust account to the Law Foundation. You should send a copy of the letter of direction to the Law Foundation for its records, and keep a copy for your own records. See Figure 8.1 for a sample of a letter of direction.

FIGURE 8.1 Sample Letter of Direction

To: The Manager

Name of Bank: [name of chartered bank, provincial savings office, credit union or caisse populaire, or registered trust company]

Branch:

Address:

Re: The Law Foundation of Ontario and Account No. _____

The above account is _____ in my name.

_____ in the name of the firm I am associated with.

In accordance with section 57 of the *Law Society Act*, I direct you, until further notice, to compute the amount earned by applying to the balance in the above account the rate of interest approved from time to time by the Trustees of The Law Foundation of Ontario. Please pay into an account held in your main office in Ontario in the name of The Law Foundation of Ontario amounts so calculated and give written notice to me at the address shown on the above account and to The Law Foundation of Ontario, 20 Queen Street West, Suite 3002, Box #19, Toronto, Ontario, M5H 3R3, when each such payment is made. This notice should show, as applicable as per the terms of the interest agreement between the LFO and your financial institution, the amount of the payment, the amounts of the daily/monthly balances, and the rates of interest used in computing the payment.

Dated the   day of   ,   .

Signed: _____

[name of signatory]

Firm name:

Address:

When you open a mixed trust account, you are required to file a report with the Law Foundation no later than 30 days after the day on which the mixed trust account was opened (Law Foundation, R.R.O. 1990, Reg. 709).

With respect to every mixed trust account you hold in a given year, an annual report must be filed with the Law Foundation on or before March 31 of the following year.

When you close a mixed trust account, you are required to file a report with the Law Foundation no later than 30 days after the day on which the account was closed.

In some cases, the Law Foundation may request that you file a supplementary report in order to confirm or clarify information. A supplementary report shall be filed with the Law Foundation no later than 30 days after you receive the request.

Opening the Account

Before opening a trust account with a financial institution, you should confirm that the institution will provide monthly bank statements and passbooks, along with cancelled cheques, including certified cheques, as required by By-law 9. These are your source documents, or records of transactions, on your trust account. A **source**

document is an original document on which a transaction is recorded. It is evidence of the occurrence of a transaction and the value of that transaction. It is also the source of the information that is entered into your books and records.

If your financial institution cannot provide the documents and records required by By-law 9, you should consider switching to a financial institution that can and will provide them.

The trust account should be opened in your name or in the name of the paralegal firm of which you are a partner or an employee. The trust account should be clearly designated as a trust account. Your trust cheques and trust bank statements must be clearly designated as such. You should consider ordering general cheques and trust cheques in different colours, so that they can be easily distinguished. General cheques and trust cheques should be prenumbered.

The service charges on the mixed trust account are a business expense, to be paid out of the general account. The agreement that you sign when opening a mixed trust account should direct the financial institution to deduct service charges on the mixed trust account from your general account.

BOX 8.3

Service Charges

If your financial institution withdraws service charges from your trust account instead of the general account in error, you must ensure that the funds are returned to trust as soon as possible. You may have to deposit funds from the general account to the trust account. Your bank statements will show the incorrect debit and the correction. However, you should consider obtaining a written statement from your financial institution for your records, confirming that the error occurred through the fault of the financial institution and explaining when and how it was corrected. ◇

Your agreement with the financial institution should also contain a term that the institution shall not remove any money from your trust account without your authorization. For example, money from the mixed trust account cannot be transferred automatically and applied by the financial institution to an overdraft on your general account. An overdraft is money owed by your firm to the bank. The money in the mixed trust account belongs to your clients. It cannot be used by the financial institution to pay debts owed by your paralegal firm.

Sharing Trust Accounts

You may share a trust account with another paralegal if you are in a partnership with that paralegal, or if you employ or are employed by the other paralegal.

If you share office facilities in association with other paralegals, you must have your own separate trust account and you must maintain separate books and records for trust transactions.

Canada Deposit Insurance Corporation

The Canada Deposit Insurance Corporation (CDIC) is a federal Crown corporation that insures Canadians' savings in case their bank or other CDIC member institution fails or goes bankrupt. Persons who hold money in trust in a member institution are required to disclose eligible deposits on the records of the member institution within 30 days of April 30 in each year. Each client whose funds you hold in trust is deemed to be a separate beneficiary whose deposit is insured up to a maximum of $100,000.00 under the *Canada Deposit Insurance Corporation Act*.

If your financial institution is a CDIC member institution, you should update the information with respect to the beneficiaries of any mixed trust accounts with your branch every year, on or before May 30 (Canada Deposit Insurance Joint and Trust Account Disclosure By-law). More information, including a list of member institutions, is available at the CDIC website (www.cdic.ca).

SEPARATE INTEREST-BEARING TRUST ACCOUNT

This type of trust account holds money for one client only. It may be used when you are holding substantial funds in trust for a client for an extended period of time. In those circumstances, you should advise the client of the option of using this type of account, ensuring that the client understands that you are not giving financial or investment advice. The client should consider the following when making a decision about whether to use this type of account (*Paralegal Bookkeeping Guide*, at 8):

- Any interest that accrues on the money belongs to the client.

- Service charges on the account are charged to the client as disbursements.

- During periods when interest rates are extremely low, the client may wish to consider whether there is any benefit in using this type of trust account.

- A separate interest-bearing trust account may not be suitable if there is a possibility that the money will be required on short notice. Some investments may have reduced or no interest upon early redemption. You should check with the financial institution about notice requirements for early redemption and the effect of early redemption on the interest paid.

- Not all types of separate interest-bearing accounts are guaranteed by the CDIC.

If the client instructs you to deposit the funds to a separate interest-bearing account, the client's instructions should be confirmed in writing (By-law 9, s. 8(1)(a)). You must discuss with the client how the interest is to be allocated for income tax purposes, and you must obtain the client's social insurance number and/or corporate number for that purpose.

The account will be in your name or your firm name in trust for the client. Separate interest-bearing trust accounts may be passbook accounts, guaranteed investment certificates (GICs), and term deposits. For bookkeeping purposes, interest on the money should be recorded as trust receipts. Service charges on the account are charged to the client, and are recorded as disbursements for the client.

You must keep complete records for money deposited to a separate interest-bearing trust account pursuant to a client's instructions, as required by By-law 9.

MANAGING TRUST MONEY

You should review the client accounts in the clients' trust ledger on a regular basis. The **clients' trust ledger** is a record that shows, separately for each client for whom trust money is held, all trust funds received and disbursed, and any unexpended balance.

Billing the Client

Matters that can be billed should be billed. For ongoing client matters, you should interim bill the client, transfer money from trust to general in payment of the interim invoice as soon as is practicable, and, if appropriate, consider requesting a further money retainer from the client.

BOX 8.4

Reminder: Billing Practices

At the outset of the retainer, you should discuss with the client your billing practices, whether you require a money retainer, and the circumstances in which further money retainers, if any, may be required. You should confirm this information in the retainer agreement or otherwise in writing. ◇

For client matters that are concluded, you should bill the client, transfer money from trust to general in payment of the invoice as soon as is practicable, and refund any balance to the client promptly.

Outstanding or Stale-Dated Trust Cheques

If you have issued trust cheques to clients or to third parties and they remain uncashed, you must follow up with the payees to find out if they have received the cheques and, if yes, why they have not been cashed. A **payee** is a person to whom money is paid.

Like regular cheques, trust cheques become stale-dated if they are not cashed within a certain time. Depending on the financial institution, the stale-date period may be anywhere from six months to one year from the date of the cheque. A stale-dated cheque will not be honoured by the financial institution because it is too old.

When dealing with a stale-dated trust cheque, you should do the following (*Paralegal Bookkeeping Guide*, at 7):

- stop payment on the cheque;

- re-establish liability for the amount of the cheque in the client account in the clients' trust ledger; and

- reissue the cheque, if appropriate—that is, if you have located the client or third-party payee.

If you have held client money in trust for at least two years, you may apply for permission to transfer the money to the Law Society if (*Law Society Act*, s. 59.6(1)):

(a) you have been unable to locate the person entitled to the money despite having made reasonable efforts throughout a period of at least two years; or

(b) you are unable to determine who is entitled to the money.

If you are granted permission to transfer the money to the Law Society's Unclaimed Trust Fund, your liability as trustee or fiduciary with respect to the money ends when the money has been transferred to the Law Society.

The application procedure for transferring unclaimed trust funds to the Law Society is set out in By-law 10. An application form can be found at the Law Society's website in the "Practice Resources" section.

TRUST RECEIPTS

You must deposit all of the following to trust (By-law 9, ss. 7(2), (3)):

- settlement funds payable to the client by an opposing party that are received by you from the opposing party;

- settlement funds payable by the client to an opposing party that are received by you from your client;

- money received by you from the client that is to be held for the client pending the client's direction or instruction;

- money that is advanced to you on account of fees for future or unbilled legal services;

- money that is advanced to you on account of future disbursements;

- money that belongs in whole or in part to the client, where it is not practical to split the payment (for example, overpayment of an invoice by a client); and

- money withdrawn from trust in error.

Client money must be deposited to the mixed trust account immediately after receipt, and no later than the end of the next banking day (By-law 9, s. 1(3)). Money deposited to trust must be allocated to specific client matters, and tracked in your books and records on that basis.

AUTOMATED BANK MACHINE

Money may be deposited to your mixed trust account by attending personally at the financial institution, or by automated bank machine. If your financial institution offers automatic bank machine (ABM) access to your trust account, you may use it for deposits only. You must ensure that your bank card for the trust account is encoded for deposits only. You should print receipts of all ABM deposits to trust and keep them with your deposit book, along with a record of the source of the funds and the client matter number (*Paralegal Bookkeeping Guide*, at 14).

> ### BOX 8.5
>
> ## Reminder: Money Not to Be Paid into Trust (By-law 9, s. 8(1))
>
> You are not required to deposit to your trust account money received in trust from or for a client if:
>
> (a) the client requests in writing that the money shall not be deposited to trust;
>
> (b) you deposit the money into an account in the client's name, or in the name of a person designated by the client, or in the name of an agent of the client other than you; or
>
> (c) you pay the money immediately upon receiving it to the client or to a person on behalf of the client, following normal business practices.
>
> When dealing with client money that is not paid into trust, you must maintain an audit trail of how it was handled. Where the client requests in writing that the money be deposited to a separate interest-bearing trust account, you must maintain proper records for that account as required by By-law 9 (s. 8(3)). ◇

Cash Receipts (By-law 9, Part III and s. 19)

DUPLICATE CASH RECEIPTS BOOK

Cash means current coin or banknotes of Canada, or current coin or banknotes of countries other than Canada (By-law 9, s. 1(1)).

Whenever you receive cash from a client, whether in trust for future legal services or in payment of an outstanding account, you must prepare a duplicate cash receipt identifying (By-law 9, s. 19(1)):

- the date on which cash is received,

- the person from whom cash is received,

- the amount of cash received,

- the client for whom the cash is received, and

- the client matter number or code.

The duplicate cash receipt is a source document, and should be prenumbered.

The duplicate cash receipt must be signed by you or a person you have authorized to receive the cash, and by the person from whom the cash is received. See Figure 8.2 for a sample of a duplicate cash receipt.

If you cannot obtain the signature of the person from whom the cash is received after reasonable efforts, the duplicate cash receipt is acceptable so long as it meets the other requirements of By-law 9, s. 19 (s. 19(2)). However, you should be wary of accepting cash from someone who does not wish to sign a document recording the transaction.

The requirement to complete a duplicate cash receipt is in addition to your other record-keeping obligations under By-law 9.

FIGURE 8.2   Duplicate Cash Receipt

DUPLICATE CASH RECEIPT

Date _____   No. 0001

Received from _____ the amount of $_____

on behalf of _____ in client matter no. _____

_____   _____
Signature of payor   Authorized signature on behalf of
[person paying cash]   [name of paralegal firm]

RESTRICTIONS ON ACCEPTING CASH (BY-LAW 9, PART III)

For any one client matter, you are not permitted to receive or accept more than 7,500.00 Canadian dollars in cash (By-law 9, s. 4(1)).

If you receive or accept cash in a foreign currency for any one client matter, you must convert it to Canadian dollars using the Bank of Canada's Daily Noon Rates for the day when you receive or accept the cash (By-law 9, s. 4(2)(a)).

If the day you receive or accept the foreign currency is a holiday, you must convert it to Canadian dollars using the official Bank of Canada conversion rate in effect on the last business day before the day when you receive or accept the cash (By-law 9, s. 4(2)(b)).

If the value of the foreign currency in Canadian dollars exceeds $7,500.00, you may accept $7,500.00 in cash and the remainder from the client by a method other than cash.

This restriction applies when you receive or pay funds, or transfer funds by any means. It does not apply when you receive cash (By-law 9, s. 6):

(a)   from a public body, an authorized foreign bank within the meaning of section 2 of the *Bank Act* (Canada) in respect of its business in Canada or a bank to which the *Bank Act* (Canada) applies, a cooperative credit society, savings and credit union or caisse populaire that is regulated by a provincial Act, an association that is regulated by the *Cooperative Credit Associations Act* (Canada), a company to which the *Trust and Loan Companies Act* (Canada) applies, a trust company or loan company regulated by a provincial Act or a department or agent of Her Majesty in right of Canada or of a province where the department or agent accepts deposit liabilities in the course of providing financial services to the public;

(b)   from a peace officer, law enforcement agency or other agent of the Crown acting in an official capacity;

(c)   pursuant to an order of a tribunal;

(d)   to pay a fine or penalty; or

(e) for fees, disbursements, expenses or bail provided that any refund out of such receipts is also made in cash.

DISBURSING CASH FROM YOUR GENERAL OR TRUST ACCOUNT

By-law 9, s. 6(e) permits you to accept cash for fees, disbursements, expenses, or bail, provided that any refund must also be made in cash. When making a cash refund from your trust or general account, you must take care to leave an audit trail of the transaction.

Using Cheques for a Cash Refund

Cheques leave the best audit trail. If you are using a cheque for the refund, you should:

1. obtain the client's written instructions with respect to the refund;

2. issue a general or trust cheque payable to yourself, noting on the cheque the client matter number and indicating that it is a cash withdrawal;

3. cash the cheque, and give the cash to the client; and

4. obtain a receipt for the cash from the client or arrange for a witness to be present to attest to the transfer.

When using a cheque for a cash refund, you shall not make the cheque payable to "Cash" or "Bearer." It must be payable to the person who will be cashing the cheque.

Withdrawing Cash for a Cash Refund

If you choose to withdraw a cash refund directly from trust or general, you should (*Paralegal Bookkeeping Guide*, at 12):

1. obtain written client instructions first;

2. obtain a duplicate of the withdrawal slip for your records;

3. give the cash to the client; and

4. obtain a receipt for the cash from the client or arrange for a witness to be present to attest to the transfer.

BOX 8.6

Dealing with Cash

Dealing with cash is a lot of extra trouble. You have to do extra record-keeping when handling cash, including maintaining the duplicate cash receipts book as required by By-law 9, s. 19. Your employees may be reluctant to handle cash.

You may wish to consider making it a policy in your firm not to accept cash, or not to accept cash over a certain amount. You must notify potential clients in writing of this requirement before accepting their retainers (*Paralegal Bookkeeping Guide*, at 28). ◇

Other Trust Receipts

In addition to receiving cash, paralegals may receive money in trust for a client by (*Paralegal Bookkeeping Guide*, at 12–14):

- electronic or wire transfer,

- credit or debit card,

- personal cheque,

- certified cheque, or

- bank draft or money order.

ELECTRONIC OR WIRE TRANSFER

If you accept trust funds by wire transfer, you must provide the trust account details to the person transferring the funds. Your financial institution must be advised that trust account details are to be used for deposit only.

USING DEBIT OR CREDIT CARDS

If you accept credit or debit card payments from clients, you must arrange with your financial institution to have trust funds paid directly to your trust account, and payments of outstanding invoices paid directly to your general account. You shall not deposit trust funds and your own money to one account and then transfer the funds that do not belong in that account to your other account. By-law 9, s. 7(1) requires you to deposit money received in trust for a client to your trust account. By-law 9, s. 8(2) prohibits you from depositing money that belongs to you or your firm, including money that is payment for fees that have been billed to the client, to the trust account.

All service charges, discounts, and other fees associated with the use of debit or credit cards in your paralegal practice are business expenses, and must be charged to the general account.

If you accept both trust receipts and general receipts by debit card, you may have to use two point-of-sale machines, one for the trust account and one for the general account, in order to comply with By-law 9 (*Paralegal Bookkeeping Guide*, at 13).

Credit Cards

When trust funds are received by credit card, "trust account" must appear on the original credit card sales slip, and the credit card sales slip must be deposited to your trust account, as required by By-law 9, s. 7(1). Normal accounting procedures apply to transfers from trust to general.

Any refund shall be by credit card voucher. The client must be credited with the full amount of the credit card invoice. The credit card company's discount or fee is a cost of doing business and must be charged to the general account.

Some credit card companies require businesses to designate one bank account for deposit of credit card payments. The company discount is automatically debited from this account.

You are required by By-law 9 to deposit trust funds directly to your trust account (s. 7(1)) and to deposit payments of outstanding invoices directly to your general account (s. 8(2)). The discount is a business expense and must be charged to your general account.

If you are considering using a credit card company that requires you to designate one account for all transactions including debits for discounts or fees, your general account must be the designated account, and you are restricted to receiving credit card payments for outstanding invoices only.

The *Paralegal Bookkeeping Guide* (at 13) suggests using an imprint machine, and depositing trust vouchers to trust using the trust receipts journal (trust deposit book), and general vouchers to general using the general receipts journal (general deposit book).

TRUST DISBURSEMENTS

Authorization to Disburse Trust Funds (Guideline 15; By-law 9, s. 11)

A trust disbursement must be initiated in writing by a paralegal licensee who is authorized to handle trust funds. The signed written authorization to disburse trust funds may be a trust cheque, a Form 9A electronic trust transfer requisition, or a written direction to transfer funds from the trust account to the general account. These documents form part of your trust accounting records.

You must control your trust account. If you are a sole practitioner, you should be the only person with signing authority for the trust account. If you are in a partnership, the managing partners will likely be the paralegals in control of the trust account.

A trust cheque shall not be signed by a non-licensee except (By-law 9, s. 11(b)):

- in exceptional circumstances, and

- when the non-licensee has signing authority on the trust account on which the cheque will be drawn and is bonded in an amount at least equal to the maximum balance on deposit in the immediately preceding fiscal year of the licensee in all of the trust accounts on which signing authority has been delegated to the non-licensee.

The Law Society has found appropriate exceptional circumstances to be very rare (guideline 15).

If you are the only paralegal in your firm with signing authority on your trust account(s), you should consider making arrangements for another licensee to have signing authority on the trust account(s) in case of an unexpected emergency, such as illness or an accident, or in the event of your absence. This can be arranged through your financial institution through a power of attorney. Your chosen attorney should be insured and should be a member in good standing with the Law Society (guideline 15).

Guideline 15 recommends that you implement the following internal controls to prevent unauthorized withdrawals from trust:

- limit access to blank trust account cheques and electronic banking software;

- never sign blank trust cheques; and

- use prenumbered trust cheques, and keep them locked up when not in use.

Hold Period

With respect to a particular client matter, you shall not at any time withdraw from the trust account more money than you are actually holding in trust on behalf of that client (By-law 9, s. 9(3)).

When you deposit funds to trust, you should designate a hold period for those funds, depending on the type of payment.

Certified cheques, bank drafts, and money orders are the equivalent of cash, because they are guaranteed or certified by the issuing institution. They are considered cleared as soon as they are deposited.

A client's uncertified personal cheque carries no such guarantees. When you deposit an uncertified personal cheque to your trust account, you should designate a hold period for the funds. The hold period should be noted on the client account in the clients' trust ledger.

During the hold, or clearance, period, you should disburse no funds from trust in the client matter, because there is no certainty that the funds will be there until the funds have cleared the bank.

For an uncertified personal cheque, you should consider designating a hold period of a minimum of ten days. If, after the hold period has expired, you are uncertain whether or not the funds have cleared, you should call your financial institution for clarification. You must not disburse funds in a client matter until you are certain that those funds are in your trust account. You cannot borrow money from other clients to meet a client's obligations (By-law 9, s. 9(3)). Doing so is a misapplication of trust funds.

If you disburse trust funds in a client matter and the client's payment is later returned for insufficient funds, this is what will follow:

- Your financial institution will reverse the deposit by debiting the trust account.

- You must ensure that any non-sufficient funds (NSF) and other charges are charged to the general account.

- You must correct the trust receipts journal, the trust disbursements journal, and the clients' trust ledger to show the reversal of the NSF funds, and give a detailed explanation for the reversal.

- You must contact anyone to whom you have sent trust cheques disbursing client funds in the client matter, to arrange for deferral of payment.

- If any of the trust cheques have been cashed, you must reimburse the trust account from your own funds—that is, from the general account.

- You must obtain replacement funds from the client, preferably by certified cheque.

In a client matter where you anticipate a lot of client disbursements at the commencement of the retainer, you should request that the money retainer be paid by certified cheque.

You should review the client accounts in the clients' trust ledger on a regular basis to ensure that there are sufficient funds in trust to meet future obligations, and if not, to determine how soon those funds will need to be replenished.

Money That May Be Withdrawn from Trust

By-law 9, s. 9(1) permits you to withdraw from trust the following money:

1. money required to make a proper payment to a client or on behalf of a client;

2. money required to reimburse your paralegal firm for proper disbursements and expenses incurred on behalf of the client;

3. money properly required to pay your fees for legal services that have been performed and billed to the client;

4. money that is directly transferred into another trust account and held on behalf of a client; and

5. money that should not have been paid into trust but was deposited to trust in error.

You may also withdraw money from trust if you have applied to the Law Society for permission to transfer client funds to the Law Society's Unclaimed Trust Fund pursuant to s. 59.6 of the *Law Society Act* and the Law Society has authorized you to do so.

You shall not withdraw money from trust unless (By-law 9, s. 9(1)):

- the client has instructed you to withdraw the money, or

- the money is properly owed to you for fees that have been billed and/or expenses that were properly incurred.

If you withdraw money from trust for any other reason, it is **misappropriation of trust funds**, contrary to rule 5.01(5).

Manner of Withdrawing Money from the Trust Account

A paralegal may withdraw money from the trust account by the following methods (*Paralegal Bookkeeping Guide*, at 11–14):

- a trust cheque signed by a paralegal who is authorized to disburse trust funds;

- a transfer to a non-trust account (in other words, the general account) kept in the paralegal's name or the paralegal firm's name, authorized by the paralegal in writing; or

- electronic transfer in accordance with By-law 9, s. 12.

These methods produce the records necessary for compliance with the Law Society's record-keeping requirements.

Automated banking machines may not be used to disburse funds from trust, because they do not provide adequate records of transactions to meet the record-keeping requirements of By-law 9.

DISBURSING TRUST FUNDS BY CHEQUE

A cheque drawn on a trust account shall not be made payable to "Cash" or "Bearer" (By-law 9, s. 11(a)). A cheque drawn on a trust account shall not be signed by a person who is not a licensee except in exceptional circumstances as outlined in By-law 9, s. 11(b).

Cancelled cheques, including certified cheques, are your records, and should be returned to you every month along with your bank statements, as arranged by you and your financial institution. Imaged cheques that are sent to you electronically are acceptable for paralegal record-keeping purposes so long as the images are of both the back and the front of the cheque, and are easy to read. If your financial institution uses imaged cheques, you should consider printing out hard copies for your records, or saving the images in a format that will be retrievable for the required ten-year period.

Guideline 15 recommends that you implement the following internal controls to prevent unauthorized withdrawals from trust through the use of trust cheques:

- limit access to blank trust cheques and electronic banking software;

- never sign blank trust cheques;

- use pre-numbered trust cheques, and keep them locked up when not in use.

DISBURSING TRUST FUNDS BY ELECTRONIC TRANSFER (BY-LAW 9, S. 12; FORM 9A)

Electronic transfers include Internet banking.

The following conditions shall be met when disbursing trust funds by electronic transfer (By-law 9, s. 12):

1. Before any data with respect to the electronic transfer is entered into the electronic trust transfer system, a paralegal or office staff shall complete a Form 9A Electronic Trust Transfer Requisition for the transaction. The Form 9A must be signed by a licensee with signing authority on the trust account, except in exceptional circumstances as outlined in By-law 9, s. 12(2)4(ii).

2. The electronic trust transfer system must require two persons, using different passwords or access codes, to enter data to complete the transaction. One person uses a password or access code to enter the data describing the details of the transfer. Another person, using another password or access code, enters the data authorizing the financial system to carry out the transfer. These persons do not have to be licensees.

3. A paralegal sole practitioner without employees may enter the data and authorize the transaction.

4. The information entered into the electronic trust transfer system must be the same as the information on the Form 9A.

5. Print the electronic confirmation of the transaction, which must include the following information:

   - your trust account number;

- the name, branch, and address of the financial institution for the account to which the funds have been transferred;

- the name of the account to which the funds have been transferred;

- the number of the account to which the funds have been transferred;

- the time and date that the transaction details and authorization were received by your financial institution; and

- the time and date that the confirmation of the transaction is sent to you from the financial institution.

6. No later than the close of the banking day immediately after the day on which the electronic trust transfer was authorized, you must compare the printed electronic confirmation with the Form 9A and verify that the money was disbursed as requested in the Form 9A.

7. Write the client name, client matter, and matter number on the printed confirmation.

8. Sign and date the printed confirmation.

The Form 9A and printed confirmation should be kept in numerical order by requisition number with your financial records. You should consider keeping copies of the Form 9A and printed confirmation in the client file as well.

You will find a sample Form 9A in Figure 8.3 and in the Appendices to the *Paralegal Bookkeeping Guide*.

RECORD-KEEPING IN A PARALEGAL PRACTICE (BY-LAW 9, SS. 18 TO 23)

General Requirements

SOURCE DOCUMENTS, JOURNALS, AND LEDGERS

A source document is an original document on which a transaction is recorded. It is evidence of the occurrence and value of a transaction. It is also the source of the information that is entered into your books and records.

A **journal** is also called a book of original entry, because it is where transactions are first recorded. It is a record of all parts of a transaction in one place, in chronological order (that is, in the order in which they take place). The process of making entries in a journal is called **journalizing**. Each transaction recorded in a journal is called an **entry**. A journal records entries for many different accounts as transactions occur.

Each entry in a journal should reference a source document.

Journal entries are transferred to individual accounts in the ledger. Transferring information from a journal to specific accounts in a ledger is called **posting** to the ledger. A **ledger** is a book where transactions are organized and recorded by account name—in other words, it is a group of accounts. An **account** is a form in which changes resulting from transactions are recorded for a particular item on a balance sheet.

The ledger is useful because account balances are updated as transactions occur in accounts.

FIGURE 8.3   Electronic Trust Transfer Requisition (Completed)

[sample]

FORM 9A

ELECTRONIC TRUST TRANSFER REQUISITION

Requisition No.: ETT103

Amount of funds to be transferred: $908.25

Re: DOUANIER Speeding
Client: Sidney Douanier
Matter no.:   0153

Reason for payment: Fees ($865.00) and GST ($43.25) billed to client

Trust account to be debited:
        Name of financial institution: Georgetown Trust
        Account number: 112233445
        Name of recipient: Beatrice Webb, General Account

Account to be credited:
        Name of financial institution: Georgetown Trust
        Branch name: Georgetown Commercial Banking Centre
        Address: 123 Shaw Avenue, Georgetown, ON A1A 2B3
        Account number: 566778899

Person requisitioning electronic trust transfer: Beatrice Webb

August 23, 20—	Beatrice Webb
Date	Signature

Additional transaction particulars:

Person entering details of transfer:

Name: Albert Assistant	Albert Assistant
	Signature

Person authorizing transfer at computer terminal:

Name: Barbara Bookkeeper	Barbara Bookkeeper
	Signature

FIGURE 8.4 Posting to the Ledger

Entering transactions manually in journals and then posting the information manually to ledgers is labour intensive and time consuming. Accounting software posts transactions as they are entered, which means that your records are always current and up to date, as required by By-law 9, s. 22. However, you need to know how to use a manual set of records, in order to understand the record-keeping process step by step.

REQUIREMENTS FOR FINANCIAL RECORDS

The minimum requirements for financial records in a paralegal practice are set out in By-law 9, ss. 18 to 23.

Trust and General Account

For your trust account, the following records are required:

- detailed duplicate trust deposit slips (s. 18(10)),
- trust receipts journal (s. 18(1)),
- trust disbursements journal (s. 18(2)),
- clients' trust ledger (s. 18(3)),
- trust transfer journal (s. 18(4)), and
- trust bank comparison (s. 18(8)).

For your general account, the following records are required:

- detailed duplicate general deposit slips (s. 18(10)),
- general receipts journal (s. 18(5)),
- general disbursements journal (s. 18(6)), and
- fees book (s. 18(7)).

Although it is not required by By-law 9, the *Paralegal Bookkeeping Guide* recommends that you consider maintaining a clients' general ledger for client accounts where there are no funds held in trust. The clients' general ledger shows (*Paralegal Bookkeeping Guide*, at 21):

- expenses and disbursements paid from the general account,
- invoices delivered to the client,
- payments made by the client on account of fees and disbursements, and
- the outstanding balance, if any.

The clients' general ledger is required for accounting purposes, because it tracks client receivables—that is, expenses paid from the general account, invoices, payments, and amounts outstanding for each client account.

> ### BOX 8.7
>
> ## Client Matters with No Trust Funds
>
> In a client matter where a money retainer is held in trust, you may pay all proper disbursements and expenses directly from the client funds held in trust (By-law 9, s. 9(1)2). After you have completed legal services and billed the client for fees, you may pay your fees from the client funds held in trust.
>
> In a client matter where there is no money retainer held in trust, you must pay all proper disbursements and expenses from your general account, out of firm money. After you have completed legal services, you will bill the client for your fees, plus disbursements and expenses paid from general. The client payment for the invoice may be deposited directly to your general account, because the payment is for fees for completed legal services and reimbursement of proper expenses paid on behalf of the client by your firm—in other words, the money belongs to you. ◈

Other Financial Records

You are also required to maintain the following:

- source documents (By-law 9, ss. 18(10), (11)),

- duplicate cash receipts book (By-law 9, s. 19), and

- valuable property record (By-law 9, s. 18(9); rule 3.07).

Maintaining Financial Records (By-law 9, ss. 21, 22)

The financial records required to be maintained by By-law 9 must be permanent records. If you choose a manual accounting system, where transactions are entered and posted by hand, the entries must be entered and posted in ink, or drafted in pencil and then photocopied.

If you use spreadsheet programs, accounting software, or other computerized systems for bookkeeping and accounting, you must ensure that you can produce hard copies of all documents for your own records and for production to the Law Society upon request. You should consider printing out your records monthly. You must implement appropriate security measures, including installation of firewalls and antivirus software, and use passwords to limit access. You should put backup and disaster recovery plans in place to ensure that your books and records can be replaced or recovered if they become damaged or lost.

Financial records shall be entered and posted so as to be current at all times, with the exception of the trust bank comparison, which is required to be completed by the 25th day of the month following the month for which the record is created.

Preservation of Financial Records (By-law 9, s. 23)

You must keep the following financial records for six full years plus the current year:

- trust transfer journal,

- general receipts journal,

- general disbursements journal,

- fees book or chronological file of client invoices, and

- duplicate cash receipts book.

You must keep the following financial records for ten full years plus the current year:

- trust receipts journal,

- trust disbursements journal,

- clients' trust ledger,

- monthly trust comparisons for all trust accounts supported by trust bank reconciliations and client trust listings,

- valuable property record,

- source documents, including

  ◇ cashed general and trust cheques, including certified cheques and imaged cheques;

  ◇ trust and general account statements, including GIC, term deposit, or other confirmations from your financial institution;

  ◇ trust and general passbooks;

  ◇ detailed duplicate deposit slips for the general and trust accounts, stamped by the teller or with the ABM deposit slip attached;

  ◇ fee invoices, if you do not keep a fees book;

  ◇ signed Form 9A requisitions for electronic trust transfers; and

  ◇ signed printed confirmations of electronic trust transfers.

Books and Records for the General Account

For your general account, By-law 9 requires the following records:

- detailed duplicate general deposit slips and other source documents (s. 18(10)),

- general receipts journal (s. 18(5)),

- general disbursements journal (s. 18(6)), and

- fees book (s. 18(7)).

You should consider maintaining a clients' general ledger to keep track of client receivables—that is, all money that is owed by clients to your paralegal firm, and information regarding how and when it is paid (*Paralegal Bookkeeping Guide*, at 21).

DETAILED DUPLICATE GENERAL DEPOSIT SLIP (S. 18(10))— TEN YEARS

You must record information about money deposited to your general (operating) account on a detailed duplicate general deposit slip. If the deposit is made at your financial institution, the teller must stamp each deposit slip. If the deposit is made at an ABM, the ABM receipt should be attached to the deposit slip.

> **BOX 8.8**
>
> ## Preservation Periods for Trust and General Books and Records
>
> As a memory aid, the preservation period for each of the required books and records for the general and trust accounts is stated in the subtitle. ◈

The general deposit slip should contain, at a minimum, the following information:

- date of deposit,

- your firm name,

- your bank account number,

- the source of each receipt,

- the client matter for each receipt from a client, and

- the amount of the general receipt.

GENERAL RECEIPTS JOURNAL (S. 18(5))—SIX YEARS

The money in the general account comes from the following sources:

- payment for completed legal services for which the client has received an invoice,

- payment you have received from the client for proper disbursements and expenses incurred in the client matter, and/or

- you, if you have made a contribution to the firm's liquidity.

Money that belongs to a client shall never be deposited to your general account.

Each receipt of money in the general account must be entered in the general receipts journal. The journal entry must include the following information:

- date of receipt,

- method of payment,

- payor, with reference to reason for payment, and

- the amount received.

A **payor** is a person who pays money to another.

GENERAL DISBURSEMENTS JOURNAL (S. 18(6))—SIX YEARS

The general account is your operating account. You use the money in the general account to pay for business expenses, such as:

- staff salaries,

- rent,

- telephone and Internet,

- bank fees,

- GST/HST, if you do not have a separate account for GST remittances,

- office supplies,

- Law Society membership fees,

- liability insurance premiums, and

- proper disbursements and expenses in client matters where you are holding no funds or insufficient funds in trust.

You also draw money from the general account to pay yourself.

Every disbursement of money from the general account must be recorded in the general disbursements journal. The journal entry must include the following information:

- date of payment,

- method of payment (for example, "general cheque"),

- number of the document used for payment (cheque number),

- amount of the payment,

- payee, and

- reason for payment.

CLIENTS' GENERAL LEDGER

By-law 9 does not require you to keep a clients' general ledger. However, it is required for accounting purposes, because it tracks client receivables—that is, expenses paid from general, invoices, payments, and amounts outstanding for each client account.

The clients' general ledger will contain a separate account for every client matter where money is owed to the paralegal firm.

Each client account in the clients' general ledger should contain the following information:

- name of account,

- date of transaction,

- particulars of transaction,

- expenses paid from general,

- GST payable on those expenses, if any,

- fees billed to the client,

- GST payable on fees,

- payments from the client, and

- balance owed.

As a general rule, you should always request a money retainer at the outset of the client matter. In a client matter where no funds are held in trust, you will pay expenses in the client matter from your general bank account. These expenses will be entered in the general disbursements journal and posted to the client's account in the clients' trust ledger. You will bill them back to the client with your invoice for fees.

FEES BOOK (S. 18(7))—SIX YEARS

By-law 9 gives you the option of maintaining a fees book or a chronological file of copies of invoices. If you maintain a fees book, each entry must contain the following information:

- date,
- invoice number,
- client matter and matter number,
- fees billed, and
- other billings charged to the client (expenses, GST/HST).

BOOKS AND RECORDS—NO CLIENT MONEY IN TRUST

You are retained by Winston Burroughs to commence an action in a Small Claims Court matter. Mr. Burroughs is a repeat client who pays his bills promptly. You do not ask him for a money retainer. The client matter number is 0567.

On January 3, 20—, you issue the plaintiff's claim. You pay the fee of $75.00 with general cheque #205. On January 3, 20—, you also pay for office supplies in the amount of $105.00, including GST/HST, with general cheque #206.

Entries in journals are made in chronological order as transactions take place. You enter both of the January 3 transactions in the general disbursements journal as follows:

		Paralegal Firm Name **General Disbursements Journal**			
Date 20—	Method of payment/ Reference number	Paid to	Particulars	GST paid	Amount
Jan. 3	Cheque #205	Minister of Finance	Burroughs Small Claims Client matter no. 5097 Issue plaintiff's claim		75.00
Jan. 3	Cheque #206	Office Supplies Depot	Stationery	5.00	105.00

You post the January 3 transaction to the client account in the clients' general ledger. Note that the entry for office supplies, along with any other journal entries for January 3, would be posted to the appropriate ledger accounts at the same time. From this point on, however, we will focus on transactions in the client matter.

Paralegal Firm Name Clients' General Ledger							
Account: Burroughs, Winston Client matter no. 0567			Re: Small Claims Court				
Date 20—	Particulars	Expenses paid	GST on expenses	Fees	GST on fees	Payment from client	Balance owing
Jan. 3	Issue plaintiff's claim Cheque #205	75.00					75.00

The defendant fails to file a defence within the required time. On January 28, 20—, you arrange for the clerk to note the defendant in default and enter default judgment. You pay the fee of $35.00 with general cheque #224.

You enter the January 28 transaction in the general disbursements journal and post the journal entry to the client account in the clients' general ledger, as shown below. Note that there would be many other entries in the general disbursements journal. The following is the entry for the January 28 transaction in this client matter only.

Paralegal Firm Name General Disbursements Journal					
Date 20—	Method of payment/ Reference number	Paid to	Particulars	GST paid	Amount
Jan. 28	Cheque #224	Minister of Finance	Burroughs Small Claims Client matter no. 0567 Default judgment	n/a	35.00

Paralegal Firm Name Clients' General Ledger							
Account: Burroughs, Winston Client matter no. 0567			Re: Small Claims Court				
Date 20—	Particulars	Expenses paid	GST on expenses	Fees	GST on fees	Payment from client	Balance owing
Jan. 3	Issue plaintiff's claim Cheque #205	75.00					75.00
Jan. 28	Default judgment Cheque #224	35.00					110.00

This concludes your retainer in the client matter. Your total fees are $500.00. The GST payable on your fees is $25.00. Your final invoice is numbered 668 and dated February 15, 20—.

You record the final invoice in the clients' general ledger and in the fees book, as shown.

Paralegal Firm Name **Clients' General Ledger**							
Account: Burroughs, Winston Client matter no. 0567			Re: Small Claims Court				
Date 20—	Particulars	Expenses paid	GST on expenses	Fees	GST on fees	Payment from client	Balance owing
Jan. 3	Issue plaintiff's claim Cheque #205	75.00					75.00
Jan. 28	Default judgment Cheque #224	35.00					110.00
Feb. 15	Invoice #668			500.00	25.00		635.00

Paralegal Firm Name **Fees' Book**						
Date 20—	Invoice number	Client	Fees billed	Disbursements billed	GST billed	Total billed
Feb. 15	668	Burroughs, Winston Re: Small Claims Court Client matter no. 0567	500.00	110.00	25.00	635.00

On February 25, 20—, you receive Mr. Burroughs's personal cheque for $635.00. The cheque number is 987.

On the same day, you fill out a detailed duplicate general deposit slip for the payment and deposit the cheque to your general bank account using an ABM. Remember that you must attach a copy of the printed ABM receipt to the duplicate general deposit slip.

DEPOSIT SLIP

BANK OF GEORGETOWN

Date:

2	0	__	__	0	2	2	5

Transit

9	8	7	6	5

Account number

2	3	4	5	6	7	8	9	9	1

CREDIT ACCOUNT OF

Current Account
Paralegal Firm Name
General Account

Depositor's
B.W.
Initials

TELLER STAMP

Teller's

Initials

Cheques and Credit Card Vouchers			Details		Cash	
Re: Burroughs			x	$5		
Invoice #668	635	00	x	$10		
			x	$20		
			x	$50		
			x	$100		
			x			
			x			
			coin			
			Cdn Cash Total			
Total >	635	00	Credit Card Vouchers and Cheques Forwarded		> 635	00

You enter receipt of the payment in the general receipts journal and in the clients' general ledger, as shown.

Paralegal Firm Name General Receipts Journal			
Date 20—	Funds received from	Amount	Method of payment
Feb. 25	Winston Burroughs Re: Invoice #668	635.00	Cheque #987

Paralegal Firm Name
Clients' General Ledger

Account: Burroughs, Winston   Re: Small Claims Court
Client matter no. 0567

Date 20—	Particulars	Expenses paid	GST on expenses	Fees	GST on fees	Payment from client	Balance owing
Jan. 3	Issue plaintiff's claim Cheque #205	75.00					75.00
Jan. 28	Default judgment Cheque #224	35.00					110.00
Feb. 15	Fees and disbursements Invoice #668			500.00	25.00		635.00
Feb. 25	Client payment Invoice #668					635.00	0.00

Trust Records

For your trust account, By-law 9 requires the following records:

- detailed duplicate trust deposit slips and other source documents (ss. 18(10), (11)),

- trust receipts journal (s. 18(1)),

- trust disbursements journal (s. 18(2)),

- clients' trust ledger (s. 18(3)),

- trust transfer journal (s. 18(4)),

- trust bank comparison (s. 18(8)),

- duplicate cash receipts book (s. 19), and

- valuable property record (s. 18(9)).

DETAILED DUPLICATE TRUST DEPOSIT SLIP (S. 18(10))—TEN YEARS

When you receive trust money from a client, you shall deposit it to trust immediately, and not later than the close of banking on the following banking day.

Information about money deposited to trust is recorded on a detailed duplicate trust deposit slip. If the deposit is made at your financial institution, the teller should stamp each deposit slip. If the deposit is made at an ABM, the ABM receipt should be attached to the deposit slip.

The trust deposit slip should contain, at a minimum, the following information:

- date of deposit,

- your firm name,

- your bank account number,

- the source of each receipt,

- the client matter for each receipt from a client, and

- the amount of each trust receipt.

TRUST RECEIPTS JOURNAL (S. 18(1))—TEN YEARS

The trust receipts journal is a record of money received into trust. Every receipt of trust money must be recorded in the trust receipts journal, in chronological order as transactions occur.

A trust receipts journal entry must include the following information:

- date of receiving the client money,

- method by which you received the money,

- person or institution from whom the money was received,

- amount received, and

- name of the client for whom you received the money.

TRUST DISBURSEMENTS JOURNAL (S. 18(2))—TEN YEARS

The trust disbursements journal is a record of money paid out of trust. Every disbursement of trust money must be recorded in the trust disbursements journal, in chronological order as transactions occur.

A trust disbursements journal entry must include the following information:

- date of the disbursement from trust,

- method of transfer (for example, "trust cheque," "electronic trust transfer"),

- number of the document used to make the transfer (for example, trust cheque number, electronic trust transfer requisition number),

- person or institution to whom the funds were paid,

- amount of the payment, and

- name of the client on whose behalf the payment was made.

If you are using a manual accounting system, you may wish to consider combining the trust receipts journal and the trust disbursements journal into one journal, called the trust cash journal (*Paralegal Bookkeeping Guide*, at 16).

CLIENTS' TRUST LEDGER (S. 18(3))—TEN YEARS

The clients' trust ledger lets you track the money you are holding in trust to the credit of each client account where trust money is held.

Whenever you enter a trust disbursement or a trust receipt into your trust journals, you must post the entry to the client account in the clients' trust ledger. As transactions are entered into the client account in the clients' trust ledger, the balance held in trust for that client account is also calculated.

The clients' trust ledger tracks how much money you have in trust in client accounts where trust funds are held. Each client account in the clients' trust ledger should contain the following information:

- name of account,

- date of trust transaction,

- particulars of trust transaction,

- whether the trust transaction was a receipt or a disbursement, and

- balance held in trust.

> **BOX 8.9**
>
> ### Reminder: Trust Accounts
>
> The clients' trust ledger tracks how much money you have in trust in client accounts where trust funds are held. You should review the clients' trust ledger regularly to ensure that you are holding sufficient trust funds in a particular client matter before disbursing funds in that matter. Do not disburse funds in a client matter until any hold periods have expired and you have confirmed that the funds are available. ◇

TRUST TRANSFER JOURNAL (S. 18(4))—SIX YEARS

The trust transfer journal is used to record transfers of trust funds from one clients' trust ledger account to another clients' trust ledger account.

When you transfer trust funds from a client's trust ledger account to another trust ledger account in a separate matter for the same client, you do not have to enter the transaction in the trust transfer journal. However, you should obtain the client's instructions before transferring the money, and you should considering confirming them in writing.

When you transfer trust funds from a client's trust ledger account to another client's trust ledger account, you must obtain the transferring client's instructions in writing before transferring the money, because the transfer has the effect of taking one client's money to pay for another client's matter.

BOX 8.10

Using the Trust Transfer Journal

Scenario

You are retained by Francesca Sayed in Matter 079. You receive $1,200.00 in trust to the credit of Matter 079. An account is opened in the clients' trust ledger for Francesca Sayed/Matter 079, recording the trust receipt of $1,200.00.

You are retained by Francesca Sayed's husband, Ahmed Sayed, in Matter 101. You receive $800.00 in trust to the credit of Matter 101. An account is opened in the clients' trust ledger for Ahmed Sayed/Matter 101, recording the trust receipt of $800.00.

Matter 079 is concluded. You deliver a final invoice to Francesca Sayed for $900.00. You transfer $900.00 from the trust account to your general account to pay the invoice. This leaves a balance in trust to the credit of Francesca Sayed/Matter 079 in the amount of $300.00.

You consult with Francesca Sayed, and she directs you to transfer the balance from Matter 079 to Matter 101, which is ongoing.

What procedures should you follow to carry out the transfer of trust funds?

Discussion

Because this is a transfer from one client's trust account to another client's trust account, you must obtain written instructions from Francesca Sayed directing that the money be transferred, and you must enter the transaction in the trust transfer journal as shown below.

Paralegal Firm Name Trust Transfer Journal				
Date 20—	Funds received from	To client account	Amount	Particulars
Mar. 30	Francesca Sayed Matter 079	Ahmed Sayed Matter 101	300.00	Unused retainer in Matter 079; funds transferred on Francesca Sayed's written direction

The transfer of funds from Matter 079 to Matter 101 would also be recorded in the trust ledger accounts for those matters. ◇

TRUST BANK RECONCILIATION, CLIENT TRUST LISTING, AND TRUST COMPARISON (S. 18(8))—TEN YEARS

The **trust comparison** compares

- the reconciled trust bank balance from your trust bank reconciliation, and
- the total amount in your trust account according to the client trust listing.

The **client trust listing** is a list of client trust ledger accounts in which trust funds were held as of the previous month end. You must complete the trust comparison by the 25th day of each month for all trust funds you held at the end of the previous month. Any shortages in the trust account must be corrected immediately. Bank or posting errors must be corrected before the end of the next month.

Trust Bank Reconciliation

The **trust bank reconciliation** is used to reconcile your trust records with your trust bank statement. It accounts for discrepancies between the mixed trust account balance as of the previous month end according to your trust bank statement as of that date, and the mixed trust account balance as of the previous month end according to your client trust listing for that date.

You need the following books and records for the trust bank reconciliation:

- your trust bank statement for the previous month,
- your trust disbursements journal and returned cashed trust cheques, and
- your trust receipts journal and deposit slips.

For the trust reconciliation, you must do the following:

1. Compare your trust bank statement and the trust disbursements journal. Make a note of any cheques recorded in the trust disbursements journal for the previous month that do not show up as cleared on the trust bank statement. List these outstanding cheques by cheque number, date, and amount. Total them.

2. Compare your trust bank statement and the trust receipts journal (deposit book). Make a note of any deposits that do not appear on the trust bank statement for the previous month. List outstanding deposits by date and amount. Total them.

3. From the balance on the trust bank statement, subtract the total amount of outstanding cheques. Then add any outstanding deposits. The result is your **reconciled trust bank balance** for the previous month end. The reconciled trust bank balance should be the same as the clients' trust listing.

Client Trust Listing

For the client trust listing, you must do the following:

1. From the clients' trust ledger, identify any client for whom you held trust funds at the previous month end.

2. List the client names in logical order, with the unexpended trust balance for each client at the previous month end. Include the last activity date for each client. This will help you monitor inactive amounts.

3. Total the client trust listing.

Trust Comparison

The trust comparison compares the reconciled trust bank balance and the client trust listing balance. The two amounts must be the same. If they are not, you must go back and check for errors, including errors in your calculations, bank errors, and/or posting errors.

BOX 8.11

Trust Comparison

Scenario

According to your trust bank statement for the month ending October 31, 20—, your trust bank balance is $6,055.00.

Using your clients' trust ledger, you identify the following accounts holding trust funds for the month ending October 31, 20—:

File name	Last activity date	Amount
SAYED, Ahmed	15 Oct. —	$1,100.00
CHANGE, David	1 Oct. —	$300.00
BATALI, Lidia	22 Oct. —	$1,500.00
DORY, John	23 Oct. —	$750.00
	Total client funds in trust:	$3,650.00

Your bank statement says that you have $6,055.00 in trust as of October 31, 20—. Your clients' trust ledger says that all you have in trust as of October 31, 20— is $3,650.00. The difference is $2,405.00. Where did the money go?

Discussion

To answer this question, you must compare the transactions recorded in your trust receipts journal and trust disbursements journal to the transactions that are showing on your bank statement.

When you do so, you note that there are three trust cheques that are recorded in your trust disbursements journal for the month of October but do not appear on the October bank statement.

Cheque #	Date	Amount
243	30 Oct. —	$145.00
244	31 Oct. —	$1,600.00
245	31 Oct. —	$660.00
	Total outstanding cheques:	$2,405.00

The balance showing in your clients' trust ledger reflects deductions made for the three outstanding cheques. The balance on the bank statement does not show deductions for the three outstanding cheques, because they had not cleared the bank as of October 31, 20—. When you subtract the total amount of the outstanding cheques from the balance on the bank statement, the reconciled bank balance is the same as the trust balance showing in the clients' trust ledger.

Your trust bank reconciliation, client trust listing, and trust comparison for the month ending October 31, 20— will look like this. Note that it must be completed on or before November 25, 20—.

Paralegal Firm Name
Trust Bank Reconciliation as at October 31, 20—

Mixed trust account:

Balance per bank statement	$6,055.00
Less: Outstanding cheques (see list below)	2,405.00
Plus: Outstanding deposits: 31 Oct. —	0.00
Reconciled mixed trust bank balance at October 31, 20—	**$3,650.00**

Outstanding cheques:

Cheque #	Date	Amount
243	30 Oct. —	$ 145.00
244	31 Oct. —	1,600.00
245	31 Oct. —	660.00
Total outstanding cheques		$2,405.00

Client Trust Listing as at October 31, 20—
(From clients' trust ledger balances)

File name	Last activity date	Amount
SAYED, Ahmed	15 Oct. —	$ 1,100.00
CHANG, David	1 Oct. —	300.00
BATALI, Lidia	22 Oct. —	1,500.00
DORY, John	23 Oct. —	750.00
Total client funds in trust:		$3,650.00

Total trust liabilities to clients at October 31, 20—	**$3,650.00**

Trust Comparison as at October 31, 20—

Total reconciled trust bank balance	**$3,650.00**
Total of unexpended balances as per clients' trust ledger	**$3,650.00**

DUPLICATE CASH RECEIPTS BOOK (BY-LAW 9, PART III AND S. 19)—SIX YEARS

Cash means current coin or banknotes of Canada, or current coin or banknotes of countries other than Canada.

Whenever you receive cash from a client, whether in trust for future legal services or in payment of an outstanding account, you must prepare a duplicate cash receipt identifying:

- the date on which the cash is received,

- the person from whom the cash is received,

- the amount of cash received,

- the client for whom the cash is received, and

- the client matter number or code.

The duplicate cash receipt should be sequentially numbered. It must be signed by you or a person you have authorized to receive the cash, and by the person from whom the cash is received.

If you cannot obtain the signature of the person from whom the cash is received after reasonable efforts, the duplicate cash receipt is acceptable so long as it meets the other requirements of By-law 9, s. 19. However, you should be wary of accepting cash from someone who does not wish to sign a receipt.

The requirement to complete a duplicate cash receipt is in addition to your other record-keeping obligations under By-law 9.

Cash receipts are discussed at pages 227 to 229. See page 228 for a sample duplicate cash receipt.

VALUABLE PROPERTY RECORD (BY-LAW 9, S. 18(9); RULE 3.07)

When you receive valuable property from a client, you shall clearly label and identify the client's property and place it in safekeeping. While in safekeeping, the client's property must be distinguishable from the paralegal's own property (rule 3.07(3)). For example, you would not store client property in the same safe deposit box that you use for your own valuables.

You are required to maintain a valuable property record in accordance with By-law 9, s. 18(9). The valuable property record is a record of all property, other than money, held in trust for clients. The valuable property record should contain, at a minimum, the following information for each item held in trust (*Paralegal Bookkeeping Guide*, at 29):

- a description of the property,

- the date when the paralegal took possession of the property,

- the person who had possession of the property immediately before the paralegal took possession of it,

- the value of the property,

- the client for whom the property is held in trust,

- the date on which each property is given away, and

- the name of the person to whom possession of the property is given.

You will find a sample valuable property record in Figure 8.5 and in Chapter 4 on page 109.

Your obligations with respect to the property end when the property is delivered or transferred to the person for whose benefit it was held, or to another person on the written direction of the person for whose benefit the property was held.

The following properties should be included in the valuable property record:

- instruments registered in the paralegal's name in trust;

- stocks, bonds, or other securities in bearer form (that is, payable to the person having possession of them);

- jewellery, paintings, furs, collector's items, or any variety of saleable valuables; and

- any property that a paralegal can convert, on her own authority, to cash.

Term deposits, deposit slips, savings accounts, or similar deposit accounts maintained for individual clients at chartered banks or registered trust companies are not included in the valuable property record. These are trust monies and must be recorded in the trust accounting records in accordance with By-law 9.

FIGURE 8.5   Valuable Property Record

Paralegal Firm Name
Valuable Property Record

Client	Description of property	Date received	Received from	Value	Delivered to	Date of delivery
KRULL, Felix	Sony laptop	5 Jan. 20—	KRULL, Felix	$2,300.00	KRULL, Felix	7 Mar. 20—
KRULL, Felix	Canon digital camera	5 Jan. 20—	KRULL, Felix	$1,279.00	EKPUNOBE, Andrew	7 Mar. 20—
DORY, John	TAG Heuer sports watch	15 May 20—	DORY, John	$4,000.00		
BATALI, Lidia	D. Lafrance painting "Les Euphoriants"	30 Aug. 20—	BATALI, Lidia	$2,500.00		

BOOKS AND RECORDS: MONEY RETAINER

You are retained by Mary Barton to commence an action in a Small Claims Court matter. At the outset of the retainer, you advise Ms. Barton of your billing practices and that you will require a money retainer. The terms you discussed are set out in the signed retainer agreement.

Ms. Barton is eager to get started, so she provides you with a certified cheque for $1,000.00 as a money retainer. The cheque number is 418. The client matter number is 0625.

On March 1, 20—, you deposit Ms. Barton's certified cheque to your mixed trust account. For this transaction, you complete a detailed duplicate trust deposit slip, enter the transaction in the trusts receipts journal, and post it to Ms. Barton's account in the clients' trust ledger, as shown below.

DEPOSIT SLIP

CREDIT ACCOUNT OF

Current Account
Paralegal Firm Name
Trust Account

BANK OF GEORGETOWN

Date:

2	0	__	__	0	3	0	1

Depositor's
B.W.
Initials

Transit

9	8	7	6	5

TELLER STAMP

Teller's
TEL
Initials

Account number

2	3	4	5	6	7	8	9	9	0

Cheques and Credit Card Vouchers			Details		Cash	
Re: Barton Small Claims			x	$5		
Client matter no. 0625	1000	00	x	$10		
			x	$20		
			x	$50		
			x	$100		
			x			
			x			
			coin			
			Cdn Cash Total			
Total >	1000	00	Credit Card Vouchers and Cheques Forwarded		> 1000	00

Paralegal Firm Name Trust Receipts Journal				
Date 20—	Funds received from	Client	Amount	Method of payment
Mar. 1	Mary Barton	Mary Barton Small Claims Client matter no. 0625	1,000.00	Certified cheque #418

Paralegal Firm Name Clients' Trust Ledger				
Account: BARTON, Mary Client matter no. 0625		Re: Small Claims Court		
Date 20—	Particulars	Receipts	Disbursements	Trust balance
Mar. 1	Retainer re: Small Claims Court action	1,000.00		1,000.00

On March 5, 20—, you issue the plaintiff's claim. You pay the court fee of $75.00 with trust cheque #325.

You enter the March 5 transaction in the trust disbursements journal and post it to the client's trust ledger, as shown.

Paralegal Firm Name Trust Disbursements Journal				
Date 20—	Method of payment/ Reference number	Paid to	Client	Amount
Mar. 5	Cheque #325	Minister of Finance	Barton re: Small Claims Client matter no. 0625	75.00

Paralegal Firm Name Clients' Trust Ledger				
Account: BARTON, Mary Client matter no. 0625		Re: Small Claims Court		
Date 20—	Particulars	Receipts	Disbursements	Trust balance
Mar. 1	Retainer re: Small Claims Court action	1,000.00		1,000.00
Mar. 5	Minister of Finance Issue plaintiff's claim Cheque #325		75.00	925.00

The matter goes to settlement conference on June 15, 20—. No settlement is reached at the settlement conference, or within 30 days thereafter. On July 17, 20—, you request a date for trial. The court fee of $100.00 is paid out of the trust account with cheque #419.

You enter the July 17 transaction in the trust disbursements journal and post it to the client's trust ledger, as shown.

Paralegal Firm Name				
Trust Disbursements Journal				
Date 20—	Method of payment/ Reference number	Paid to	Client	Amount
Mar. 5	Cheque #325	Minister of Finance	Barton re: Small Claims Client matter no. 0625 Issue plaintiff's claim	75.00
Jul. 17	Cheque #419	Minister of Finance	Barton re: Small Claims Client matter no. 0625 Request trial date	100.00

Paralegal Firm Name				
Clients' Trust Ledger				
Account: BARTON, Mary Client matter no. 0625		Re: Small Claims Court		
Date 20—	Particulars	Receipts	Disbursements	Trust balance
Mar. 1	Retainer re: Small Claims Court action	1,000.00		1,000.00
Mar. 5	Minister of Finance Issue plaintiff's claim Cheque #325		75.00	925.00
Jul. 17	Minister of Finance Request trial date Cheque #419		100.00	825.00

On July 20, 20—, you deliver an interim invoice to Ms. Barton. Your fees, excluding GST, are $775.00. The total amount of invoice #713, including GST, is $813.75. You enter the amount of the invoice in the fees book and in the clients' general ledger (receivables).

Paralegal Firm Name Fees' Book						
Date 20—	Invoice number	Client	Fees billed	Disbursements billed	GST billed	Total billed
Jul. 20	713	Barton, Mary Re: Small Claims Court Client matter no. 0625	775.00		38.75	813.75

Paralegal Firm Name Clients' General Ledger							
Account: BARTON, Mary Client matter no. 0625			Re: Small Claims Court				
Date 20—	Particulars	Expenses paid	GST on expenses	Fees	GST on fees	Payment from client	Balance owing
Jul. 20	Fees Invoice #713			775.00	38.75		813.75

On July 25, 20—, you transfer funds from trust to general in payment of invoice #713 by electronic trust transfer #0323. You complete the electronic trust transfer requisition, enter the transaction in the trust disbursements journal, and post it to the clients' trust ledger.

FORM 9A

ELECTRONIC TRUST TRANSFER REQUISITION

Requisition No.: ET 0323

Amount of funds to be transferred: $813.75

Re: BARTON Small Claims
Client: Mary Barton
Matter no.: 0625

Reason for payment: Fees ($775.00) and GST ($38.75) billed to client

Trust account to be debited:
          Name of financial institution: Georgetown Trust
          Account number: 2345678990
          Name of recipient: Paralegal firm name, General Account

Account to be credited:
          Name of financial institution: Georgetown Trust
          Branch name: Georgetown Commercial Banking Centre
          Address: 123 Shaw Avenue, Georgetown, ON A1A 2B3
          Account number: 2345678991

Person requisitioning electronic trust transfer: Beatrice Webb

July 25, 20—	Beatrice Webb
Date	Signature

Additional transaction particulars:

Person entering details of transfer:

Name: Albert Assistant

	Albert Assistant
	Signature

Person authorizing transfer at computer terminal:

Name: Barbara Bookkeeper

	Barbara Bookkeeper
	Signature

	Paralegal Firm Name Trust Disbursements Journal			
Date 20—	Method of payment/ Reference number	Paid to	Client	Amount
Mar. 5	Cheque #325	Minister of Finance	Barton re: Small Claims Client matter no. 0625 Issue plaintiff's claim	75.00
Jul. 17	Cheque #419	Minister of Finance	Barton re: Small Claims Client matter no. 0625 Request trial date	100.00
Jul. 25	ET #0323	Paralegal Firm Name	Barton re: Small Claims Client matter no. 0625 Invoice #713	813.75

	Paralegal Firm Name Clients' Trust Ledger			
Account: BARTON, Mary Client matter no. 0625		Re: Small Claims Court		
Date 20—	Particulars	Receipts	Disbursements	Trust balance
Mar. 1	Retainer re: Small Claims Court action	1,000.00		1,000.00
Mar. 5	Minister of Finance Issue plaintiff's claim Cheque #325		75.00	925.00
Jul. 17	Minister of Finance Request trial date Cheque #419		100.00	825.00
Jul. 25	Transfer to general ET #0323		813.75	11.25

You enter the transfer of funds from trust to general in the general receipts journal and post the entry to the clients' general ledger.

Paralegal Firm Name General Receipts Journal			
Date 20—	Funds received from	Amount	Method of payment
Jul. 25	Mary Barton re: Invoice #713	813.75	ET #0323

Paralegal Firm Name Clients' General Ledger							
Account: BARTON, Mary Client matter no. 0625			Re: Small Claims Court				
Date 20—	Particulars	Expenses paid	GST on expenses	Fees	GST on fees	Payment from client	Balance owing
Jul. 20	Fees Invoice #713			775.00	38.75		813.75
Jul. 25	From trust ET #0323					813.75	0.00

At this point in the matter, with a trial approaching and no funds in trust, you should consider requesting a further money retainer from Mary Barton.

CHAPTER SUMMARY

Complete, accurate, and up-to-date books and records provide the information you need to make financial decisions in your paralegal practice. They also help you fulfill various reporting and filing obligations to the Canada Revenue Agency, the Law Society, and the Law Foundation of Ontario.

By-law 9 sets out minimum requirements for books and records in a legal services practice.

The financial records that you are required to maintain must be permanent records. You must ensure that you can produce hard copies of all documents related to bookkeeping and accounting for your own records and for production to the Law Society upon request. You must implement appropriate security measures to protect data, and should have backup and disaster recovery plans in place to ensure that your books and records can be replaced or recovered if they become damaged or lost.

The general account is your operating account. It is a business account, and should be separate and apart from any personal accounts you may hold. You use this account to pay for business expenses, to pay your Law Society membership fees and liability insurance premiums, to pay proper disbursements and expenses in a client matter if you are holding no client money or insufficient money in trust, and to pay yourself. There should be no client money in the general account.

The trust account is used for client money. If you do not ask for money retainers or otherwise deal with client money in your paralegal practice, you are not required to have a trust account. If you require clients to pay you money in advance for future legal services, expenses, or disbursements, or if you act in client matters that may involve handling settlement funds, then you should have a trust account. The trust account should be used for client money only.

When you receive money that belongs to a client or is to be held on behalf of a client, you must deposit those funds to your trust account immediately, and by no later than the end of the next banking day.

The mixed trust account is an account into which money belonging to many different clients is deposited and held.

You should review the client accounts in the clients' trust ledger on a regular basis. Matters that can be billed should be billed. For ongoing client matters, you should interim bill the client, transfer money from trust to general in payment of the interim invoice as soon as is practicable, and, if appropriate, consider requesting a further money retainer from the client. For client matters that are concluded, you should bill the client, transfer money from trust to general in payment of the invoice as soon as is practicable, and refund any balance to the client promptly.

Whenever you receive cash from a client, you must prepare a duplicate cash receipt. You are prohibited from accepting more than $7,500.00 in Canadian funds from a client. You may also receive money in trust for a client by electronic or wire transfer, credit or debit card, personal cheque, certified cheque, and bank draft or money order.

You must control your trust account. If you are a sole practitioner, you should be the only person with signing authority for the trust account. If you are in a partnership, the managing partners will likely be the paralegals in control of the trust account.

A trust disbursement must be initiated in writing by a paralegal licensee who is authorized to handle trust funds. The signed written authorization to disburse trust funds may be a trust cheque, a Form 9A electronic trust transfer requisition, or a written direction to transfer funds from the trust account to the general account. These documents form part of your trust accounting records.

With respect to a particular client matter, you shall not at any time withdraw from the trust account more money than you are actually holding in trust on behalf of that client. You should check the clients' trust ledger to ensure that you are holding sufficient trust funds in a particular client matter before disbursing funds in that matter. Do not disburse funds in a client matter until any hold periods have expired and you have confirmed that the funds are available.

You shall not withdraw money from trust unless the client has instructed you to withdraw the money, or the money is properly owed to you for fees that have been billed and/or expenses that were properly incurred. Withdrawing money from trust for any other reason is misappropriation of trust funds, contrary to rule 5.01(5).

If you accept a cash receipt, you must provide any refund in cash. There are special rules for disbursing cash.

The minimum requirements for financial records in a paralegal practice are set out in By-law 9, ss. 18 to 23.

Although not required by By-law 9, the *Paralegal Bookkeeping Guide* recommends that you consider maintaining a clients' general ledger for client accounts where there are no funds held in trust. You are required to maintain a clients' general ledger for accounting purposes, in order to track receivables.

KEY TERMS

general account	journal
liquidity	journalizing
general retainer	entry
fiscal year	posting
trust funds	ledger
audit trail	account
source document	payor
clients' trust ledger	trust comparison
payee	client trust listing
cash	trust bank reconciliation
misappropriation of trust funds	reconciled trust bank balance

REFERENCES

Canada Deposit Insurance Corporation Act, RSC 1985, c. C-3.

Canada Deposit Insurance Joint and Trust Account Disclosure By-law, SOR/95-279, as amended.

Canada Revenue Agency, Goods and Services Tax/Harmonized Sales Tax (GST/HST) (2009); available online at http://www.cra-arc.gc.ca/tx/bsnss/tpcs/gst-tps/menu-eng.html.

Canada Revenue Agency, GST/HST Policy Statement P-209R—Lawyers' Disbursements; available online at http://www.cra-arc.gc.ca/E/pub/gl/p-209r/README.html.

Law Foundation, RRO 1990, Reg. 709.

Law Society Act, RSO 1990, c. L.8, as amended.

Law Society of Upper Canada (LSUC), By-Laws (Toronto: LSUC, 2005); available online at http://www.lsuc.on.ca/regulation/a/by-laws.

Law Society of Upper Canada (LSUC), *Guide to Opening Your Practice* (Toronto: LSUC, 2008); available online at http://rc.lsuc.on.ca/pdf/guideOpeningYourPractice/guideToOpeningYourPractice_complete.pdf.

Law Society of Upper Canada (LSUC), *Paralegal Bookkeeping Guide* (Toronto: LSUC, 2008); available online at http://rc.lsuc.on.ca/jsp/bookkeepingGuide/paralegal.jsp.

Law Society of Upper Canada (LSUC), Paralegal Professional Conduct Guidelines (Toronto: LSUC, 2008) ("the Guidelines"); available online at http://www.lsuc.on.ca/paralegals/a/paralegal-professional-conduct-guidelines.

Law Society of Upper Canada (LSUC), Paralegal Rules of Conduct (Toronto: LSUC, 2007, as amended) ("the Rules"); available online at http://www.lsuc.on.ca/paralegals/a/paralegal-rules-of-conduct.

REVIEW QUESTIONS

1. What are two reasons for keeping complete, accurate, and up-to-date books and records?

2. What steps should you take to ensure that your books and records are permanent?

3. "You may delegate responsibility for your books and records to your accountant." Discuss.

4. What is the general account, and what is it used for?

5. When is a paralegal required to have a trust account? What is the trust account used for?

6. What financial institutions shall you use for your trust account?

7. What terms should you discuss with a financial institution before opening a trust account there?

8. What are permissible methods of receiving trust money?

9. a. What procedures must you follow when receiving cash from a client?

    b. What are the restrictions on cash receipts?

10. a. Which books and records must you preserve for six years?

    b. Which books and records must you preserve for ten years?

11. You receive a cheque from a client in payment of an outstanding invoice. Which bank account will you deposit the cheque to, and why? What books and records will you use to record the transaction?

12. a. You receive a money retainer from a client by personal cheque. Which bank account will you deposit the money to, and why? What books and records will you use to record the transaction?

    b. You want to get started on the matter. There are some proper disbursements you would like to pay from trust. What should you consider before doing so?

13. You deliver an interim invoice for $900.00 to a client. You are holding $950.00 in trust to the credit of that client matter. How may the invoice be paid, and what books and records will you use to record the transaction?

14. a. What is the purpose of the trust comparison?

    b. What is the purpose of the trust bank reconciliation? What books and records do you use for the trust bank reconciliation?

    c. How do you produce the client trust listing, and what books and records do you use?

15. According to your trust bank statement for June 30, 20—, your trust bank balance is $5,225.00. Your outstanding trust cheques for the June month end total $3,500.00. There is one outstanding trust deposit for the June month end in the amount of $900.00.

    a. What is your reconciled trust bank balance?

    b. What should the total amount of your client trust listing as of June 30, 20— be?

16. According to your trust bank statement for November 30, 20—, your trust bank balance is $3,660.00. Your outstanding trust cheques for that period total $2,100.00. There are two outstanding trust deposits, one for $600.00 and the other for $1,100.00.

    a. What is your reconciled trust bank balance?

    b. The total amount in your client trust listing as of November 30, 20—is $3,375.25. What should you do?

Glossary

accommodation an action taken or a change made to allow a person or group protected by the Ontario *Human Rights Code* to engage in any of the activities covered by the Code—for example, employment

account a form on which changes resulting from transactions are recorded for a particular item on a balance sheet

accredited legal services program a paralegal program in Ontario that is approved by the Minister of Training, Colleges and Universities and accredited by the Law Society of Upper Canada

acting in good faith making legitimate and honest efforts to meet your obligations in a given situation, without trying to mislead or attempting to gain an unfair advantage over other persons or parties, through legal technicalities or otherwise

acting with courtesy and civility being polite, respectful, and considerate of others

adjudicative body a body—such as a federal or provincial court, an administrative tribunal, a statutory board, or an arbitrator—that hears evidence or legal argument and makes a decision affecting the legal interests, rights, or responsibilities of a person (*Law Society Act*, s. 1)

adjudicator a person who hears or considers a proceeding before a tribunal and makes a decision with respect to that proceeding

adverse impact discrimination *see* constructive discrimination

advocate a person who assists, defends, or pleads for others before a tribunal

affidavit a written statement of facts that is confirmed under oath or by affirmation by the person making it

affiliated entity any person or group of persons other than a person or group authorized to provide legal services in Ontario; a non-licensee or group of non-licensees

affiliation an arrangement whereby a paralegal services firm provides legal services to the public jointly with a non-legal entity whose members practise a profession, trade, or occupation that supports or supplements the paralegal's provision of legal services

alternative dispute resolution resolution of a dispute through negotiation, mediation, arbitration, or similar means, instead of litigation

ancestry family descent

audit trail a set of original documents and other records that provide information about a transaction

authorized areas of practice areas of legal services that are authorized for P1 (paralegal) licensees

best efforts a paralegal's effort to do what he can to ensure that an undertaking is fulfilled, without assuming personal responsibility

billable time time that is charged to the client on an invoice

binding authority a judicial decision by a higher court that must be followed by lower courts; also known as a binding precedent

breach of undertaking failure to fulfill an undertaking

candid being forthright and sincere, and looking at both sides of each issue without bias

cash current coin or banknotes of Canada, or current coin or banknotes of countries other than Canada (By-law 9, s. 1(1))

client a customer; any person who seeks the professional advice or services of a paralegal firm, or who discloses confidential information to a paralegal, regardless of whether the person hires the paralegal; includes any client of the paralegal firm of which a paralegal is a partner or employee, regardless of whether the paralegal actually handles the client's work (rule 1.02)

client identification information that By-law 7.1 requires a licensee to obtain from a client about who the client is and what he does

client property a wide range of items, including money, other valuables, physical items, and information

client settlement funds money paid by another person to a client in settlement of a client matter

client trust listing a list of client trust ledger accounts in which trust funds were held as of the previous month end; used for the trust comparison

client under disability   an individual who lacks legal capacity to perform certain acts—for example, to understand legal advice and give instructions based on that understanding, and to enter into binding contracts

client verification   information that By-law 7.1 requires a licensee to obtain in order to confirm that the client is who he says he is

clients' trust ledger   a record that shows, separately for each client for whom trust money is held, all money received and disbursed, and any unexpended balance

competent paralegal   a paralegal who has and applies the relevant skills, attributes, and values appropriate to each matter undertaken on behalf of a client

complainant   a person who alleges that he was the victim of a crime, and who takes part in the prosecution of the person(s) accused of committing the crime

compromise and settlement   an arrangement whereby a party to a dispute agrees to waive some part of what is owing or make other concessions in order to resolve a matter without the additional costs, delay, and uncertainty of continuing a legal proceeding

conduct unbecoming a paralegal   conduct in a paralegal's personal or private capacity that tends to bring discredit upon the paralegal profession

confidential information   any information touching on the business and affairs of a client acquired in the course of the paralegal–client relationship; a paralegal has a duty to hold all such information in strictest confidence and not to disclose it to any other person, unless authorized to do so by the client or required to do so by law (rule 3.03(1))

conflict-checking system   a list of all clients (including prospective clients), opposing parties, and related parties, if any, that is checked to ensure that there are no conflicts of interest on any client files

conflict of interest   an interest, financial or otherwise, that may negatively affect a paralegal's ability to fulfill her professional and ethical obligations to a client

constructive discrimination   a requirement, qualification, or factor that is not discrimination on a prohibited ground but that results in the exclusion, restriction, or preference of a group of persons who are identified by a prohibited ground of discrimination (*Human Rights Code*, s. 11(1)); also known as adverse impact discrimination

contingency fee   an arrangement whereby payment of part or all of the fee is contingent on the successful disposition or completion of the matter in respect of which legal services are provided; may be calculated as a percentage of any amount recovered by the client

continuing client   a client for whom a paralegal acts in several different matters or transactions over a period of time

continuing relationship   a paralegal–client relationship where a paralegal acts for the same client in several different matters or transactions over a period of time

Convocation   the governing body of the Law Society of Upper Canada

creed   religion or faith

deponent   a person who makes an affidavit

diarize   to note a deadline or other important date in your tickler system, along with a series of bring-forward dates to remind you that the deadline is approaching

disbursements   expenses related to the client matter that are paid by the paralegal on behalf of the client and for which the paralegal is entitled to be reimbursed, if the expenses are paid from the paralegal's general account

discrimination   unfair treatment by one person of another person or group on any of the prohibited grounds under the *Human Rights Code*

dispute   an argument or disagreement between two or more parties in which the interest of one side is adverse to that of the other side

docket   a manual or electronic record of all time spent on a client matter

docketed time   the total time recorded to a client matter

due diligence   in a legal context, exercising prudence and vigilance in determining the facts

duty of confidentiality   the requirement that a paralegal shall not share client information (even information that is generally known to the public) with anyone, unless authorized to do so by the client or required to do so by law

elected bencher   a licensee who is elected to sit on Convocation

elements of the offence   the components of an offence that must be proven beyond a reasonable doubt by the prosecution in order to obtain a conviction

engagement letter   a letter to the client from the paralegal that confirms the retainer and the terms of the retainer; *see also* retainer agreement

entry   a record of a transaction recorded in a journal

error   an action by a legal representative that may cause harm to a client

errors and omissions insurance   insurance intended to reimburse clients for loss or damage suffered as a result of negligence or wrongdoing by a legal representative

ethnic origin   cultural background

examination out of court   a procedure during which a party or witness is examined under oath or affirmation by opposing parties or their representatives with a view to obtaining facts and information that will assist the parties to prepare their case

express (or explicit) consent   spoken or written authorization given by the client to the paralegal permitting disclosure of confidential information to specified third parties

family status   parent and child relationships (*Human Rights Code*, s. 10(1)); a parent may be a biological parent, an adoptive parent, or a legal guardian

fee splitting   a paralegal's act of sharing or splitting her fee with another person

fees   the amount charged to a client by a paralegal for legal services provided by the paralegal to the client, including advice, correspondence, drafting pleadings and other documents, and time spent in court

fees based on an hourly rate   an arrangement whereby a paralegal is paid for actual time spent on the client matter; calculated by multiplying the paralegal's hourly rate (or that of others who have completed work on the file) by the amount of time spent on the client matter to the date of the invoice

fees by stages   an arrangement whereby the client matter is broken down into stages and the client is charged based on a reasonable estimate of the fee for each stage or step in the matter

fiduciary   a person who must act with scrupulous good faith, honesty, and candour for the benefit of another person, who places absolute trust and confidence in the fiduciary

fiduciary relationship   a relationship of trust and confidence between two persons in which one person (the fiduciary) is required to act with scrupulous good faith, honesty, and candour for the benefit of the other person

fiscal year   an accounting period of 12 months used for producing annual financial statements in businesses; may not coincide with the calendar year

fixed, flat, or block fee   a fixed amount charged for a particular task or client matter

fresh evidence   evidence of something that has happened since the first hearing, or that has come to the knowledge of the applicant since the hearing and could not by reasonable means have come to her knowledge before that time

frivolous and vexatious objection   an objection that has no legal merit and is made to annoy, harass, or embarrass the other side

fulfill an undertaking   to complete the requirements of the undertaking

funds   cash, currency, securities, negotiable instruments, or other financial instruments that indicate a person's title or interest in them

general account   the operating account in a legal services practice, used to pay for business expenses such as rent, staff salaries, insurance premiums, and Law Society membership fees

general retainer   money paid by a client to a legal services firm to secure its services; there is no obligation to account for a general retainer

guarantee   an agreement to make oneself liable or responsible to a lender for the payment of a debt if the debtor defaults in payment

harassment   engaging in a course of vexatious comment or conduct that is known or ought reasonably to be known to be unwelcome (*Human Rights Code*, s. 10(1))

implied consent   unwritten or unstated client authorization, implied by the paralegal–client relationship, for the paralegal to disclose confidential information to third parties

independent legal advice   impartial, confidential advice obtained from competent counsel with no personal interest in the matter; also called ILA

independent legal representation   legal advice and assistance from a competent paralegal or lawyer with no personal interest in the matter

independent paralegal   before regulation of the paralegal profession in Ontario, a non-lawyer agent who provided legal advice and other legal services to the public for a fee

informed consent   consent based on information that is sufficient to allow a person to make an informed decision

instructions   directions or authorizations from a client to a paralegal with respect to a particular course of action to be taken in a matter

interim invoice   an invoice that is delivered to the client before the client matter is completed, for fees and disbursements to the date of the interim invoice

joint clients   the clients in a joint retainer

joint retainer   an arrangement whereby a paralegal is hired to represent more than one client in a matter or transaction

journal   a record of all parts of a transaction in one place, in chronological order (that is, in the order in which they take place); also known as a book of original entry

journalizing   the process of entering transactions in a journal

judicial notice   when a tribunal notices, or accepts as true, certain notorious facts or matters of common knowledge without hearing evidence and without inquiry; other lesser-known facts may be noticed after inquiry

justified disclosure   mandatory disclosure of confidential information without the client's authority

Law Society of Upper Canada   a self-governing body that regulates the legal and paralegal professions in Ontario in the public interest, according to Ontario law and the rules, regulations, and guidelines of the Law Society

lay bencher   a non-licensee who sits on Convocation

ledger   a record of transactions organized and recorded by account name; a group of accounts

limited scope retainer   a retainer where the client hires a paralegal to perform one specific task, such as drafting a demand letter

liquidity   the amount of cash, or assets that can be easily converted to cash, that the firm has available to meet its short-term (one year or less) financial commitments

litigation guardian   a person who makes decisions for a person under disability in a court proceeding

marital status   for purposes of the Ontario *Human Rights Code*, the status of being married, single, widowed, divorced, separated, or living with a person in a conjugal relationship outside of marriage

marketing   includes advertisements and similar communications in various media, as well as firm names (including trade names), letterhead, business cards, and logos (rule 8.03(1))

material change in circumstances   a change in the applicant's circumstances that has occurred since the previous hearing and that may justify a variation of the original order

mediation   a non-adversarial process in which a qualified and impartial third party (the mediator) helps the parties to a dispute resolve their differences

mediator   a qualified and impartial third party who helps the parties to a dispute resolve their differences through mediation

merits of the case   the legal principles upon which a party's assertion of rights is based

minor   in Ontario, any person under 18 years of age

misappropriation of trust funds   appropriation by a paralegal of client funds held in trust or otherwise under the paralegal's control for a purpose not permitted by By-law 9

misrepresentation   a statement or conduct by a person that is misleading or false, and that is intended to deceive another person; includes a deliberate failure to disclose correct information

mixed trust account   a trust account that holds money for more than one client

money retainer   payment for future legal services, which must be held in trust for the benefit of the client until part or all of those services have been provided and invoiced to the client

multi-discipline practice   a business arrangement that permits paralegal licensees to provide to clients the services of a non-licensee who practises a profession, trade, or occupation that supports or supplements the provision of legal services; also called MDP

negotiable instrument   an unconditional order or promise to pay an amount of money, which can be transferred—for example, cheques or banknotes (paper money)

nepotism   favouritism based on family relationships

non-billable time   time that is docketed to a client matter but is not billed to the client

non-engagement   Failure to enter into a contract or agreement for legal services

non-engagement letter   a letter written by a paralegal to a client confirming that the paralegal will not be providing legal services to the client in a particular matter

objection   an argument by a party that a particular piece of evidence, line of questioning, or other matter is improper or unlawful and should not be allowed by the court

omission   a failure to act by a legal representative that may cause harm to a client

outside interest   any profession, business, occupation, or other outside interest, including holding public office, engaged in by a paralegal concurrently with the provision of legal services

paralegal   in Ontario, a non-lawyer agent who provides legal services to the public and who must be licensed to do so unless he falls within one of the categories of exemptions; the paralegal profession is governed by the Law Society of Upper Canada

paralegal–client relationship   a professional relationship that is established between a prospective client and a paralegal, usually during the initial consultation

paralegal–client retainer   the contractual relationship between the client and the paralegal, which establishes the scope of the retainer, what the client will be charged for the legal services provided, and other terms of the agreement; *see also* retainer

paralegal in good standing   a paralegal licensee who has fulfilled all membership requirements and who is not suspended or disbarred

paralegal licensee   a person licensed to provide legal services in Ontario

payee   a person to whom money is paid

payor   a person who pays money to another

permitted disclosure   discretionary disclosure of confidential information by a paralegal without the client's authority

person   any entity that is recognized by law as the subject of legal rights and obligations, including the right to sue and be sued

phantom client   a person who believes that a paralegal is representing him, even though the paralegal has not been formally retained and may be unaware of the person's belief

place of origin   for purposes of the Ontario *Human Rights Code*, a person's country or region of birth, including a region in Canada

posting   transferring information from a journal to specific accounts in a ledger

private company   a corporation whose shares are not publicly traded; also called a closely held company

pro bono legal services   legal services provided for the public good, at no charge or for a reduced fee

procedural law   the rules for judicial enforcement of a person's legal rights and obligations as set out in substantive law

professional judgment   the competent paralegal's capacity to assess situations or circumstances carefully and to make sensible decisions about client matters and her own conduct

professional misconduct   conduct by a paralegal that tends to bring discredit upon the paralegal profession

prohibited grounds   grounds upon which discrimination is prohibited by the Ontario *Human Rights Code* (s. 1)— race or colour, ancestry, place of origin, ethnic origin, citizenship, creed, sex, sexual orientation, age, marital or family status, or disability; for purposes of employment, record of offences is also a ground of discrimination

prospective client   A client who consults a paralegal regarding a legal issue but has not yet hired the paralegal as her legal representative

provide legal services   to engage in conduct involving the application of legal principles and legal judgment to the circumstances or objectives of another person

public company   a corporation whose shares are for sale to the general public and that is subject to rigorous disclosure requirements under securities legislation

receivable   money owed to a business by its clients

reconciled trust bank balance   the balance on the trust bank statement minus any outstanding cheques plus any outstanding deposits; should be the same as the clients' trust listing

record of offence   for purposes of the Ontario *Human Rights Code*, a *Criminal Code* conviction that has been pardoned, or a provincial offence

recusal   removing yourself from participation in a matter to avoid a conflict of interest

referral fee   a fee paid by a paralegal to another licensee for referring a client to the paralegal, or a fee paid to a paralegal by another licensee for the paralegal's referral of a person to the other licensee

remedy   a way of enforcing a right, or preventing or compensating for a wrong

representing a person in a proceeding   representation includes making decisions about service and filing of documents relating to a proceeding; deciding what persons to serve a document upon or with whom to file a document; deciding when, where, or how to serve or file a document; and/or engaging in any other conduct necessary to the conduct of the proceeding

retained   to be hired to represent a person in a legal matter

retainer   *see* paralegal–client retainer

retainer agreement   a written agreement between the client and the paralegal that confirms that the paralegal has been hired to provide legal services to the client, and confirms the terms upon which she has been hired

scope of the retainer   the nature and extent of the legal services to be provided by the paralegal pursuant to the paralegal–client retainer

serious loss of confidence   a situation in which the paralegal and the client no longer trust and rely on each other, making it impossible to have a normal paralegal–client relationship

sharp practice   dishonourable taking of advantage; trickery

shell corporation   an incorporated business with no assets

source document   an original document on which a transaction is recorded; it is evidence of the occurrence of a transaction and the value of that transaction

statement of account   a statement (that is, an invoice or bill) that tells the client how much is owed to the paralegal for fees, disbursements, and GST or HST as of the date of the account

statute-barred   a proceeding that is prevented by the expiry of the statutory limitation period

statutory limitation period   a period of time established by a statute for commencing a proceeding

substantive law   the statutory law and jurisprudence that creates, defines, and interprets the rights and obligations of those who are subject to it

supervised paralegal   before the regulation of the paralegal profession in Ontario, a non-lawyer working under the supervision of a lawyer in a role similar or identical to that of a legal office assistant or a law clerk

sympathetic witness   a witness who gives evidence that supports a party's cause

tickler system   a paper or electronic system that gives notice of upcoming deadlines (including limitation periods) or tasks to be completed

tribunal   includes courts, boards, arbitrators, mediators, administrative agencies, and bodies that resolve disputes, regardless of their function or the informality of their procedures

trust account   a bank account in which client money is held

trust bank reconciliation   a reconciliation of paralegal trust records with the paralegal trust bank statement, which accounts for discrepancies between the mixed trust account balance as of the previous month end according to the trust bank statement as of that date, and the mixed trust account balance as of the previous month end according to the client trust listing for that date

trust comparison   a comparison of the reconciled trust bank balance and the client trust listing balance for the previous month end; if the two amounts are not the same, the paralegal must check for and correct errors, including posting errors, errors in calculations, and bank errors

trust funds   funds held in a paralegal's trust account for or on behalf of a client

undertaking   an unequivocal, personal promise by a paralegal to perform a certain act

unsympathetic witness   a witness who gives evidence that supports an opposing party's cause

valuable property record   a record of all property, other than money, held in trust for clients, as required by By-law 9, s. 18(9).

write off time   not bill a client for time that was spent on the client matter

Index